The Cult of Jagannātha

Myths And Rituals

The Cult of Jagannātha

Myths And Rituals

José Carlos Gomes da Silva

MOTILAL BANARSIDASS PUBLISHERS
PRIVATE LIMITED • DELHI

Reprint : Delhi, **2016**
First Edition : Delhi, **2010**

ISBN : 978-81-208-3462-0

MOTILAL BANARSIDASS
41 U.A. Bungalow Road, Jawahar Nagar, Delhi 110 007
8 Mahalaxmi Chamber, 22 Bhulabhai Desai Road, Mumbai 400 026
203 Royapettah High Road, Mylapore, Chennai 600 004
236, 9th Main III Block, Jayanagar, Bengaluru 560 011
8 Camac Street, Kolkata 700 017
Ashok Rajpath, Patna 800 004
Chowk, Varanasi 221 001

Printed in India

by RP Jain at NAB Printing Unit,
A-44, Naraina Industrial Area, Phase I, New Delhi–110028
and published by JP Jain for Motilal Banarsidass Publishers (P) Ltd,
41 U.A. Bungalow Road, Jawahar Nagar, Delhi-110007

For Teresa, Barbara and Sara

CONTENTS

ACKNOWLEDGEMENTS

The Gulbenkian and Orient Foundations have, at different times, supported my ethnographic research in India. I am indebted to both of them for their invaluable help.

Thanks are due also to Purna Chandra Mishra for his assistance and friendly collaboration during my field work in Orissa.

Madeleine Biardeau and Luc de Heusch read and commented on a first version of this book, substantially different from its final form. Although these pages often contain ideas that differ from theirs, they are unequivocal testimony of my heartfelt acknowledgement.

ABBREVIATIONS

Indian Texts

AV	*Atharva Veda*
BrP	*Brahma Purāṇa*
DT	*Deuḷa Tolā*
KP	*Kūrma Purāṇa*
MāP	*Mādaḷā Pāñjī*
Mbh	*Mahābhārata*
MP	*Matsya Purāṇa*
PB	*Pañcaviṃśa Brāhmaṇa*
RV	*Ṛg Veda*
ŚB	*Śatapatha Brāhmaṇa*
ŚP	*Śiva Purāṇa*
SkP	*Skanda Purāṇa*
TS	*Taittirīya Saṃhitā*

Other Abbreviations

AITMS	*Ancient Indian Tradition and Mythology Series*
BEFEO	*Bulletin de l'École Française d'Extrême Orient*
CIS	*Contributions to Indian Sociology*
CJRTO	*The Cult of Jagannatha and the Regional Tradition of Orissa [A. Eschmann, H. Kulke, G. C. Tripathi (ed.)]*
EzV	*Ezourvedam*
HR	*History of Religions*
IIJ	*Indo-Iranian Journal*
JA	*Journal Asiatique*
JAOS	*Journal of the American Oriental Society*
ORP	*Orissa Research Project*
SBE	*Sacred Books of the East*

LIST OF ILLUSTRATIONS

PREFACE

The transition from the coastal to the inland regions of Orissa is characterised by sharp demographic and sociological discontinuities (Bailey 1957; 1960). Such regional differences are probably a reflection of aryanisation. Indo-European communities once settled in the fertile plains of the coastland (those of the Mahānadī delta, in particular), forcing the local tribal populations to migrate progressively to poorer and less irrigated areas. Ethnological accounts have most commonly relied on the historical reconstruction of this process. It has been assumed that native communities exercised a decisive influence on the traditions that flourished in the delta plain, especially those related to its vital centres – the city of Puri and the temple of Jagannātha. "Puri", Alexander MacDonald wrote, "is *par excellence* a meeting place between the Aryan and non-Aryan elements of the population" (1975: 46). In the words of Charles Fabri, "practically every temple... in Orissa" bears the mark of "non-Aryan beliefs" (1974: 12). This is questionable. The temples built in Orissa between the early 7th and the 14th century are examples of typical Hindu architecture, sharing "features in common with other northern temple styles such as the group of Khajuraho in Madhya Pradesh and those in Rajasthan" (Dehejia 1979: 1; see also Donaldson 1985-1987).

Some authors have also argued that autochthonous communities had a striking influence on the Jagannātha cult, namely as regards certain ritual performances and the unexpected prominence of Śūdra ritualists of "tribal origin" (see Eschmann 1978c; Tripathi 1978b). The persistence of native religious iconography has been equally emphasised in the relevant literature. Eschmann, Kulke, Tripathi, and Stietencron, among others, saw in the image of Jagannātha an anthropomorphic transformation of a tribal (Khond) post. In many Orissan villages, the presence of a wooden post in front of a sanctuary seemed to confirm this point of view. According to Madeleine Biardeau, however, the existence of similar objects in South India weakens the plausibility of the tribal explanation in the Orissan context. In her opinion, autochthonous conceptions exerted no significant influence on the emergence of Hinduism in the region (Biardeau 1989: 65-66).

The wooden post commonly found in South India plays an important role in strictly Hindu rituals. It has been considered by Biardeau a transformation of the *yūpa*, the sacrificial post of the Vedic period (see also Hiltebeitel 1988, 1991, 1999). The ancient *yūpa* occupied a central place in the stage of sacrificial performances, and was closely associated to the brick fire altar, the primeval model of the Hindu temple. The same symbolic relationships are crucial elements of the traditions related to the Jagannātha cult. Myths and rituals show that sacrificial symbolism is at the core of Puri's religious system. Explicitly associated with an inaugural *aśvamedha* (the Vedic horse sacrifice), the building of the great temple is still seen as a transformation of the brick fire altar. These correlations are further supported by an impressive web of orthodox representations, both Vedic and Hindu.

This acknowledgement of orthodoxy takes us back to the so-called singularities of local traditions. How to interpret the iconographic "specificity" of Puri's deities? What status should be attributed to the Śūdra ritualists of the great temple? The present book provides new answers to these old questions. Puzzling as it may appear, the "strangeness" of Orissan ethnography is a particular – yet extremely coherent – expression of Indian traditions.

PART I

THE BEGINNING BEFORE THE BEGINNING

CHAPTER ONE

INTRODUCTION: BETWEEN HISTORY AND MYTH

I

Set on the coast of Orissa, in the Bay of Bengal, Puri is one of the major pilgrimage centres on the subcontinent:

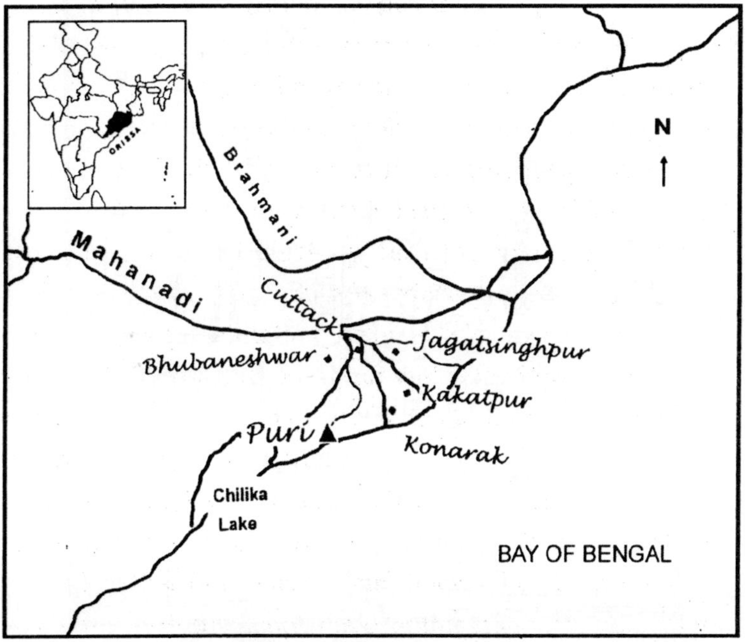

FIG. 1. The Mahānadī Delta.

In the heart of the city, there rises the great Temple of Jagannātha (the "Lord of the Universe"), begun by Coḍagaṅga in 1135. The original structure included the sanctuary (*rekhā deula*) crowned by a curvilinear tower, and a portico or audience hall (*jagamohana*). The *rekhā deula* comprises the *bāhāra pokhariā* or outer sanctum, and the *bhitara pokhariā* or inner sanctum, with the *siṃhāsana*, the throne of the gods.

The *jagamohana*, a sixteen-pillared hall, is located to the east of the *rekhā deula*. Various subsidiary buildings and two concentric walls were erected around the old complex at a later date:

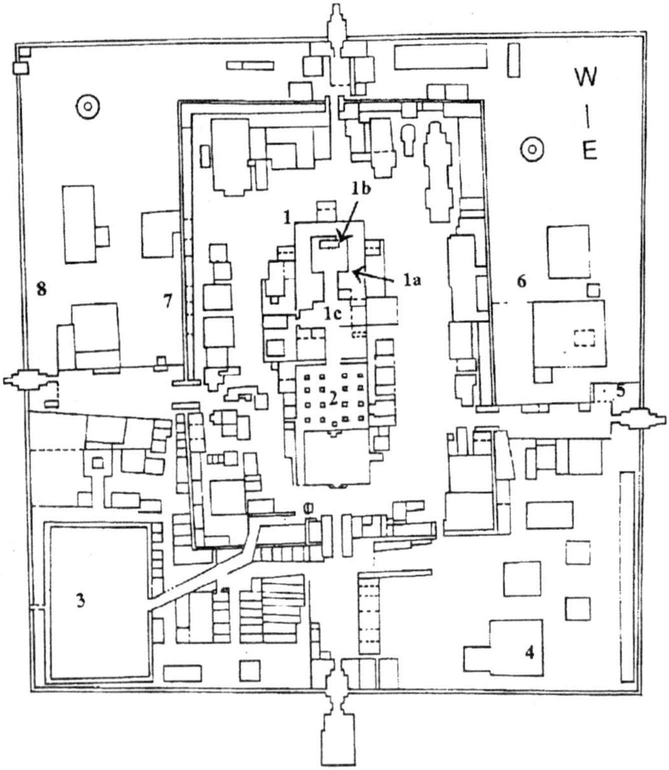

1. Rekhā Deula:
   1a. *Bhitara pokhariā* (the inner sanctum)
   1b. *Siṃhāsana*, "the Lion's Seat" (the throne of the gods)
   1c. *Bāhāra pokhariā* (the outer sanctum)
2. *Jagamohana*, (the sixteen-pillared hall)
3. The kitchen
4. *Snāna maṇḍapa* (the bathing platform)
5. The Golden Well
6. The burial ground
7, 8. Concentric walls

FIG. 2. Plan of the Jagannātha Temple.

The impressive character of the Jagannātha Temple – in T. E. Donaldson's words (1985: 403) "the most stupendous architectural undertaking during the early Gaṅgā period" – and the extraordinary execution of its sculptures contrast nevertheless (or so it seems) with the humble, unexpected nature of the four wooden images found within the sanctuary. Jagannātha, Balabhadra, Subhadrā and Sudarśana[1] were frequently described as "strange", "grotesque", "peculiar". They are "exceedingly ugly", remarked R. Mitra (1875, II: 123); they "do not bear the least resemblance to any deity of the Hindu pantheon," added M. M. Ganguly (1912: 405). The same idea was underlined by S. Kramrisch: "The image of Jagannatha, Lord of the World – in his temple of the twelfth century in Puri, an imposing structure built in the Great Tradition and of lavish sophistication – is a log of wood. Just that and nothing else" (1968: 72).

FIG. 3. Balabhadra, Subhadrā, Jagannātha.

[1] Subhadrā and Balabhadra are the sister and brother of Jagannātha. Sudarśana (the word generally designates the *cakra*, one of Viṣṇu's weapons) is here the wooden post to the left of Jagannātha.

Carved in *nīm* wood (*azadirachta indica*), the images are periodically renovated. Whilst stressing their particularity, T. A. Gopinatha Rao emphasised the enigmatic nature of the renewal rituals themselves, a "log being every time brought mysteriously from some unknown land" (1914, I, 1: 273). The same view reappears in later texts: the history of the temple "is shrouded in mystery" (Chatterji 1966: 70); the icons within the monument are "mysterious deities" (Mishra 1971: xi). "Generations after generations have tried to solve [Jagannātha's] mystery, but he looks as if sarcastically smiling at the vain efforts of the mortals" (Tripathi 1978c: 490).[2]

It is therefore hardly surprising that, for many authors (archaeologists, anthropologists, historians, and art historians), the origin of the cult should be sought outside Hinduism. By the middle of the nineteenth century, A. Cunningham sustained "the absolute *identity in form* of... Jagannatha... with the Buddhist monogram or symbol of Dharma" (1854: 359).[3] His theory, he believed, was confirmed by the "suspension of caste" occuring during the *ratha yatrā* (the annual festival of Puri). This, he further noted, is "so utterly repugnant to the deeply inwoven spirit of caste which pervades Brahmanism, that we may safely refer it to a Buddhist origin" (*ibid.*: 360). Mitra (1875) and Ganguly (1912) shared these views. In Gopinatha Rao's opinion, the Temple of Jagannātha might have "belonged to the Buddhists at one time," (1914, I, 1: 273), an idea expressed also by A. K. Coomaraswamy (1927: 115, note 1).

As just shown, the alleged particularity of the icons and the cult was related by Cunningham to sociological "singularities", such as the periodic suspension of caste distinctions. Also, more recently, stressing "total disregard of caste restrictions", S. K. Chatterji attributed

[2] More than a century later, Tripathi reproduces, in almost the same terms, Ganguly's statement about the "strangeness" of the images: "Nowhere else is [their] iconography... so strangely different from the traditional representation of these Deities described in the Vaiṣṇava Āgamas" (2004: 121).

[3] Buddhism was introduced in Orissa by Aśoka in 261 B.C.E.

this specificity to a kind of "protestant Hinduism" inspired by Buddhism (1966: 70). This idea, however, must be qualified. The prevalent norm up until independence prohibited Untouchables going into the temple, and it is by direct reference to purity and impurity (or to auspiciousness and inauspiciousness) that behavioural rules are defined among the ritualists themselves.

Without dismissing the Buddhist influence, some authors – for example W. W. Hunter 1872; A. W. Macdonald 1953; K. C. Mishra 1971 – believed that a major role had been played also by the tribal societies of Orissa.[4] But the syncretic nature attributed to the Jagannātha cult faded gradually and Buddhism was obliterated by the tribal perspective. In H. Zimmer's perception, the "primitive, doll-like, gaily colored figures of Jagannātha..., his brother Balarāma [Balabhadra], and their sister Subhadrā... remind one of the masks of the Red Indians and of the Eskimos of Alaska" (1955: 258-259). Kramrisch spoke in turn of "a temple-craft based on tribal tradition" (1968: 72). The earliest images of religious art in Orissa, Ch. L. Fabri wrote,

> are not those of Vedic deities or of Buddhist faith: they are popular village gods, spirits and nymphs of the Orissan jungle. And however powerful the priesthood becomes in later days, it may be emphasized here, the strong undercurrent of pre-Aryan faith is powerful in Orissa, probably much more powerful here than in many other parts of India (1974: 12).

A sudden change in aesthetic sensibility seems to have taken place: Jagannātha is no longer a "hideous caricature", to use Mitra's expression (1875, II: 123), or "an ill-shaped log of wood", in the words of Gopinatha Rao (1914, I, 1: 273). Its image becomes "an outstanding

---

[4] There is an extraordinary ethnographic diversity in Orissa: over sixty tribal societies (about a quarter of the State's population) coexist with the caste system. The situation varies considerably between regions, but a clear dividing line separates the strongly Hindu coastal area from the inland region. It is in the heart of the province that the tribal societies are currently settled, making up approximately 50% of the local population in certain districts.

example of a non-Aryan, aborigine divinity, carved with the barbarous beauty of primitive art" (Fabri 1974: 12). Yet, the old viewpoint remains: it is not through Hinduism that the origin of the cult can be explained.

The tribal thesis, however, evaded an essential fact. As V. Elwin had already seen, tribal communities did not generally ascribe anthropomorphic traits to their divinities: "In tribal India anthropomorphic images of the gods are rare... In Orissa, the Gadabas, Didayis, Parengas, Jhorias and Bondos do not make images of any of their gods, certainly not of any tribal hero or Creator" (1955: 178).

At first sight, the Saora (from the *muṇḍa* linguistic family) would be an exception: they "occasionally make rude little images of their deities" (*ibid.*)

The author's monograph on the Hill Saora of Orissa (of the Ganjam and Koraput districts) begins with a note of caution:

> The Saoras [of Orissa] are a fragment of a great tribe to which there are many, if confused, references in the ancient literature of India, and which today is widely distributed in groups of different traditions and manners.
>
> It is possible that the word Saora (Sabara, Savara), or something like it, was used in ancient times much as people in India today use the words "aboriginal", "Bhumijan" or "Adibasi", for it seems to have been synonymous with such names as Matanga, Kirata, Janangana, Pulinda and Bhilla, and can hardly have been employed in any ethnographic sense (*ibid.*: 1).

In spite of such judicious remarks – and notwithstanding the scantness of religious anthropomorphic representations, "rarely found in the Saora hills" (*ibid.*: 181) – Elwin himself engaged in unsound speculation: "The Jagannath images, in their curiously stunted form, look as if they might have come down from the Ganjam Hills" (*ibid.*: 29). He even alluded to a "curious parallel" between the Jagannātha figures and "the image of the maimed Kittung" (1951: 119, Fig. 129), one of the many "classes" of Saora gods. "This parallel", O. M. Starza rightly pointed out, "is not a particularly close one": the Kittung figure reproduced by Elwin is just "a burnt stump of wood which hardly resembles the image of Jagannatha" (1993: 65).

The Saora influence over Jagannātha has been largely accepted. Such a hazardous step was encouraged by a loose affinity between the words *Saora*[5] and *Śabara*, the latter being generally applied to the ancestors of the Daitās, Śūdra ritualists in the temple of Puri. This identification had devastating consequences. Mishra, for example, assumed unhesitatingly that "Nilamādhava, which, according to tradition, was worshipped by the Śabara chief Viśvāvasu, was ultimately transformed into Puruṣottama Jagannātha". And he concluded without further ado that Jagannātha-Nilamādhava had been "worshipped by Śabaras on the Mahendra Mountain" (1971: 24).

The Orissa Research Project (ORP) at the University of Heidelberg contributed to the same thesis in an unexpected way. Stating that "the Jagannātha cult is of tribal origin", A. Eschmann wrote:

> The legend of the Puri temple, the Indradyumna legend, narrates that the deity was originally worshipped by the aboriginal *Śabara* chief Viśvāvasu in the woods, and only later on miraculously appeared in Puri. Accordingly, the Jagannātha figures still display what seems to be a "tribal look" (1978b: 99).

But what might be the "tribal look" of a Hindu god in Orissa, if tribal deities are not, in this context, anthropomorphically represented? Eschmann was fully aware of the minor role of Saora images, which do not seem "to have been incorporated into a Hindu cult" (*ibid.*: 100). She also did not ignore the fact that in the meridional areas of Orissa, Saora temples sometimes only harbour a wooden post. The same happens with the Dravidian Khond (or Kond):

---

[5] As Elwin ironically observed, the word Saora, "has been spelt in almost as many different ways as the name Shakespeare. I have noted the following: Sabar, Sabara, Sahara, Sahra, Saonr, Saor, Saora, Saoura, Sar, Saur, Saura, Saurah, Savar, Savara, Savaralu, Savra, Sawara, Sayar, Sobor, Soeri, Soiri, Sora, Sor'a, So:ra, Soura, Sourah, Sowra, Sowrah, Suir, Swiri"... (1955: xx).

> A typical shrine of a Khond village... consists of an open mud house with thatched roof and an enclosure fenced by posts of *sāl* wood. Whereas within the enclosure there is always a stout post of *rohiṇī* wood..., the shrine may be completely empty as well as contain another post of *māhula* wood. At these shrines, once in a while buffaloes are sacrificed... At the time of such festivals, the priest (*dehuri*) worships the post... in a process which, sometimes, resembles the giving of the five *upacāras*, typical for the Hindu *pūjā* (1978 c: 267-268).[6]

In Eschmann's opinion, one of these posts – but not an anthropomorphical icon – could have been the origin of the current images:

> The peculiar shape of the Jagannātha figures is certainly a result of their tribal origin... not because such figures are typical of tribal religion, but because such figures are typical products of the process of Hinduization. At a certain stage, the original uniconical symbol is anthropomorphized in order to comply basically with the needs of Hindu image (1978b: 100).

The argument turns into a paradox: it was, basically, due to the demands of Hinduism that the figure ended up with a tribal look – or what seems to be a tribal look.

Unanimous as regards their initial presupposition (the tribal origin of the images), the ORP authors diverge on important issues. Eschmann's relative scepticism is not shared by Tripathi: "the peculiar iconography of the wooden images", he contends, betrays "its tribal origin and character even to a layman" (1978c: 477). H. von Stietencron,

[6] Eschmann suggested in particular that the wooden post renovation, carried out by the Khond, might be at the origin of the *naba kalebara*, the ritual renewal of the main images in the Puri temple. *Cf.* Stietencron (1978b: 66). The hypothesis was received with sceptcism by Starza: "Eschmann's description of Kond renewal rites is not based on direct observation" (1993: 114). Starza set the data obtained at second hand by Eschmann against B. Boal's direct ethnographic testimony. As it is also stressed by A. Hiltebeitel, the "documentation... gathered by the Orissa Research Project needs to be reexamined in its entirety from a detribalized perspective. The operating assumption of that collaborative effort turns on the notion of the 'Hinduization' of originally tribal rituals and ritual paraphernalia. But the result is really an unsuccessful scholarly tribalization of Hinduism" (1991: 99).

in turn, argues that the Śaivite figuration of Ekapāda Bhairava displays obvious analogies with the oldest known sculptural representations of Jagannātha, like those in the temple of Koṇārak (13th cent.): for example, the lower part of the image reduced to a simple pillar, a single leg, in the shape of an inverted cone (1978c: 120). The form of Ekapāda Bhairava would then explain that of Jagannātha:

FIG. 4. Ekapāda Bhairava: Mārkaṇḍeśvara Temple, Bhubaneshwar (8th century?).

One can therefore say that the Jagannātha image

- *seems to be* of tribal origin (according to Eschmann);
- *is clearly* of tribal origin (according to Tripathi);
- *can be* explained by Śaivite iconography (according to Stietencron).

The last of these propositions makes the second meaningless and justifies the hesitant nature of the first. It also raises doubts about the differences between the Jagannātha images and those worshipped in other Hindu temples (*cf.* Eschmann 1978b: 99).[7] Surprisingly, Stietencron's arguments did not disturb the initial thesis in the slightest. He believes that the hypothetical wooden post (worshipped by an unidentified tribal community) was the origin of Ekapāda Bhairava which, later on, determined the iconographic lines of the Puri gods. The tribal origin of the representation of Jagannātha is thus taken for granted, despite

1. the non-existence of analogous tribal images; and
2. the presence of (at least) one other Hindu image, acknowledged as identical.

II

The ancient state of Orissa was the result of the Somabaṃśī unification policy. The Utkala region was annexed by Yayāti I (922-955) to the small kingdom of Kośala (Sambalpur, Balāṅgīr, Kalāhāṇḍi) founded by Janmejaya (882-922). There is no consistent information about the period up until the coronation of Yayāti II (1025), but it seems that the territories under his control included Kaliṅga, Koṅgoda, Dakṣiṇa Kośala and Utkala. He also moved the kingdom's capital to

---

[7] The cult of Ekapāda Bhairava seems to have been particularly widespread between the 8th and 10th centuries (Panigrahi 1961: 82-84, 144-5; Williams 1984).

the Mahānadī Delta. The Somabaṃśī were ousted from the country by a branch of the Gaṅgā: Anantavarman Coḍagaṅga Deva (1078-1147) founded a new dynasty and built the great temple at Puri.

Painstakingly reconstructed on the basis of scanty epigraphic sources, the history of this period remains obscure. In order to fill the gaps, historians have often made use of the *Mādaḷā Pāñjī* (*MāP*), the "chronicle" of the Puri temple (in its different versions). Repeatedly recopied in the traditional palm leaf manuscripts, the text underwent significant changes.

For Panigrahi, the chronology of various passages in the *MāP* is "wholly untrustworthy": the parts of the narrative concerning Coḍagaṅga and his sucessors are just "a tangled mass of mythology, untruths, distortions and vilifications" (1981: 124). Paradoxically, many other pages in the same text seem credible to him. After all, "there is no reason to doubt a genuine tradition which preserves a historical truth though in a distorted form as all traditions do" (*ibid.*: 106). The historian now appears to be sceptical about his own scepticism: "there is no reason to doubt"...

The ORP researchers are equally complacent as regards the *MāP*. H. Kulke acknowledges its "general unreliability in a strict historiographical sense" (Kulke 1978b: 140). Yet, he asserts outright (following Panigrahi): "the legendary account of the temple chronicle about 'Yayāti Keśarī' remains of great importance for the study of the political aspect of the Jagannātha cult" (*ibid.*: 141). Panigrahi's phrase – "there is no reason to doubt" – corresponds to Kulke's: "it will be possible to utilise those portions of the legend for a historical study which can be verified through other historical sources" (*ibid.*: 140).

Panigrahi's "there is no reason to doubt", and the need to validate a text of dubious value "through other historical sources" come together in Stietencron:

> The... reliability [of the *MāP*] in matters of political history has rightly been questioned. But there is no need to reject its statements about the history of the god as long as they are corroborated by other independent sources (Stietencron 1978b: 64).

What are these "independent sources"? Like Panigrahi, Stietencron relies on the *MāP* to validate a passage about Yayāti Keśarī. According to the chronicle, this Sovereign – a mythical figure, to be sure – built an ancient temple of Jagannātha which, after falling into ruin, was replaced by the present monument. Stietencron accepts the historical verisimilitude of this account, which is corroborated by an episode in the foundation myth: King Indradyumna conquered Utkala and ordered the construction of the Puri temple, which was later to sink beneath the sands. From the author's viewpoint, the myth is the "independent source" fully confirming a "fact" registered by the *MāP*. Indradyumna thus becomes a synthesis of several historical Sovereigns – Yayāti I, Yayāti II and Coḍagaṅga (*ibid.*: 67):

1. Indradyumna masters the Mahānadī Delta and orders the building of the great temple of Jagannātha (Yayāti I);
2. He settles in the region with his subjects (Yayāti II); the temple falls into ruin. The image of the divinity disappears under the sand (the final period of the Soma dynasty);
3. A new temple is built (Coḍagaṅga Deva).

But a myth which mirrors itself in another myth is still a myth – by no means a historical source. Stietencron's reconstruction does not stand up to scrutiny.

The foundation myth describes the conquest of the present region of Puri (Puruṣottama kṣetra), the submission of the Śabara, and the disappearance of the sapphire they held in their power (an ancient representation of Viṣṇu, later replaced by wooden icons). All these episodes have been related to historical facts.

In Kulke's opinion, the heterodox nature of the cult and its images should be seen as a Hindu power strategy:

> To impose a "foreign" cult upon the population of the conquered area usually would be contrary to the political aim and against the Hindu tradition. The enlargement and elevation of an already existing autochthonous cult, on the other hand, glorified the new ruler and legitimized his power in the domain of the deity (1978b: 142).

A temporal nexus is thus introduced between the building of the temple (12th century), the "specificities" of the cult and the consolidation of Hindu power in the region. The Temple of Jagannātha, however, is only one among numerous examples of the impressive architectural tradition which had been flourishing in the Mahānadī Delta. Built in the late 6th century, the earlier monuments mark the emergence of a vital creative process and confirm a solid Hindu implantation from then on (Dehejia 1979: 173). Rightly again, Starza noted the tendency to see the history of Orissa

> in terms of contemporary European parallels, to see the area as one dominated by the rise of tribal chiefs to royal status. It is easy to forget that when the temple was built the region had been settled by Aryans since before the pre-Asokan period (1993: xi).

The myth of Indradyumna tells us that the Śabaras are the ancestors of the Daitās, a group of *sebakas* (functionaries or ritualists) at the Jagannātha Temple.[8] This hypothetical relationship, posited by the myth, reinforced again the historical argument.[9]

The Daitās are part of the *pāṇi açuā* (a group of Śūdra castes from whom Brahmins do not accept water) and, except for certain periods of the ritual cycle, they are forbidden to come into direct contact with

---

[8] The regular functioning of the temple requires the presence of a large number of *sebakas* (from *sebā*, "service"). Certain "services" (namely those of the Brahmins, who are the officiating priests, cooks etc.) derive from caste generic responsibilities; other "services" imply highly precise tasks: opening and closing the temple doors; guaranteeing the well-being and entertainment of the divinities – reciting passages of the *Purāṇas*; offering flowers, music and dances; lighting and extinguishing lamps at the appropriate times; preparing the beds at the end of the day; providing coconuts before sleep; wielding the ceremonial umbrellas; etc., etc.

[9] The Daitās have been seen as "priests of tribal origin" (Eschmann 1978c: 266), a vestige of a "purely tribal" cult (Tripathi 1978b: 264). Even today, the links between the tribal communities of Orissa and the Jagannātha cult are largely assumed. They are confirmed by "the continued practice of a special priesthood bestowed upon the *Daita*" (Nayak 2001: 28). For a different perspective, *cf.* Marglin: "The *daitās* of Puri have no actual connection with tribal peoples of Orissa except in [a] mythical sense" (1985b: 69).

the images. Nonetheless, they "represent" Jagannātha in various circumstances, being considered his blood relatives (*rakta samparka*). Every year, at the end of the hot season, "disease" strikes Jagannātha, who "dies" periodically (when his wooden icon is replaced). On both occasions, it falls to the Daitās – and to them alone – to provide appropriate care and to mourn the god's death publicly.

III

The singularity attributed to the Puri images and cult is linked to the conception of Jagannātha as a "tolerated" divinity in Hinduism – "accepted by the Brahmans" according to Fabri (1974: 12); "out of place in the pantheon of Hindu gods", for Tripathi (1978c: 488); an "intruding god" in Stietencron's terms (1978a: 27).

Jagannātha, Orissa's sovereign god (*raṣṭradevatā*), is however a manifestation of Kṛṣṇa, an *avatāra*, a "descent" of Viṣṇu. As Eschmann herself was compelled to acknowledge, he is worshipped in a "complex mode... which belongs to the highest level of Brahmanical Hinduism" (1978c: 266). The cult's foundation myth, as we shall see, is also an expression of Hindu conceptions, stemming from the oldest Vedic views on sacrifice. All the alleged local peculiarities must be reexamined in this context. The ritual prominence of the Daitās is neither a paradox nor a sociological scandal. It does not suggest the least conflict with the essence of Hinduism; on the contrary, it manifests that very essence.

The Indradyumna myth is a whole which needs to be seen on its own terms. The attempt to single out a particular version – trusted for its supposed earlier date or higher degree of coherence – reveals a view of myth that has long been suspect (Lévi-Strauss 1958; 1964; 1971; O'Flaherty 1973; 1988; Ramanujan 1999). Be that as it may, the criteria adopted to justify the primacy of one variant over all others can always be contested. Starza admits that "the oldest comprehensive account of Jagannatha... is found in the *Brahma Purāṇa*" (*BrP*), which was written, according to R. C. Hazra (1940: 153), between the middle of the 12th and the end of the 13th century. It is, however, the *Skanda Purāṇa* (*SkP*) version that Tripathi favours.[10] In his opinion, "it forms the basis of, or has at least strongly influenced, all the later versions" (2004: 8).

This last statement calls for discussion. The two versions included in the Oriya *Mahābhārata* (Sāraḷā Dāsa, 15th cent.) differ from one another on important points and both diverge significantly from the *SkP*'s version, privileged by Tripathi. It would be rash to assume that the former took the latter as a fundamental reference. We will see that, on the contrary, certain aspects of the Purāṇic versions are even clarified by the vernacular texts. The story of Indradyumna – like myth in general, according to Lévi-Strauss – is the "sum of its variants". Interpretation cannot therefore be linear. The overlapping narrative structure, probably inspired by the similar structure of the Vedic rituals, resists presentation as a rigorous progressive sequence: myth confronts us with subtly implicated movements, a metaphor for the transformation process inherent in the Indian model of the Universe.[11]

---

[10] Hazra believes that the *Puruṣottamakṣetra-māhātmya* of the *Skanda Purāṇa* "contains chapters which must be dated earlier than 1300 A. D." (1940: 165). But opinions diverge. "In this world of ever-shifting Purāṇic sands", W. Doniger writes, "the *Skanda Purāṇa* is surely the shiftiest, or perhaps the sandiest, of all.... Even the formidable Ludo Rocher despairs of dating this text" (1993 b: 59-60). In fact, Rocher does not reject the point of view of Binayak Misra: the *Puruṣottamakṣetra-māhātmya* "may have been incorporated in the Skanda[-Purāṇa] before the time of the supremacy of the Gaṅgas in Orissa, possibly in the eleventh century A. D." (Rocher 1986: 231); he also refers (without further remarks) to Gopinatha Mohapatra, who "concludes that the text was composed about A. D. 700" (*ibid.*).

[11] "The Hindu universe is a kind of four-dimensional Möbius strip, finite but unbounded, negatively curved (as our own universe is now said to be, according to some scientists)" (O'Flaherty 1984 a: 241).

* * *

A passage from the *Śatapatha Brāhmaṇa* (VI, 1, 1, 9-15; VI, 1, 2, 1-12) states that, having created the waters at the beginning of time, Prajāpati penetrated them and produced an egg, whose embryo was the fire (Agni) and whose shell was the earth; in the form of Agni, he penetrated the earth and produced an egg, whose embryo was the wind (Vāyu) and whose shell was the air; in the form of Vāyu, he penetrated the air and produced an egg, whose embryo was the Sun and whose shell was the sky; in the form of the Sun, he penetrated the sky and produced an egg, out of which the moon, the stars and the cardinal points were born:

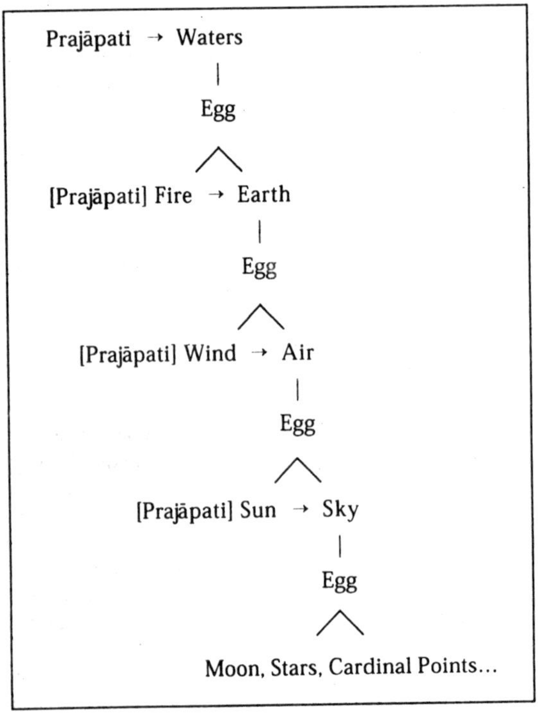

FIG. 5

Indian art, religion and philosophy offer us innumerable examples of objects which, unfolding in replicas of themselves, reproduce like the primordial egg of Prajāpati. There are temples whose façades obsessively repeat the model of their own architecture on a smaller scale; surfaces where the obverse and reverse – or spaces where the exterior and the interior – mirror each other and interweave; rituals which multiply indefinitely; narratives which frame (or are framed by) other narratives. Similarly, every moment in the transformation process is the replica of a preceding one. The exquisite web of the Jagannātha cult illustrates the same principles.

There is a striking resemblance between these intricate structures and David Bohm's holographic model of the Universe – an "implicate order" where "everything is enfolded in everything" (Bohm 1980: 177). Now, since the part reproduces the whole, the understanding of reality excludes any linear relation, or "point-to-point correspondence" between elements. From this perspective, the Indradyumna myth does not constitute a single narrative, but rather a plurality of narratives. It is a complex "hyper-narrative", comparable to a multidimensional board on which various games of chess take place simultaneously. By the same token, characters in the story may be appropriately described as "hyper-characters"– figures who reflect and imply the attributes of all those with whom they perform. "Hyper-narratives" and "hyper-characters", however, demand particular ways of telling which, in turn, presuppose particular ways of reading or listening.

CHAPTER TWO

A PROLOGUE ABOUT A PROLOGUE: TEXTUAL SELF-AWARENESS

How many *Rāmāyaṇas*? Three hundred? Three thousand? At the end of some *Rāmāyaṇas*, a question is sometimes asked: How many *Rāmāyaṇas* have there been? And there are stories that answer the question.

. . . .

Part of the aesthetic pleasure in the later poet's telling derives from its artistic use of its predecessor's work.... To some extent all later *Rāmāyaṇas* play on the knowledge of previous tellings: they are meta-*Rāmāyaṇas*.... In several of the later *Rāmāyaṇas*..., when Rāma is exiled, he does not want Sītā to go with him into the forest. Sītā argues with him. At first she uses the usual arguments: she is his wife, she should share his sufferings, exile herself in his exile, and so on. When he still resists the idea, she is furious. She bursts out, "Countless *Rāmāyaṇas* have been composed before this. Do you know of one where Sītā doesn't go with Rāma to the forest?"

A. K. Ramanujan

I

Nīlagiri, Nīlācala, Nīlādri - literally, the "Blue Mountain" - are some of the names by which the city of Puri is known. Although there is no mountain in the region, this is a sacred place with which a sacred mountain is associated as a symbol of the *nābhi*, the "navel" of the Universe. Nīlagiri, a replica of Meru, the fabulous Indian mountain above which shines the polestar, is thus conceived of as the *summit* and *center* of the world: here, as elsewhere, "elevation is centrality" (Butterworth 1970: 88-89).

According to local traditions, there was formerly a huge banyan tree (*nyagrodha, ficus indica*)[1] on the mountain peak. Therefore, both mountain and tree define the Cosmic Pillar,[2] the *axis mundi*, which simultaneously unites and separates heaven and earth:[3] they express the intimate connection that will be established later between the stone temple and the wooden image of Jagannātha.

Kramrisch showed that the Cosmic Mountain is the model of the Hindu temple:

> Meru, Mandara and Kailāsa are the first three names amongst the twenty types of temples described in the early texts, the 'B ṛhat Sa ṃhitā' and the 'Matsya Purāṇa'; all three are the names of the Mountain, which is the axis of the world; that is Meru, the pole of this earth; Mandara as churning rod, planted on Viṣṇu, the tortoise, during the Satya Yuga...; and Kailāsa, as seat of Śiva, in the Himālaya (1946: 161).

---

[1] The banyan tree, with its aerial prop roots hanging down and turning into new trunks, is a symbol of cyclicity and perpetual renovation.

[2] As Eliade has noted, "the symbolism of the World Tree is complementary to that of the Central Mountain. Sometimes the two symbols coincide; usually they complete each other. But both are merely more developed mythical formulations of the Cosmic Axis (World Pillar, etc.)" (1964: 269). See also Oguibénine 1973, Chapter IV.

[3] For a different perspective, *cf.* Stietencron 1978: 25.

This relationship is reflected in the temple's architectural features. The term *śikhara*, referring to the building's curvilinear superstructure, was first applied to the peak of a mountainous outcrop, and the "false storeys" distributed in stairs along the *śikhara* are called *bhūmi* (earth or soil), "as if to further reinforce this mountain symbolism" (Michell 1977: 69).

But the mountain is also the prototype of the god's image.[4] According to the myth of Indradyumna, it is a blue stone (*indranīla*), a metonymical expression for the Blue Mountain (*nīlagiri*, etc.), which initially represented the divinity:

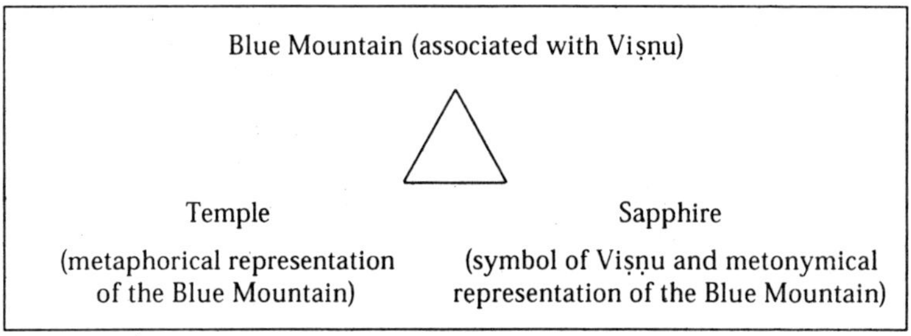

FIG. 6

The relation between the Blue Mountain and the blue stone (later replaced by wooden icons) thus foretells the isomorphism postulated by the architectural "treatises" between the apparent structure of the building and the image set in the sanctuary.

It is well known that the Hindu temple is an anthropomorphic replica of the Cosmic Man (Puruṣa,[5] Mahāpuruṣa), i.e. Viṣṇu (*puruṣottama*) in the Puri context. Some of its basic features – the columns supporting the tower, the tower itself, the cupola and several of its details –

[4] On the association between Viṣṇu and the Mountain, *cf.* Gonda 1954: 73-76.

[5] Puruṣa (the Universal Being, the Primeval Man), is one of the various designations of the Absolute.

are equivalent, in the terminology adopted in Orissa, to different parts of the body: *jaṅghā* (the "leg"); *gaṇḍi* (the "trunk"); *mastaka* (the "head"); *khapuri* (the "cranium"); *beki* (the "throat") (Bose 1932; Kramrisch 1946; Donaldson 1985; Dagens 2005). There is harmony between the exterior and interior configuration of the temple – its hidden plan, conceived of as a geometrical diagram, is a square divided into a variable number of smaller ones (9 x 9; 8 x 8...), each corresponding to a part of Puruṣa's body. Moreover, the form of the building prefigures the god's image in the *sanctum sanctorum*.[6]

Now, the isomorphic connection between the exterior and interior of the temple is not restricted to mountain symbolism. It applies also to the sacred tree. Let us start by remarking that

> The word *caitya* sometimes means no more than a sacred tree, or a tree with an altar; such are designated *caitya-vṛkṣas* in the Epics, and it is stated in the *Mahābhārata*... that such holy trees should not be injured inasmuch as they are the resorts of Devas, Yakṣas, Rākṣasas, etc. (Coomaraswamy 1928:18).

But *caitya* is a "sanctuary" in religious architectural terminology.[7]

Different versions of the myth of Indradyumna state that, in the past, a banyan tree protected Viṣṇu's sapphire under its branches. The long aerial roots of the *nyagrodha*[8] define an interior, almost closed

---

6 "The body, the temple, and the universe being... analogous, it follows that whatever worship is outwardly and visibly performed can also be celebrated inwardly and invisibly (Coomaraswamy, "An Indian Temple: The Kandarya Mahadeo" [1947], in Coomaraswamy 1977, I: 4). In the words of Kramrisch, "The wall of the Orissan temples is a three dimensional substance replete with an interknit movement based on small, repetitive units up and downwards, laterally, backwards and forwards, of solids and voids with their darkness.... The wall as an articulate integument bodied forth on the outside of the temples is a monumental equivalent to the modelling of the images. There, the gradation of planes holds the subtle body of divinity and makes it manifest. The temple also is the "body of God" (1947: 180-181).

7 *Cf.* Kramrisch 1946: 138.

8 "*Nyagrodha* means 'downward growing' not merely insofar as this is actually represented by the growth of aerial roots, but because the Tree itself is thought of as inverted" (Coomaraswamy, "The Inverted Tree" [1938], in Coomaraswamy 1977, I: 385).

space, over which they cast a protective shadow. The banyan sometimes evokes the *brahman* (the Absolute, cosmic energy), sometimes the *yūpa*[9] (the ancient sacrificial post), or even the "body of Viṣṇu". It thus appears simultaneously as the prefiguration of the temple and an evocation of the god:

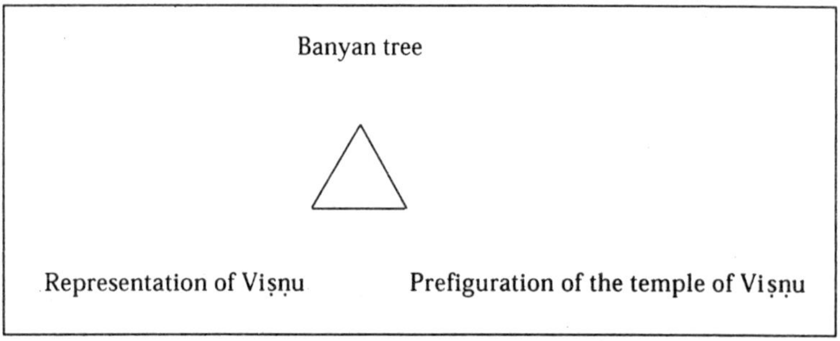

FIG. 7

Prominent elements of the mythical landscape, the mountain and the tree manifest the presence of the god, whose name also designates the city of Puri: Puruṣottama (the supreme Puruṣa) or Puruṣottama kṣetra (the "field" of Puruṣottama). They are permanent features of a universe ruled by perpetual expansion and retraction.

Cosmic time in Hinduism is thought of as a regular succession of four "aeons" (or *yugas*): *kṛta* (or *satya*), *tretā*, *dvāpara*, *kali*. The first lasts longer than the second, which lasts longer than the third, which lasts longer than the final one, and this gradual diminution corresponds to a progressive weakening of *dharma* (the cosmic order).

---

[9] Conceived of as a guarantee of cohesion, the *yūpa*, symbol of the *axis mundi*, was seen as a mediation between gods and men. Carved in wood, it depicted the Cosmic Tree (Gonda 1954: 81), just as, in the texts, the Cosmic Tree represented the *yūpa*.

Calculated in divine years (1 divine year = 360 human ones), each *yuga* is bordered by two "twilights" (*sandhyā*):

Cosmic period:	**Divine years:**
Kṛta yuga	400 (*sandhyā*) 4,000 400 (*sandhyā*)
Tretā yuga	300 (*sandhyā*) 3,000 300 (*sandhyā*)
Dvāpara yuga	200 (*sandhyā*) 2,000 200 (*sandhyā*)
Kali yuga	100 (*sandhyā*) 1,000 100 (*sandhyā*)
Total	12,000

FIG. 8

A cycle of 12,000 divine years is a "great *yuga*" (*mahā yuga*) and a thousand of these cycles is a *kalpa*, at the end of which a fire and a flood of immense proportions destroy the Universe. The Puruṣottama kṣetra survives nonetheless. This, at least, is what the *SkP* tells us, in a kind of 'prologue' to the myth of Indradyumna.

II

Prologue to the story of Indradyumna
(*SkP, II, Puruṣottama māhātmya,* 1-5)

A group of hermits gathered around a sage, Jaimini. They wanted to know who had created the Puruṣottama kṣetra and why Viṣṇu was worshiped there in the form of a wooden image. The answer took them back to the last recreation of the Universe:

> A lotus, Jaimini told them, grew out of Viṣṇu's navel and from its corolla sprang Brahmā who, once more, took up the task of creation. Exhausted, he cherished the hope that birth and death could be abolished once and for all: this would spare him the exorbitant labour of new demiurgical action. Viṣṇu explained to him that this aim would never be achieved whilst ignorance *(avidyā)* continues in the world. He, nevertheless, invited him to visit Puruṣottama, the only place in the Universe which resists, intact, the cyclical processes of emission and reabsorption.
>
> Brahmā set off. On arrival, he surprised Viṣṇu in the form in which he had seen him before leaving. Approaching the image of Mādhava (Viṣṇu) and diving into the Rohiṇī tank[10], a crow achieved freedom from cycles of rebirth. This, for the demiurge, established definitively the sacred nature of the place. Shortly afterwards, Yama arrived. He was concerned that he would no longer be able to perform his functions in Puruṣottama, as the god of death. Śrī-Lakṣmī (Viṣṇu's wife) guessed what was in his mind and, in Brahmā's presence, decided to tell the following story:
>
>> In former times, during a period between two *kalpas*, the Brahmin Mārkaṇḍeya was lost in the immensity of the waters of dissolution. Suddenly, he caught sight of the Puruṣottama kṣetra, where a banyan tree, similar to a sacrificial post, was emerging from the ocean. Viṣṇu, in the likeness of a child, lay on one of its branches: 'Come, Mārkaṇḍeya; take shelter in me and be free of your misfortune.' The Brahmin climbed up the trunk and, reach-

---

[10] *Rohiṇī kuṇḍa* is the name of a tank in the temple precinct, to the south of the *rekhā deula*.

ing the very top of the fig tree, slipped between the god's lips, who absorbed him. Within Viṣṇu, he discovered the entire Universe, the Earth with its oceans and continents, and each of the continents with its kingdoms, cities and sacred places. When he later left the interior of Viṣṇu, whose limits he could not fathom, he surprised him again in the form of a child lying on the same branch of the tree. All around, the waters of dissolution were rising. Mārkaṇḍeya was confused: how could reality reappear to him, wholly recreated, in the course of a *pralaya?* Viṣṇu explained that the Puruṣottama kṣetra is immune to the duality of life and death, to cosmic reabsorption and reemission. Knowing he was protected from the threats of Yama, the sage decided to remain at that place, and having propitiated Śiva (here expressly associated with Viṣṇu), he received from him triumph over death.

Śrī then announced that King Indradyumna would soon arrive at the Puruṣottama kṣetra, where he would order a thousand *aśvamedhas* (the horse sacrifice) to be performed: a single tree would divide in four parts from which the divine images would originate.

* * *

Jaimini adds that, after listening carefully to Śrī's words, Yama and Brahmā, feeling blissed, left Puruṣottama. He goes on to tell the hermits the following narrative:

Ignoring the study of the Veda and sacrificial practice, Puṇḍarīka and Aṃbarīṣa – a Brahmin and a Kṣatriya – had strayed from the path of duty. One day, they heard of the Puruṣottama kṣetra. Resolving to leave the unworthy existence they had led until then, they went to the city and entered the temple but, inexplicably, were unable to distinguish the image of Jagannātha. At the end of seven days' fasting and meditation, the god revealed himself. Dominated by the *māyā* of Viṣṇu, however, they imagined that what they had seen was no more than a dream. In contrast, they could now perceive the four wooden icons (Jagannātha, Balabhadra, Subhadrā and Sudarśana) with absolute clarity. They understood that, more than simple ephemeral representations, they were the God himself. Puṇḍarīka and Aṃbarīṣa decided to stay in that sacred place, where they eventually achieved liberation.

Who created the Puruṣottama kṣetra? Why is Viṣṇu worshipped at this place in the form of a wooden image?

The answer is in Indradyumna's story. Jaimini, however, did not think it appropriate to focus the hermits' attention immediately on the foundation myth: the very idea of a *direct answer* would have appeared foreign to the narrator's aims. On the contrary, what he started by offering them was a number of short narratives related to the myth of Indradyumna through a subtle, complex game of mirrors. They are not an "introduction" in the usual sense of the term; instead, they compose a geometrical figure, like a diagram or a *maṇḍala*.

The themes of "ignorance" (*avidyā*) and "illusion" (*māyā*)[11] run through the episodes we have just read. From Jaimini's opening words it follows that Viṣṇu, on the one hand, Brahmā and Yama on the other, do not coexist in the same plane of reality and do not represent the same level of consciousness. The first is here identified with the Supreme Being, to whom the demiurge himself owes his origin. He is the *brahman*, the inexhaustible source of the energy which pervades the Universe, the ultimate expression of reality. The last two[12] are the illustration of a fragmented world. Ready to abdicate from his demiurgic role, Brahmā would have been pleased if the Universe were to survive forever, in the form of his last creation. But Yama was not willing to suspend the exercise of his own authority... Victims of *māyā*,

---

[11] The term refers to the metamorphoses of apparent reality, to the incomprehensible effects of an act of magic or superior wisdom. It alludes to the false dualities engendered by a spirit immersed in ignorance as well as to the mysterious, divine proceedings which conceal the *brahman* (*cf.* Gonda 1965: Ch. VI).

[12] The opposition between Brahmā and Yama is the expression of manifest reality. As Kramrisch says, "Two is the number of the pairs of opposites. Two is the number of relation of the One to itself. Two is the number that unites while it separates. The Two has two stages, that of the Dual and that of the Two. The Dual carries into creation the dyadic potentiality of the monad. It is charged with the tension of the opposites. Two is the principle of the manifest cosmos which is patterned by the dialectic of the Two" (1962: 110).

Brahmā and Yama are still attached to the world of dichotomies and divergences:

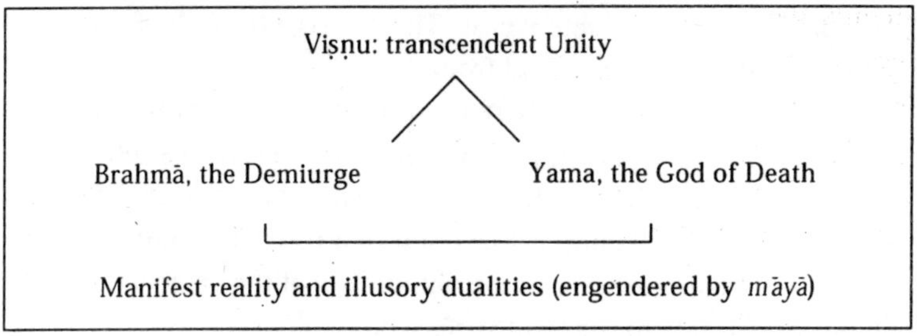

FIG. 9

The apparent discontinuity between these two planes is here emphasised by the subtleties of the narrative technique. Indeed, an unexpected turn diverts the listeners' attention from the main narrative to a sub-narrative (attributed to Śrī-Lakṣmī):

> The hermits' initial questions: "Who created the Puruṣottama kṣetra? Why is Viṣṇu worshiped there in the form of a wooden image?"

> **Main narrative:**
>
> > To answer the hermits' question, Jaimini tells a story whose action goes back to the last creation of the Universe. As a character of this story, Yama muses about the impossibility of fulfilling his duties.
>
> **Sub-narrative:**
>
> > To answer Yama's (implicit) question, Śrī tells him a story which goes back to a preceding creation of the Universe.

FIG. 10

Apparently unrelated questions act as a trigger for consecutive narratives, each presupposing a receding movement to an earlier period in the history of the world. Every movement backwards favours an enlargement of consciousness. The passage from the first to the second level of discourse (and from the second to a third...) does not reduce the angle of vision; there is no sub-perspective implied in the sub-story (just as a sub-sub-story would not require a sub-sub-perspective). In the following figure, representing a structure of nested stories, level III does not correspond to a restricted point of view; rather, it symbolises the *maximum* withdrawal of the observer: a higher plane comparable to the total surface of a hologram.

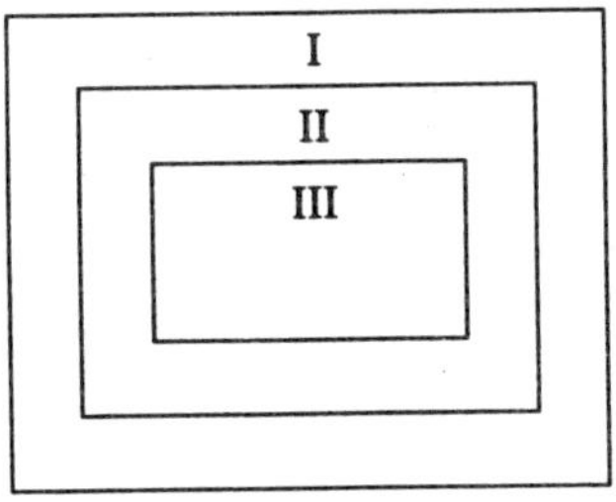

FIG. 11

The narrator's replacement (from the first to the second level of discourse) is therefore particularly significant. *Consubstantial* with Viṣṇu, Śrī (for whom Jaimini makes way) is herself an expression of transcendent unity. Brahmā and Yama (in the first level) appear enmeshed in a superficial vision, and it falls to the goddess (in the second level) to reveal the illusive nature of their conception of reality.

* * *

The relationship between an outer frame-narrative and an inner narrative may be highly complex. In certain examples, as Ramanujan pointed out, "not only does the outer frame-story motivate the inner sub-story; the inner story illuminates the outer as well. It often acts as a microcosmic replica for the whole text" (1999: 42).

But the nested narratives are inextricable strands of a single thread, indissociable features of the hyper-narrative. The two embedded stories of Jaimini's prologue belong to the same spatial framework (the city of Puri) and, as we have seen, the protagonists of the first become the listeners to the second.

On arriving at the Puruṣottama kṣetra (first level), Brahmā again meets the Supreme Being, whose form had not changed. The episode reflects a motif involving Mārkaṇḍeya (second level): as he leaves the "interior" of Viṣṇu's body, where he had wandered endlessly, the Brahmin surprises him, immobile and impassive, as if frozen in the same position for thousands of years (an expression of the absence of both time and space in Viṣṇu's realm).

Outer frame-narrative and inner narrative thus compose a system of communicating vessels: Mārkaṇḍeya's awareness reacts on the awareness of Brahmā and Yama – Śrī's aim, after all. This is the surplus of information provided by the sub-narrative. In fact, it is not enough to highlight the replacement of the narrator. The passage from one narrative to another also implies a significant change as regards the experience of the protagonist. In the first case, Brahmā is eager for a permanent Universe – indeed, an eagerness for release – and that motivates his journey to the top of the Blue Mountain. Guided by the Supreme Being, the ascendant trajectory is, undoubtedly, the search for a plane of reality to which the demiurge seems to aspire. However, in the second narrative, Mārkaṇḍeya is invited to go beyond the limit attained by Brahmā. Having reached the peak of Nīlagiri, he will continue his ascending route and, still guided by the Supreme Being, will rise to the top of the Cosmic Tree. Accordingly, this last ascent leads to a still higher form of comprehension. "Outside" and "inside" Viṣṇu's body, the puzzled Brahmin witnesses the "destruction" and "recreation" of reality. He wonders about the coherence of his own perception, finally realising the illusive character of duality.

Mārkaṇḍeya is a Bhārgava, a descendant of Bhṛgu, a Vedic sage. The Bhārgava are a group of seers who played an important, if "ambiguous" role in Vedic and post-Vedic literature. R. Goldman pointed out that their mythology "is to an extraordinary degree concerned with the themes of death and resurrection" (1977: 92). The idea is clearly expressed in stories about a second birth, in which "a figure is swallowed and then disgorged".

But there is more at stake here. Referring to one of the oldest versions of Mārkaṇḍeya's odyssey (*Matsya Purāṇa*, 167-168), Zimmer (1946: 39) observed that it can be seen as "a kind of commentary on the idea of Māyā, the problem of 'What is real?' as conceived by the Hindu". As O'Flaherty wrote, the sage seems to oscillate

> back and forth between the two worlds until he ends up seeing the double image of both at once. The two images merge for him when he realizes that he and Viṣṇu are one and the same, the soul and God (1984a: 112).

The same observations apply to the *SkP* version. Mārkaṇḍeya, the good disciple, understands that the oneness of the Supreme Being is hidden behind his "diverse" manifestations and concludes that the distinction between Śiva and Viṣṇu is also illusory.[13] Śrī-Lakṣmī thus makes use of a parable about false dualities, in order to transcend those inherent in the perspectives of Brahmā and Yama. Encouraging them to go beyond the level of reality in which they feel opposed, she inverts the process which had led from the undifferentiated whole to multiple and deceptive reality:

---

[13] The *BrP* version of the story also emphasises the sage's decision to remain in Puruṣottama kṣetra to teach men the absolute identity of Śiva and Viṣṇu.

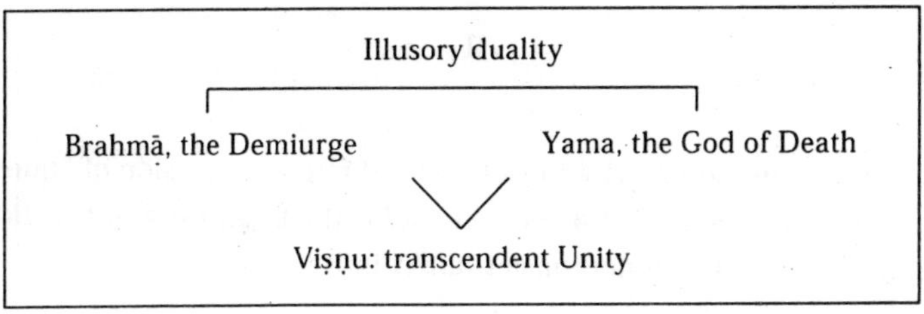

FIG. 12

Mārkaṇḍeya, the protagonist of the second discursive level, illustrates and resolves a form of tension analogous to that which, in the first, had set Brahmā and Yama in opposition:

1st Level of discourse: Brahmā is happy and Yama concerned to discover that the Puruṣottama kṣetra is a shelter from cyclical destruction and recreation.

> **2nd Level of discourse:** Mārkaṇḍeya is led to conclude that "creation" and "destruction" are illusory appearances.

1st Level of discourse: Having heard Mārkaṇḍeya's story, Brahmā and Yama leave the Puruṣottama kṣetra in a state of perfect happiness.

FIG. 13

The first story is a blurred "copy" of the second, just as any fragment of a hologram is an impoverished version of the global image.[14]

---

[14] As Bohm remarks, "if you use only a part of the holograph, you'll still get an image of the whole object, but you'll get a less detailed image, and you'll see it from a more limited set of angles. The more of the holograph you use, the more of the object you can see, and the more accurately you can see it (1985: 10).

III

The text just summarised resolves itself into a succession of "questions" and "answers". Let us now consider the beginning of the *BrP* version in which Brahmā replaces Jaimini:[15]

Beginning of the story of Indradyumna
(*BrP, II, Puruṣottama māhātmya,* 41-43)

A group of Brahmins surrounded Brahmā, so as to hear him tell the story of how the Jagannātha cult was founded:

> Seeking liberation, Indradyumna, king of Malwa during the *kṛta yuga*, set off for the Puruṣottama kṣetra, accompanied by his priests and a powerful army. On catching sight of the ocean, however, the Sovereign decided to break his journey.

[Here, the Brahmins interrupted Brahmā: 'Was there already, at that time, any image of Viṣṇu in the Puruṣottama kṣetra?' The demiurge's answer presents itself as a second narrative:]

> One day, Śrī-Lakṣmī asked Viṣṇu: 'How can men achieve liberation in a world dominated by illusion?'
>
> [Viṣṇu's answer mentioned the existence of the Puruṣottama kṣetra, a place where liberation is within reach of all beings. He referred to the events which took place at the end of the previous *kalpa*:]
>
>> After the recreation of the Universe, Viṣṇu addresses Brahmā. He describes the Puruṣottama kṣetra, which continuously resists the processes of cosmic reabsorption and reemission. Such circumstances, however, concerned Yama. Seeing that his powers were summarily revoked in that place, the god of death asked Viṣṇu to hide the sapphire in the sands – a request that was immediately satisfied.
>
> [Brahmā carries on with the story of Indradyumna, interrupted by the Brahmins.]

---

[15] The *Nārada Purāṇa* (*Uttarabhāga*, 52-61) has a very similar version to that of the *BrP*.

Organised in the form of cascading questions and answers, the narration reveals a technique similar to that of the *SkP* prologue. To the Brahmins' initial question – *Was there already, at the time of Indradyumna's arrival, any image of Viṣṇu in the Puruṣottama kṣetra?* – the demiurge "responds" with the answer Viṣṇu gave to a question from Śrī – *By what means can men achieve definitive liberation?* Śrī's question seems to have nothing in common with that of the Brahmins. But this set of questions and answers leads to retrogression – as far back as a previous creation of the Universe, a point in time and space that encloses within itself the key to all the enigmas:

> Brahmā starts telling a group of Brahmins the story of Indradyumna. The Brahmins interrupt him to ask a question to which the demiurge "responds" with an answer Viṣṇu gave to a question from Śrī...
>
> > Śrī's question: "How can men free themselves from their illusions?"
> >
> > Viṣṇu's answer: "In the Puruṣottama kṣetra liberation is within the reach of all beings."
> >
> > Śrī's question evokes the one asked by Brahmā, after the last recreation:
> >
> > > Brahmā's question: "What is the nature of the Puruṣottama kṣetra?"
> > >
> > > Viṣṇu declares that the place is immune to cyclical destruction. The answer prompts Yama's question: "How shall I carry out my functions there as the god of death?"
> > >
> > > Yama wants Viṣṇu to hide the sapphire and the Supreme Being satisfies his request.
>
> ... Brahmā returns to Indradyumna's story, at the point where he had been interrupted.

FIG. 14

The Brahmins' curiosity is only satisfied at the end. However, the answer to their question (*yes-no*, in a way) could have been given at the very beginning: *there was an image* of Viṣṇu in the region – the sapphire, *hidden in the sand*.

In Hazra's opinion,

> The story that there had been at Puruṣottama an image of Viṣṇu made of sapphire and that it had been buried in golden sand by the god himself, before Indradyumna went to the place, is most probably fabricated to give the place an air of greater sanctity and antiquity (1940: 153).

But the episode at issue does not seem to be a mere addition to the core of the narrative. As we will see, it plays a key role in the story. It is not by chance that Brahmā is interrupted exactly when he is referring to... the interruption of Indradyumna's journey: the pause in the action corresponds to the pause in the narrative flow, as if the cadence of the narrator is bound up with the rhythm of the narrated events. As did the *SkP*, the *BrP* postulates the isomorphism between the "exterior" and "interior" (or between the "form" and "content") of the narrative.

The same device can be illustrated in yet another way. Asked at the moment when Brahmā alludes to the interruption of Indradyumna's journey, *on the sandy shores* of the Orissan coast, the Brahmins' question already implies, so to speak, Viṣṇu's answer: it was *beneath the sand* – inside the Blue Mountain – that the god hid the sapphire.

"Exterior" and "interior", "form" and "content" thus coincide. Hence, the Brahmins' initial question (in the first narrative) can be translated in terms of a question asked by Śrī-Lakṣmī (the pretext of a sub-narrative), which, in turn, can be translated in terms of the question which Brahmā himself had already posed (the object of a sub-sub-narrative). Not surprisingly, the demiurge alternately appears "outside" and "inside" the story, first as narrator, and then as a character in events whose narration he attributes to Viṣṇu.

It would be absurd to impute any kind of formalist obsession to the authors of these narratives. The technique they use simply shows that they were fully aware of how the *mode* of narrating is inseparable from the *object* of the narration: the fallacy of the opposition between "form" and "content" is no more than an example of the fallacy of dualities in general, a fundamental theme in the myth of Indradyumna.

This is also why, in the "prologue" to the *SkP*, the *inserted narrative* (about Mārkaṇḍeya) is related to the *inserted phase* which is the *pralaya*. The congruence of space and time is here added to the conformity between "form" and "content": the protagonist, whom we have seen move from "outside" to "inside" and from "inside" to "outside" Viṣṇu's body, even moves from "inside" to "outside" and from "outside" to "inside" the great cosmic periods.

The same regular movement – the flow in which all distinctions vanish – ultimately commands the succession of questions and answers. From the questions of the hermits – *Who created the Puruṣottama kṣetra? Why is Viṣṇu worshipped here in the form of a wooden image?* – to Yama's question – *How shall I carry out my functions as the god of death in a place where all beings have been promised an eternal existence?* – and from this to Mārkaṇḍeya's – *How to understand that reality appears, wholly recreated, during a phase of dissolution?* – attention is attracted to the same horizon. However different they might seem to an unprepared listener (or reader), the successively formulated questions call for a single answer, which subsumes and transcends them: the same subtle reality, the same secret unity underlies apparent dualities – stone and wood, eternity and death, creation and destruction.

Viṣṇu's words – an emanation of the Absolute where contingent perspectives are diluted – contain the answer to all questions. They transform not only Mārkaṇḍeya's consciousness (in the second narrative) but also Yama's (in the first) and that of the hermits (outside the discursive space of the embedded stories).

In fact, there is no real discontinuity between the "exterior" and the "interior" of the narrative planes: the question the hermits ask Jaimini is equivalent to the one asked in the stories they are told – and so are the answers they obtain.

What, after all, is a "question" (and what is an "answer") in this context? As we have seen, "questions" and "answers" form a coherent succession, and it is that succession – the movement suggested and the point aimed at – which we need to consider. "Questions" are imprisoned in the oppositions that bring them up ("stone" and "wood", "life" and "death", "creation" and "destruction"). But, as reflections of a clouded consciousness, they are no more than pretexts for transposition onto a higher plane. We can now see why the "answer" never matches exactly the terms in which the "question" is asked: their intricate relationship traces the ascendant trajectory for which the Absolute – the *brahman* – is the horizon. In the chain thus constructed, each answer is destined to turn into a new question; the process implies a movement towards an inaccessible, "ultimate" plane – the answer of the Supreme Being.

CHAPTER THREE

THE STRUCTURE OF THE MYTH, THE STRUCTURE OF THE TEMPLE

The Supreme Identity is neither merely silent nor merely vocal, but literally a no-what that is at the same time indefinable and partially defined, an unspoken and a spoken Word.

A. K. Coomaraswamy

I

Let us resume the myth of Mārkaṇḍeya. The version from the *SkP*, summarized in the previous chapter, is similar to those found in the *Mahābhārata* (*Mbh*) and the *Matsya Purāṇa* (*MP*). But the narrator, the listeners and the spatial coordinates of the story have changed. In the *SkP* Mārkaṇḍeya is tightly bound to the Puruṣottama kṣetra, a place which both the *Mbh* and the *MP* seem to ignore. Inscribed now within Jaimini's account, the narrative is mainly addressed to Yama. This new scenario largely recreates the text, giving it an immense allusive power. Śrī's story concludes with the following:

> Mārkaṇḍeya decides to remain in the Puruṣottama kṣetra, where
> 1. he feels safe from Yama's threats, and where,
> 2. propitiating Śiva, he attains victory over death.

These statements are remarkable in more than one way. Yama listens to a story in which he himself appears as a character – albeit in a trifling role, his powerlessness being again underscored. Moreover, Śiva is here introduced to bestow on Mārkaṇḍeya a definitive triumph over death (and, of course, over Yama). The fact is totally unexpected – and rather "inconsistent" – since, as we (and Mārkaṇḍeya) already knew, Puri is beyond "life" and "death". This is probably one of the "scars", as Witzel puts it, from the insertion of one story within the frame of another,[1] or a vestige of implicit associations between related

[1] According to Witzel, the origin of the "frame story" should be sought in the "constant competition" between Vedic ritual specialists, always in search of "new, more 'ingenious', or simply baffling explanations" for some of their own procedures (1987: 406). In order to do so, Witzel further remarks, the "Br¯ahmaṇa authors... take whatever mythical, pseudo-historical matter they have at hand. They do not tell stories for the sake of story-telling, *l'art pour l'art*, but they arrange their stories according to their (ritual) purpose, adding whatever they think necessary" (*ibid.*: 410). Such arrangements left sometimes visible "scars".

narratives. For the new elements added to the earlier versions evoke a well-known episode in Mārkaṇḍeya's youth:

Mārkaṇḍeya: from premature death to eternity (Gopinaha Rao II, 1: 156-158)

Mārkaṇḍeya had been predestined to an ephemeral existence. On becoming sixteen years old – and having heard that his life was coming to an end – he entered a temple to worship the Śiva-*liṅga*. His meditation was interrupted by the god of death. The outraged Śiva punished Yama by kicking him violently. As for Mārkaṇḍeya, he was given eternal youth...

Avoiding any direct reference to these events, Śrī's words do however suggest that Yama's present claims are a replica of those which, in the past, had exposed him to the wrath of Śiva:

[1st level of discourse:] Yama ackowledges the impossibility of carrying out his functions as the god of death at the Puruṣottama kṣetra...

> **[2nd level of discourse:]**... and hears the story of Mārkaṇḍeya...
>
> > **[3rd level of discourse:]**... which evokes an earlier story: long ago, Mārkaṇḍeya himself sought refuge within a temple, a place set beyond the duality of "life" and "death," where Yama's functions could not be carried out.
>
> ...who, during a *pralaya*, seeks refuge at Puruṣottama kṣetra. In this place, set beyond the duality of "life" and "death", he feels protected from the threats of Yama.

... and eventually leaves the place, in the company of Brahmā.

FIG. 15

An implicit third narrative thus insinuates itself into the second. Surprisingly, it plays a decisive role: this untold sub-sub-story is the true kernel of the hyper-narrative:

> [2nd **narrative:**] During a *pralaya*, Mārkaṇḍeya finds a safe haven from the threats of Yama at the Puruṣottama kṣetra (beside Viṣṇu)...

... just as...

> [3rd **narrative:**]... in the past, he had found (in a temple dedicated to Śiva) effective protection against the god of death.

FIG. 16

The events concerning the 16-year-old Brahmin (3rd narrative) clearly prefigure the sage's later action (2nd narrative). But the untold sub-sub-story is also an obvious "model" for the first narrative:

> [1st **narrative:**] Yama intends to carry out his duties as god of death at the Puruṣottama kṣetra...

... just as...

> [3rd **narrative:**]... he had formerly intended to do with Mārkaṇḍeya when he was meditating inside a temple.

FIG. 17

Yama (a character in the first narrative) and Mārkaṇḍeya (the protagonist of the second) come together in the sub-sub-narrative, an indispensable tool for the interpretation of the whole: the first story is "explained" by the second just as the link between the first and second is "explained" by the third... The sub-sub-story is, in itself, a perfect illustration of the holographic relationship between the part and the whole. Let us look at it more attentively.

Entering the temple (at the close of the lifespan initially granted to him) and leaving it (to enjoy thereafter an eternal life), Mārkaṇḍeya seems to "die" and be "reborn". The idea is inherent in the temple's symbolism, whose sanctuary is appropriately called *garbhagṛha*, "home of the embryo" or "of the uterus".

It could be tempting to say that the experience within the sanctum introduces a sharp divide between past and future. But the sanctuary, the inviolable place where Yama's actions are suspended, transcends time and space.[2] The initial part of Mārkaṇḍeya's existence – the 16 youthful years – is already an expression of the whole.

The number 16 appears, from the earliest times, as an expression of totality. The *Śatapatha Brāhmaṇa* (*ŚB*) states, for example, that "Prajāpati is composed of 16 parts," and, "since... Prajāpati is... the Totality..., the number sixteen is characteristic of the Totality" (Gonda 1965: 121). Hence, we cannot oppose the period before and the period after Mārkaṇḍeya's entrance into the temple (as it is inappropriate to oppose "death" to "rebirth," or "destruction" to "recreation").

* * *

In Vedic times, an important role had been accorded to silence – which "belongs to Prajāpati", the ineffable Supreme Being.[3] It is there-

[2] *Cf.* Kramrisch 1946: 163; O'Flaherty 1976: 232; Shulman 1980: 23.

[3] Certain Vedic rituals were performed in silence, "for what is silent is undetermined, and the undetermined is everything" (*ŚB* VII, 2, 2, 14); or "what is silent is undefined, and the undefined is everything" (*ŚB* VII, 2, 3, 3) (Eggeling,

fore highly significant that the "nuclear narrative" – interior, central and unuttered – refers to events unfolding in a secret place, the *garbhagṛha*. Unnoticed – or merely suspected – by most readers or listeners, the untold sub-sub-story does prefigure the transition from "outside" to "inside" and from "inside" to "outside" Viṣṇu's body (or the Blue Mountain) – which, like a temple, takes in and protects Mārkaṇḍeya.

We are thus entitled to assume a symbolic correspondence between different expressions of pure innerness: the most secret part of the temple (the sanctuary where the young Brahmin had become immune to the threats of destructive time), and the interior of Viṣṇu's body, or the heart of the Blue Mountain, places where the old sage would later shelter during a *pralaya*:

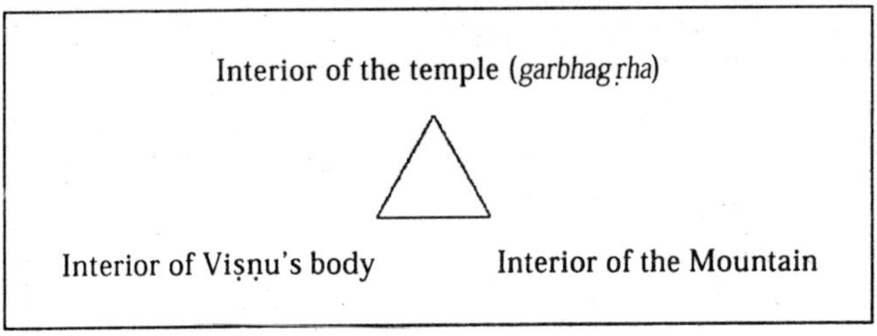

FIG. 18. Expressions of the Void (innerness, darkness and silence)

To these *spatial* manifestations of the void correspond a *temporal* expression of vacuousness. Due to the cyclical structure of cosmic periods, the "dissolution" marks the moment in which the "last" *yuga* precedes the "first". Subverting the cosmic flux, as it were, the *pralaya* is beyond space and time:

III); "Prajāpati is both declared (*niruktaḥ*) and undeclared, bounded (*parimitaḥ*) and unbounded" (Coomaraswamy, "The Vedic Doctrine of 'Silence'" [1937], in Coomaraswamy 1977, II: 200). See also Renou 1978: 71-72.

Kali yuga (the shortest of the cosmic cycles)

Pralaya: temporal and spatial emptiness

Kṛta yuga (the longest of the cosmic cycles)

FIG. 19

In other words, the emptiness of the *garbhagṛha*[4] where Mārkaṇḍeya's 16 years merged into eternity, reflects the *pralaya*, when both the shortest and the longest cosmic cycles were annihilated. Briefly, there is a striking identity between the mystical experiences of the devotee – inside the temple (i.e. inside the god, or the Blue Mountain) and during the "dissolution" of the Universe.

II

Puri (also called Śaṅkhakṣetra) is commonly conceived as a conch-shell (*śaṅkha*), one of Viṣṇu's emblems. A beautiful illustration of this conception, found in the main *jagamohana* of the Jagannātha Temple, has been reproduced by Starza (1993, plate 40). The conch-shell is here the outer frame of seven concentric figures composing a *yantra* (a geometrical device often used for meditation).[5] According to the Viṣṇurahasya of the *BrP*, the middle of these seven enclosures is occupied by the Blue Mountain's cave, "an abode... full of conscious-

[4] The *garbhagṛha* is a "secluded spot", totally "independent of time and place" (Kramrisch 1946: 163).

[5] *Cf.* Zimmer 1946.

ness" (quoted by Starza, *ibid.*: 9); Viṣṇu himself, the center of the *yantra*, is the *praṇava*, the sacred syllable Om (*ibid*).[6]

At the heart of Puri's symbolic topography – the centre of the spiral formation of the conch-shell – lies the Jagannātha Temple. Now, a temple plan is itself a *yantra*, "an artifice in which the ground (bhūmi) is converted into the extent of the manifested universe" (Kramrisch 1946: 12). Finally, the god's image inside the holy of holies is again the outcome of a sacred geometry – a new *yantra*. The god's image inside the temple and the temple inside the Puri's conch-shell compose therefore a *yantra* within a *yantra* within a *yantra*...

Invariably, the *garbhagṛha*, the innermost part of a Hindu temple, is a small, gloomy space with barren walls. It contrasts with the profusely decorated areas outside:

> The outer periphery, which represents *saṃsāra*, is rich in detail; from it the worshiper passes through a series of courtyards, which diminish in both size and detail, until finally he enters the inner sanctum or "womb-house" (*garbha-gṛha*), which may be empty or may contain a small aniconic image, symbolic of *mokṣa*. And although one has moved from a large physical space to a small physical space, the feeling is that one has been moving outward all the time, spiritually, into larger and larger spaces, until one encounters, in the still center, the stark symbol of the totality of the universe (O'Flaherty 1984a: 242).

A similar experience can be found in the mental trajectory of the reader (or listener) through the nested structures of Jaimini's "prologue". Abandoning peripheral narratives, consciousness is "enlightened" by the "nuclear narrative", whose eloquent silence calls to mind the sanctuary's superluminous darkness, in Kramrisch words.[7]

---

[6] *Cf.* also Mishra (1971: plate 56).

[7] In the same way, the succession of questions and answers (an ascendant trajectory of consciousness) seems to reproduce the temple's exterior design, the receding tiers (*bhūmi*) symbolising "the spiritual ascent of the devotee" (Kramrisch 1946: 184).

The passage from the "exterior" to the "interior" and from the "interior" to the "exterior" of a temple (the god's body) is tantamount to the transition from an outer-frame story to an inserted story (and vice-versa).[8] It is therefore clear that the nested structure at the beginning of the *SkP* version is, to some extent, a replica of the nested spaces in the Hindu temple. The kernel of the hyper-narrative corresponds symbolically to the central, reserved space of a *garbhagṛha*:

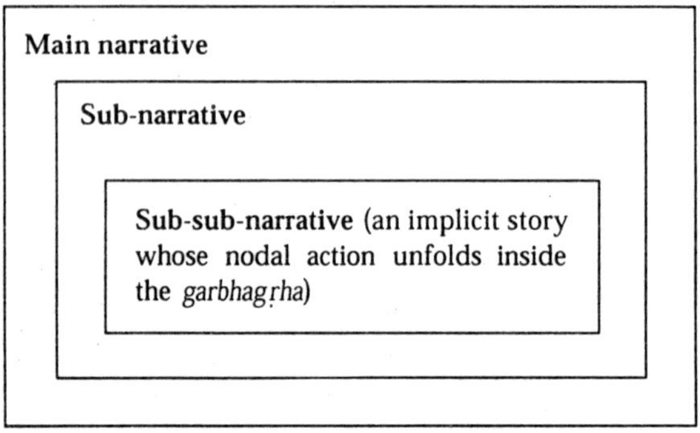

FIG. 20. The hyper-narrative structure

Not surprisingly, the last narrative of Jaimini's "prologue" – the story of Puṇḍarīka and Ambarīṣa – leads to the sanctum of the Jagannātha temple, focusing the reader's attention on the point where all things converge. Clouded by the darkness of ignorance, the Brahmin and the Kṣatriya are unable to see the wooden images lined up in the sanctuary; but thanks to meditation and abstinence, they suddenly catch a clear view of God. Is this a dream, an effect of Viṣṇu's *māyā*? Opening their eyes as if just awakening, they recognise the

[8] As Hiltebeitel expresses it, Mārkaṇḍeya illustrates "the epic's new type of bhakti Ṛṣi who ranges even beyond the Vedic Ṛṣis in traversing divine and earthly worlds, and, more than this, in moving in and out of the artifices of the text" (2001: 45).

Supreme Being in the wooden icons. Like Mārkaṇḍeya (at the beginning of his stay at the Puruṣottama kṣetra), Puṇḍarīka and Aṃbarīṣa had assumed a difference between dreaming and being awake; like him, they eventually understand that the oneness of God is contained in the apparent multiplicity of his manifestations. This short parable is, in fact, a synthesis of the whole prologue and, of course, a synthesis of Indradyumna's myth.

The inserted narratives in the *SkP* "prologue" compose a concentric configuration, a linguistic equivalent to the higher concentric structure formed by the god within the temple and the temple within the city... Organising itself – as, indeed, it does – in the most cryptic way, the "prologue" mirrors the myth, mainly concerned, as we shall see, with the hidden presence of God. As Puṇḍarīka and Aṃbarīṣa understand – and the readers are invited to grasp – Viṣṇu simultaneously conceals and reveals himself. The "prologue" is a riddle about the ultimate riddle – the inner essence of the Supreme Being.

III

In the Purāṇic literature, as in the epics according to Hiltebeitel, "nothing ever really begins... or ends. 'Vortex times' follow one upon another" (2001: 38). A similar perspective was inherent to the Vedic cosmogony, where we are faced with an "accumulation of false starts", as Malamoud puts it:

> Creating the world through a sacrifice presupposes the previous existence of a sacrificer, of offerings, of a sacrificial model, of the words to announce it. The Vedic poets make this prehistory of the genesis the theme of repeated questioning, formulated so that the answer would impose itself: the creators themselves are created beings; the ultimate origin is a mystery which escapes us, disguised by the performance of secondary creations (1990: 188, *author's translation*).

Sir John Woodroffe once rightly observed that "the English word 'creation' does not truly express" Indian conceptions (1922: 2). In the words of Kramrisch, "creation" is an ambiguous event, "an act of violence that infringes upon the Uncreated, the undifferentiated wholeness that is before the beginning of things" (Kramrisch 1988: 3-4). As a matter of fact, the Puruṣa "created"... through "destruction": he sacrificed himself. From his dismembered body – according to the *Puruṣa sūkta* (*RV* X, 90) –, the other gods were born, as well as the stars and points of the compass, the strophes and melodies. Brahmins sprang from his mouth, Kṣatriyas from his arms, Vaiśyas from his thighs, and Śūdras from his feet.

The demiurgic act of Prajāpati – the "Lord of Creatures", identified with the Puruṣa by the *ŚB* – is an unfinished process. Drained of energy after self-immolation, Prajāpati addresses Agni in particular and the gods in general, asking them to rebuild the unity of his body (*ŚB* VI, 1, 2, 13). To do so, the gods put their oblations (*iṣṭa*) in the fire which bakes and turns them into bricks (*iṣṭakā*) (*ŚB* VI, 1, 2, 22). With the bricks, they pile up a "fire altar" (*agni*) representing the restored body of the Supreme Being. In other words, the creator is recreated by his own creatures, a manifestation of reversibility promptly underlined by the text:

> Now that father [Prajāpati] is (also) the son: inasmuch as he created Agni, thereby he is Agni's father; and inasmuch as Agni restored him, thereby Agni is his [Prajāpati's] father; and inasmuch as he created the gods, thereby he is the father of the gods; and inasmuch as the gods restored him, thereby the gods are his fathers.
>
> Twofold verily is this, – father and son, [Prajāpati] and Agni, Agni and [Prajāpati], [Prajāpati] and the gods, the gods and [Prajāpati] – (for) whosoever knows this (*ŚB* VI, 1, 2, 26-27).[9]

Some of the clues to the understanding of Indradyumna's story lie in the symbolism of the ancient "fire altar".

[9] Eggeling, III.

In Vedic times, the structure of the area devoted to animal sacrifices included a trapezoidal enclosure – the *mahāvedi* (or "great altar") – to the east of a *prācīnavaṃśa*, the hut where the three fires of the sacrificer (*yajamāna*) were gathered:

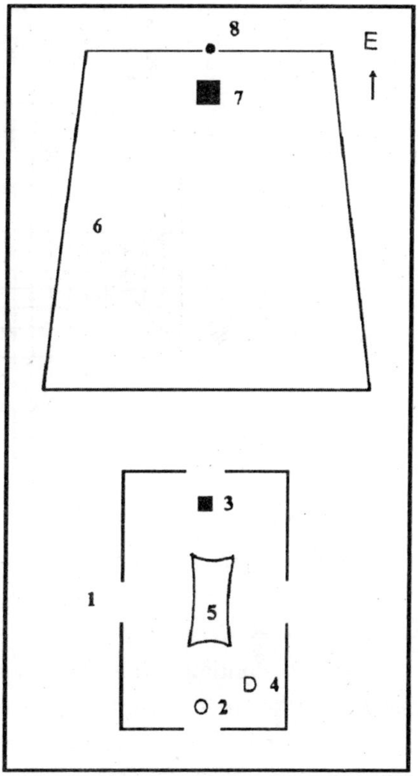

1. *prācīnavaṃśa*
2. *gārhapatya*, domestic fire
3. *āhavaṇīya*, oblation fire
4. *dakṣiṇāgni*, 'southern' fire
5. *vedi*, the altar reserved for oblation materials
6. *mahāvedi*, the "great altar" for animal sacrifices
7. *uttaravedi*, the new offering altar (literally: the "high" or "southern" altar)
8. *yūpa*.

FIG. 21. Basic structure of the sacrificial area.

This basic configuration underwent partial transformation when the building of a "fire altar" (*agnicayana*) was required. The usual square-shaped *uttaravedi* was then replaced by a structure in the form of a bird of prey, a *śyena* facing east and spreading its wings:

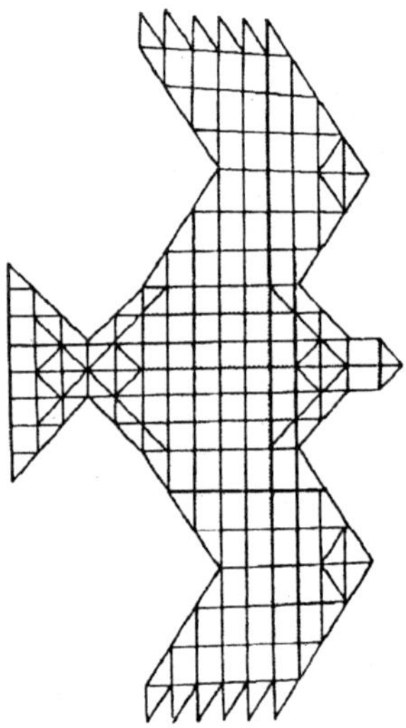

FIG. 22. The "bird of prey" in the *mahāvedi*

After the initiation (*dīkṣā*) of the sacrificer, the *mahāvedi* and the *agnikṣetra* (the "field of Agni", at the eastern border of the *mahāvedi*) were measured and layed out by the *adhvaryu*, one of the most important ritualists. Next, the *agnikṣetra* was ploughed and sowed. The *agnicayana* being closely associated with the *soma* sacrifice, a "*soma* buying" ritual would then be held. The role of the "seller" was undertaken by a Brahmin or a Śūdra with whom the *adhvaryu* would argue over the price to be paid.

A layer of sand was spread over the place intended for the construction of the "bird of prey". In the middle of this area, facing east, a "golden *puruṣa*" (*hiraṇyapuruṣa*), a statuette representing both the demiurge and the sacrificer, rested on a lotus-leaf. A live tortoise was walled in between the bricks of the first stratum (Dumont 1927: 83). Related to Prajāpati (and Viṣṇu), the reptile represented the stability of the Universe: the base of its body symbolised the earth; its shell the sky (*ŚB* VII, 5, 1-2). The last stratum of clay bricks was covered with earth (Dumont 1927: 85).

The symbolism of the *agnicayana* must be acknowledged. The clay bricks (*iṣṭakā*) possessed not only the essence of water and fire (VI, 2, 1, 8-9) but also that of the word itself (*vāc*), infused through the recitation of magic formulas (VI, 1, 2, 28). The *iṣṭakās* composing the "fire altar" expressed cosmic cohesion. Each clay brick corresponded to an hour of the (solar) year, symbolised by Prajāpati. The whole was divided into five strata, evoking the five seasons of the year (because Prajāpati is the year), or the five cardinal points (because Prajāpati is the space) (VI, 1, 2, 19). The strata also referred to the earth, air, sky and the two intermediate zones.

A stone called *svayamātṛṇṇa* (a "naturally perforated" brick) was placed in the centre of the first, third and fifth strata in order to form, along the interstices or porous spaces, an artery through which blew the vital breath of the *hiraṇyapuruṣa*. In front of the altar, on the eastern line of the *mahāvedi*, half in, half out of the sacrificial space, the *yūpa* – the post to which the victims were tied before being sacrificed by asphyxia – was finally erected.[10] It represented the sacrificer,[11] the demiurge, and the Cosmic Tree.

The first rituals took place inside the sacrificer's hut, but the *mahāvedi* was the stage of the main performances: the *soma* offerings were poured over a fire brought from the *āhavanīya* – in the *prācīnavaṃśa* – to the bird-shaped altar.

---

[10] In the case of an *aśvamedha*, 21 posts were lined up along the eastern border of the *mahāvedi*.

[11] The height of the *yūpa* was set according to the stature of the sacrificer.

* * *

The Hindu temple, itself a replica of the Puruṣa-Prajāpati, retains some of the symbolic features of the Vedic altar. The empty spaces formed by the *svayamātṛṇṇa* stones at the centre of the first, third and fifth layers of bricks in the "fire altar", correspond to the successive voids that vertically cross the temple (Kramrisch 1946: 370). The mystical function formerly attributed to the bricks also survived into Hinduism – the materials used in the temple construction being called and conceived as *iṣṭakās* (*ibid.*: 27, 149). The new foundation ceremonies still include a ritual called *iṣṭakā nyāsa*, the "installation of the bricks" (*ibid.*: 105). Certain texts mention the "sustaining stone" (*ādhāraśilā*) on which a jar (in stone or copper) is placed; this is the receptacle for alternating representations of the lotus leaf and the tortoise – in stone, silver and gold (*ibid.*: 110). It is true that the ancient burying ceremony was abolished: "No golden man forms part of the symbols in the foundation of the temple". Its identity, however, pervades the Vāstupuruṣa, the place of the old statuette being "now occupied by the Vase, full of power (śakti)" (*ibid.*: 111).

IV

We are now in a better position to approach the Indradyumna myth. Puri – so the story goes – passed, unscathed, through successive phases of cosmic destruction, due to the presence of Viṣṇu's sapphire. But the texts also mention the disappearance of the blue stone. Claiming his own rights, Yama once demanded its concealement and Viṣṇu granted his request: the image was eventually buried during a sand storm.

Is this a paradox? Should we understand that, in hiding the sapphire, the Supreme Being agreed to introduce death into the region from that moment onwards? To answer this question, we must reconsider the *agnicayana*, since the burying of the *hiraṇyapuruṣa* under the "fire altar" strongly suggests the dissimulation of the sapphire after the sand storm. The sand covering the statuette symbolised the dispersal of the *brahman*. But, simultaneously, it announced a socio-cosmic reorganisation (Ś*B* VII, 3, 1, 42). It is still the Supreme Being who, sacrificed at the outset of the *agnicayana* in the form of a "golden man",[12] arises, restored and immortal, in the altar's structure.

Without explicitly referring to the *agnicayana*, the Indradyumna myth clearly resorts to its symbolism. In this connection, a version recorded in the 18th century Ezourvedam (*EzV*)[13] seems particularly significant. On one hand, it mentions the existence of an ancient *golden temple*, hidden by sand – the work of one of Indradyumna's ancestors; on the other, it points out that it was there, right above the buried *golden temple* (evidently a stopgap for the Vedic *golden man*), that Indradyumna himself ordered the current temple to be built in stone.

* * *

Vanishing under the sands, the sapphire is not only a multiform version of the *hiraṇyapuruṣa*, buried under a "fire altar". The motif refers also to the symbolism of the temple as a transformation of the

[12] The "golden man" was already an expression of immortality: "gold is immortality" (Ś*B* VII, 4, 1, 1-15).

[13] It is generally admitted today that the *EzV*, a French manuscript edited by Ludo Rocher (1984), is a forgery, a disguised Christian composition intended for the conversion of the Brahmins. "Not only would a missionary be the only one to be interested in composing such a means of conversion; he would probably, at that time, also be the only one to make the effort of learning enough about Hinduism to be capable of writing this... ingenious composition" (*ibid.*: 60). The text is conceived as a dialogue between Biach (Vyāsa), who conveys the "traditional" Hindu viewpoints, and Chumantou (Sumantu), who refutes them. To better fulfill his mission, the author tried to be as faithful as possible to Hindu tradition. That may explain the fact that his account of the myth of Indradyumna is highly consistent with many other versions of the story.

Mountain. Indeed, the lurking place for the blue stone – the heart of the Mountain – is the very origin of the *garbhagṛha*:

> In the quest for secrecy, the enclosure of the shed in Vedic rites, or also of the dolmen for purposes of the Hindu temple, was one way of attaining it. Another way less widely and only comparatively later resorted to in architectural form by the Hindus, led to cutting into the interior of the mountain, the living rock. The final solution is the Garbhagṛha within the Prāsāda with its superstructure like a mountain (Kramrisch 1946: 171).[14]

The *garbhagṛha* of the Jagannātha Temple, placed in the middle of the *Saṅkhakṣetra*'s concentric enclosures, is thus equivalent to the "abode full of consciousness" inside the Blue Mountain's cave.

Like the ancient "fire altar", the mountain-temple expresses the mirroring relationship between the "hidden" and the "visible" aspects of God (which are one and the same). One may thus conclude that, pretending to submit to Yama's will, Viṣṇu tricked him in a new manifestation of his *māyā*:

Concealing his own representation, the sapphire, a metonymic substitution of the Blue Mountain,...

...Viṣṇu guarantees...

... his reappearance in the form of the temple, a metaphorical substitution of the Blue Mountain.

FIG. 23

[14] Built underground, the sanctuary has sometimes the very nature of a crypt: "'guhā' (cave) and 'gupta', secret, both from the same root, appear also as verbal equivalents of the 'crypt'" (Kramrisch 1946: 171, note 108).

Hiding and revealing simultaneously his own presence, the Supreme Being reaffirms the perfect identity between "inside" and "outside" – the Blue Stone in the Blue Mountain, Viṣṇu within himself.[15]

[15] According to Bidyut Lata Ray, the disappearance of the sapphire reveals Yama's sudden pre-eminence: the god of death finally imposes his power in the Puruṣottama kṣetra and, from then on, "people cannot get direct salvation by visiting the place" (1998: 8). From this point of view, however, both the sacred character of Puri and the indisputable superiority attributed to Jagannātha-Viṣṇu become incomprehensible.

PART II

FROM RITUAL TO MYTH

CHAPTER FOUR

VEDIC RITUAL AND POST-VEDIC MYTHS

I

The story included in the *EzV* introduces a suggestive link between Mārkaṇḍeya and King Indradyumna. When the Universe was consumed by fire, the sage tried to protect himself under the boughs of the great Cosmic Tree on the Blue Mountain. Discovering nonetheless that the fig tree gave not the slightest patch of shade, he burned it to ashes in one breath.[1] The tree, however, was Viṣṇu and, as such, imperishable: its half-burnt trunk eventually reappeared[2] on the Puri shore, where it was recaptured by Indradyumna. A collaborative relationship is thus suggested between the Brahmin, who begins the felling of the sacred tree, and the Sovereign, who later ordered it to be carved. This cooperation is infused with obvious allusions to sacrifice. Here is a new example of a similar alliance.

The story of Indradyumna
(*Mbh* III, 191)

One day, during their exile in the forest, the Pāṇḍavas are visited by Mārkaṇḍeya, whom they ask: "Do you know anyone who has lived longer than you?" "Yes," says the Brahmin, "Indradyumna, a royal seer, who lost his virtue and fell from heaven." And he tells them the following story:

> Indradyumna fell from heaven when his virtue was exhausted. But he would be allowed to return if someone could recall his former merits. I [Mārkaṇḍeya], was unable to recognise him, when he approached me: "Do you know anyone who has enjoyed a longer life than yours?" Indradyumna asked me. I knew of an Owl (Prākārakarṇa)

---

[1] "[V]oyant que cet arbre ne donnoit point d'ombre, [il] en fut indigné, souffla sur luy et le reduisit en cendres" (*in* Rocher 1984: 190).

[2] "[C]ependant comme cet arbre etoit *Vichnou* l'être suprême, et que par lá il devoit être immortel de sa nature, il ne fut pas tout reduit en cendres et il en resta encore le tronc" (*ibid.*).

> that had passed through countless lives. Transforming himself into a horse, the Sovereign carried me to the bird, who lives on the peaks of the Himalayas: "Do you know me?" Faced with a negative response, he asked: "Is there anywhere in the world a creature older than you?" "Yes, by Indradyumna's tank there lives an old Crane: Nāḍījaṅgha". Accompanied by myself and the Owl, Indradyumna questioned Nāḍījaṅgha in vain. And he again asked: "Do you know anyone who has enjoyed a longer life than yours?"
>
> Nāḍījaṅgha mentioned an old Tortoise, Akūpāra, who lives in the waters of the same lake. Invited to present himself before the King, Akūpāra almost collapses in a swoon: his eyes fill with tears; his heart races. This time, the efforts of the King are finally rewarded – Akūpāra knew the Sovereign, famous for the sacrifices he had carried out: "A thousand times, he ordered his 'fire altars' built upon my back. This lake was dug out by the innumerable cows he gave to the Brahmins, in payment for the rituals they performed at his request." Immediately, a celestial chariot arrived to bear the King away, to reoccupy his place in heaven.[3]

Do you know anyone who has lived longer than you? These words are the essence of a parable which, from beginning to end, turns on the question: *Do you know anyone who has lived longer than you?* Indradyumna's question is exactly that which the Pāṇḍavas asked Mārkaṇḍeya, who appears both as narrator and actor. As for Indra-

---

[3] A similar narrative appears in the *SkP*. The merits of Indradyumna had earned him heaven, from where, nonetheless, the Sovereign was expelled at the close of a hundred *kalpas*: time had swept his name from the memories of men. Having returned to earth, he realised that no one knew him. Mārkaṇḍeya, whom he approached first, recommended he visit the Crane Nāḍījaṅgha, who lived in the Himalayas. Nāḍījaṅgha has not the faintest recollection of the King but suggests the Owl, who suggests the Vulture, who suggests the Tortoise. Each of the helping animals had been subject to a curse whose effects lasted until the moment they met the King. The Tortoise finally says that he remembers Indradyumna: the sacrifices he ordered carried out had left an indelible scorch mark on his back. A celestial chariot then appears in order to bear Indradyumna off to heaven. This time, however, the King does not want to leave his friends, who have decided to join Śiva. He remains in the world of men and establishes, as an object of worship, the *liṅga* of Indradyumna or *Mahākāla* (*SkP*, *Kaumārikākhaṇḍa*, 7-13). It is, once more, to protest against forgetfulness, against the erosion of memory by the nefarious effects of time, that Indradyumna decides to build the *liṅga Mahākāla*, the *liṅga* of the "Great Time", evoking eternity.

dyumna, lost in the abyss of memory, he becomes the audience for the performance of his own drama: he is led, step by step, to some of the places where he may have lived, until he finally reaches... Indradyumna's lake. Here, he learns from Akūpāra the story of his distant past.

The King's journey can be seen as a succession of questions and answers:

> The Pāṇḍavas ask Mārkaṇḍeya: "Do you know anyone who has enjoyed a longer life than yours?"
>
> > Mārkaṇḍeya tells them that one day he was visited by Indradyumna (whom he did not recognise). The King asks him: "Do you know anyone who has enjoyed a longer life than yours?"
> >
> > > Mārkaṇḍeya mentions an Owl who lives in the Himalayas. The Owl is unable to recognise Indradyumna, who asks him: "Do you know anyone who has enjoyed a longer life than yours?"
> > >
> > > > The Owl mentions the Crane who does not recognise Indradyumna. The King asks him: "Do you know anyone who has enjoyed a longer life than yours?"
> > > >
> > > > > The Crane mentions the Tortoise who, finally, recognises Indradyumna. The Tortoise tells a story in which the King himself played the leading role.

Like Jaimini in the *SkP*, Mārkaṇḍeya does not focus his listeners' attention on a direct reply. "Do you know anyone who has enjoyed a longer life than yours?" the Pāṇḍavas had asked. Instead of just mentioning the name of Indradyumna, the Brahmin tells them the Sovereign's story, adding Akūpāra's testimony to his own.[4] The reminiscences of the Tortoise – a kind of "definitive" version of Indradyumna's myth – are inserted in Mārkaṇḍeya's frame-discourse.

---

[4] Akūpāra, one of the main characters in this story, plays in the *Mbh* the role ascribed to Viṣṇu's second *avatāra* in the Rāmāyaṇa and Purāṇic literature (*Viṣṇu Purāṇa*, I, 9; *Bhāgavat Purāṇa*, VIII, 7, etc.).

Probably inspired by the structure of Vedic rituals (Chapter 3, note 1), the technique of the frame story goes back, according to Witzel, to the period of the *Saṃhitās* and the *Brāhmaṇas*. As Minkowski also observed, "the ritual technique of embedding one rite in another provided the model for [different legends] in the form of concentric rings or frames" (1989: 402). This practice can easily be found in the great epic: "the monumental *Mahābhārata* is put together using a compositional strategy which mirrors that of Vedic rituals, especially *sattras*" (*ibid.*: 403). Hiltebeitel noted as well:

> The *Mahābhārata* is artfully designed as a story about a ritual – a collective *sattra* sacrifice performed by the Ṛṣis of the Naimiṣa Forest – in whose intervals is told the story about another *sattra* – the snake sacrifice of King Janamejaya – in whose intervals is told the story *of* (that is, in both senses, the story *by* and *about*) the author Vyāsa that is also his story about the heroes, a story that embeds many other stories and centers upon an emboxed narrative of a great 'sacrifice of battle' (2001: 38).

The frequency of this pattern is quite remarkable. But let us see how the Vedic ritual reflects itself in the story of Indradyumna, as told by Mārkaṇḍeya. We should begin by recalling the stages of Prajāpati's "demiurgic process" described by the *ŚB* (VI, 1, 1, 9-15; VI, 1, 2, 1-12),

Water (...) → Earth (...) → Heaven.

This is clearly inverted by Indradyumna's trajectory in the guise of a horse,

Heaven (Himalayas) → Earth (shores of the lake) → Water (Lake of Indradyumna).

We know the reason underlying these receding movements. The vision of the whole (or the answer to an essential question) can only be obtained by going back, as far as possible, to previous phases of cosmic transformation. It is therefore the Tortoise – a frequent representation of the Supreme Being (Prajāpati or Viṣṇu) – who holds the key to the mystery surrounding Indradyumna. More, though, than a mere witness of the Sovereign's past, the Tortoise is part of the drama. Stressing that, long ago, countless "fire altars" were built upon his back, the myth assigns him the symbolic role of the reptile walled in during the preliminary rituals of the *agnicayana*. Like the dark and exiguous *sanctum* in the Hindu temple, the innermost place of the "fire altar", the almost non-existent space between the bricks where the animal was kept imprisoned, is the unlimited abode of the "Unbound" i.e., Akūpāra.

A similar function is ascribed to the Owl and Crane, which, with the Tortoise, make up a coherent system. In fact, the helping animals are associated with three spatial points set on a vertical axis:

Owl – Higher space (Himalayas)
Crane – Intermediate space (the vicinity of Indradyumna's lake)
Tortoise – Lower space (sub-aquatic world).

The owl, a nocturnal bird of prey, is certainly reminiscent of the altar's exterior form – that of a *śyena*. Its name in the myth (Prākārakarṇa, literally "Wall-Ear") is highly significant. *Karṇa*, the "ear", is also "a moulding, any side-object, a corner-tower" (Acharya 1934: 116). *Prākāra*, in turn, designates "a wall, an enclosure, a fence, a rampart" (*ibid.*: 388). The *prākāra* (equally called *vedi*, *vedikā*), the enclosing wall "around the whole sacred precinct" (Kramrisch 1946: 146, note 45), was an "almost essential feature of Hindu and Buddhist shrines" (Coomaraswamy 1928: 22). As a "surrounding wall elevated on a mound of earth" (Acharya *ibid.*), it suggests the high place occupied by the bird in the symbolic geography of the myth.

Between the Owl's superior position and the Tortoise's inferior world, we find the perfect mediator, the Crane, a long distance migrator. The crane is a wading bird living by rivers and lakes. It can often be found resting on one leg – a fact which justifies its name in the text:

Nāḍījaṅgha, "stalk-legged". Long[5] and thin, the crane's "leg" (*jaṅgha*) is here conceived as homologous to a *nāḍī*, a term applied to tubular instruments or organs, the stalk or stem of a plant, the vein or artery of a body, as well as the channel along which flows the vital energy (*prāṇa*) of subtle physiology. But *jaṅghā* also designates the "pillar" or "column" in the jargon of religious architecture. Nāḍījaṅgha thus evokes the axis which vertically crosses the "fire altar", whose structure is organised around the empty space constituted by the "naturally perforated" bricks. It is through this channel that the sacrificer, represented within the building by the golden image, finally reaches a higher world.

Having collected the hitherto dispersed animals over the course of his journey, and gathered them together on the shores of the lake, Indradyumna symbolically restores the structure of the altar (i.e., the dismembered parts of Prajāpati's body, an idea seemingly implied in words such as *karṇa*, "the ear", or *jaṅgha*, "the leg", in Prākāra*karṇa* and Nāḍī*jaṅgha*).

In turn, the trajectory of the Sovereign who, *in equidus form*,[6] crosses the distance between the Himalayas and the tank,[7] is clearly an allusion to the wanderings of the Horse during the twelve months

---

[5] The crane stands about 1.5 meter high.

[6] There are many shamanic hints in this story – the mystical journey, the mastery of fire, the victory over death by Indradyumna, the metamorphosis of the King into a horse. Eliade stressed the symbolic meaning of the horse "in shamanic mythology and ritual". The animal is "employed by the shaman, in various contexts, as a means of achieving ecstasy, that is, the 'coming out of oneself' that makes the mystical journey possible" (1964: 467).

[7] According to the narrative, the lake (or tank) called Indradyumna (*Indradyumna saras*) was the result of soil erosion, caused by a great number of cows given to the Brahmins in remuneration for their ritual services. (The same explanation is given by the *SkP*). There is an *Indradyumna saras* in Puri (close to the Jagannātha Temple), one of the city's main centres of pilgrimage (*tīrtha*). "It contained several big old tortoises", the Puri District Gazetteer tells us: "The whereabouts of these tortoises are not known. Tradition has it that the labourers who carried stone for the construction of the great temple were, because of hard work, turned into tortoises and remained here ever since" (Senapati & Kuanr: 789).

preceding the sacrifice at the *aśvamedha* ceremonies. It is significant that it falls to Mārkaṇḍeya – he who tirelessly explored the cosmos in the "interior" of Viṣṇu – to supervise and accompany the Sovereign's itinerary. As a priest, he is a symbol of sacrificial efficacy, through which life and death are transcended.[8] The strong connection between Mārkaṇḍeya and Indradyumna, the celebrated old Brahmin and the prestigious old King, symbolises the indissoluble link between the two main figures in the sacrificial drama: priest and sacrificer.

II

The *aśvamedha*, the most theatrical of the Vedic rituals, included a multiplicity of activities: not only other rituals (such as the *agnicayana*, i.e. the building of the "fire altar", and a *soma*[9] sacrifice) but also the performance of musical pieces, the presentation of canticles praising the sacrificer, and the recitation of mythical tales. According to P.-E. Dumont, this ritual was "the highest manifestation of royal authority," and "only a victorious king, gifted with indisputable power [could] offer it to the gods" (1927: I). The ceremonies were not restricted to sanctioning a political hegemony. They guaranteed, at the right moment, rain, fertility and the prosperity of the kingdom, and, above all, the transformation of the sacrificer's identity. They reenacted the primordial self-immolation. Chosen according to strict criteria – youth, robustness, colour, etc. –, the Horse was seen as the Universe because

[8] According to a Vedic tradition which survives into the *Mbh*, the Bhārgavas were the traditional *purohitas* of sovereigns claiming to be "the descendants... of the legendary first king, Manu" (Goldman 1971: 97).

[9] The liquor of immortality, extracted from the plant of the same name (*soma*), was drunk during the sacrifice by priests and sacrificer.

Prajāpati is the Universe; its body represented the solar year because Prajāpati is the solar year...

The ceremonies began in *phālguna* (February-March), in *jyeṣṭha* (May-June), or even *āṣāḍha* (June-July). First, the *adhvaryu* would address the animal as follows: "You are the world", or "You are what surrounds [space]". The *ŚB* (XIII, 1, 2, 3) explains that, acting in the sacrificer's name, the priest in this way conquered the *four cardinal points*. The Horse was then left free for a year (in fact, its movements were observed from a distance by an escort of four hundred young men) and its wandering corresponded to a genuine military expedition. The young men accompanying the stallion used armed force against anyone who dared to challenge royal authority; if their progress was not interrupted, the land they crossed would be considered part of the King's dominions. The *four points* of space were thus appropriated by the Horse (i.e. by the Sovereign symbolically associated with the animal).

When the Horse returned, the sacrificer should undergo the initiation ceremony (which would last twelve days). The second (and most important) of the three days of the *soma* sacrifice coincided with the crucial phase of the *aśvamedha*, the ritual staging of Prajāpati's immolation. At that moment, not only the demiurge but the sacrificer himself (the representative of the demiurge on earth) would "die" and be "reborn". The *yajamāna* would then conquer eternity, his ascension to the world of the gods being the first aim of the rituals.

The Horse's erratic path leading up to the sacrifice – and the sacrifice itself – simulated the dispersal of the Supreme Being's vital energy, and of course, the restoration of his body: the *agnicayana*.

* * *

According to the myth, the prodigious longevity of Indradyumna had been assured by the countless number of *aśvamedhas* he had performed and "fire altars" he had ordered built: the horse sacrifice is the *leitmotiv* of the whole narrative. Furthermore, it is clear that, as the narrator of an *inserted* story, Akūpāra plays a role homologous to that previously imposed on him as an actor – the walled-in victim, literally "inserted" between the bricks at the altar's base. The Tortoise symbolises here the higher consciousness that awoke Indradyumna to a full perception of himself, to an existence beyond "life" and "death". Significantly, when the narrative of his life ends, the King returns to heaven – an epitome of *agnicayana*'s fundamental aims. For, the gathering of the helping animals – metaphoric elements of the altar's structure, as we have seen – is a last restaging of the sacrificial drama that had earned King Indradyumna a place in heaven. In other words, it is not only the syntax of Indradyumna's hyper-narrative that replicates the formal structure of a Vedic ritual. The very semantic of the story also mirrors the pattern of a horse sacrifice:

> **1st narrative:** Mārkaṇḍeya describes the wanderings of the Horse (into which Indradyumna had transformed himself)...
>
> > **2nd narrative:** Akūpāra recounts that Indradyumna ordered the building of countless "fire altars" (necessarily following the wanderings of the Horse in *aśvamedha* rituals).
>
> **1st narrative:** ... Having achieved the construction of a "fire altar" – which symbolically corresponds to the gathering of the Owl, the Crane and the Tortoise – Indradyumna returns to heaven.

FIG. 24

III

The symbolic connections between Indradyumna, the Tortoise and the Vedic "fire altar," reappear in epic and Purāṇic accounts. Let us consider the well-known story of the churning of the Milky Ocean by *devas* and *asuras*. Inspired by the traditional churning technique, this operation aimed at obtaining the *amṛta*, a substitute for the *soma*.[10]

The churning of the Milky Ocean
(*Mbh* I, 16)

Once, gods (*deva*) and demons (*asura, daitya*) had agreed to collaborate in order to obtain the *amṛta*, the "nectar of immortality". Mount Mandara was uprooted by the serpent Ananta (generally identified with Vāsuki) and placed by Indra upon the back of the Tortoise Akūpāra. Mandara was enlaced by the serpent, whose body was used as a churning rope. Under Brahmā's impartial eye, the gods (catching hold of the tail) and the demons (catching hold of the heads) pulled the serpent backwards and forwards alternately. Thus turning the mountain in both directions, they churned the Ocean of Milk. This action, the cause of an immense turbulence, produced a number of beings and essential goods: the moon, the goddess Śrī-Lakṣmī, wine and the white stallion Uccaiḥśravas, among others. As for the *amṛta*, the *asuras* desired to keep it. But, taking on the form of a stunning woman, Viṣṇu approached them and took their part.

[10] In the Vedic tradition, Gonda writes, "Soma and amṛta are in principle not identical, but are sometimes associated or even identified with each other" 1965: 63.

FIG. 25. The churning of milk

FIG. 26. The churning of the Milky Ocean

Akūpāra reappears in this story, supporting on his back Mount Mandara, the churning-staff whose rotational motion underlies, in Held's opinion, "the Indian's conception of the Universe and the cosmo-plastic laws that governed its moulding into concrete form" (1935: 141). But the Tortoise-under-the-Mountain motif is also an allusion to the Vedic "fire altar", the reptile being placed under the bricks in the ancient rituals of the *agnicayana*.

The churning of the Milky Ocean, in which the Tortoise is given a prominent function, is directly associated with Indradyumna according to the *Kūrma Purāṇa (KP)*, a text which deserves particular attention. In this context, it is Kūrma the Tortoise, who, as Viṣṇu's second *avatāra*, bears the mountain on his back, thus playing the role often attributed to Akūpāra. He also tells a short version of Indradyumna's story.

In a hoary past, it is stressed from the outset of the *Kūrma Purāṇa*, the sages of the Naimiṣa Forest asked Lomaharṣaṇa to recite... the *Kūrma Purāṇa*. Before he started, however, Lomaharṣaṇa introduced a remark: Viṣṇu, in his *Kūrmāvatāra*, had already narrated it to other gods and sages, during the operation for the acquisition of *amṛta*. Like the sages of the Naimiṣa Forest, the listener to the *KP* recited by Lomaharṣaṇa is led to a previous "creation":

The story of Indradyumna
(KP, I, 1, 27-131)

Arising from the Milky Ocean during the *amṛta manthana* (the churning out of *amṛta*), Śrī became Viṣṇu's *śakti*. Nārada and other sages wanted to know more about her. Viṣṇu in the form of the Tortoise explained that she was his own *māyā*, whose nature is wrapped in mystery even to the other gods. The sages ask the Tortoise another question: "What happens at the end of time?"

[Indradyumna's story starts here:]

Long ago, the high virtues of King Indradyumna had been rewarded with rebirth in a Brahmin caste. Due to the merits earned in the course of his new life, he once found himself in the presence of

> Śri and wanted to know who she was. "I am the supreme *māyā*", the goddess told him; "I am one with Viṣṇu, I am the *brahman*". She endowed the Brahmin with a still higher spiritual knowledge, allowing him to contemplate Viṣṇu and to learn from the god that the *brahman* is the ultimate, supreme truth. Then, a magical, aerial chariot drove Indradyumna through the skies, where he visited Brahmā. Obtaining eternal release, he finally grasped the unspeakable subtleties of *māyā*.

An intimate relationship is posited between Indradyumna's story and the *KP* itself. This "vital connection", Hazra asserts, is deducible from the introductory chapters of the *KP*, which "strike the keynote of the whole work" (1940: 58).[11] The story of Indradyumna lies again at the heart of a nested structure:

[1st level:] The sages of the Naimiṣa Forest ask Lomaharṣaṇa to tell them the *Kūrma Purāṇa*. Lomaharṣaṇa informs them that it had been narrated by the Tortoise, long ago...

[2nd level:]... at the time of the churning of the Ocean of Milk. As Śrī arises from the Ocean, the sages want to know more about her. The Tortoise explains that the goddess is his own *māyā* and tells them the story of Indradyumna.

[3rd level:] Indradyumna, a King reborn as a Brahmin, meets Śrī. "Who are you?" he asks. "I am the supreme *brahman*", she answers. She helps him to achieve liberation. Indradyumna is led to the presence of Brahmā.

FIG. 27

[11] The *Matsya*, the *Agni* and the *Nāradīya Purāṇa* also "testify to the traditional connection of the story of Indradyumna with the narration of the [Kūrma-]Purāṇa" (Hazra 1940: 59).

The question Indradyumna puts to Śrī "*Who are you?*" mirrors the one *indirectly* put by the sages to the Tortoise, "*Who is she?*" The narrative structure produces an echo, or even the echo of an echo. The words uttered by Indradyumna (at the third level) replicate those of the sages (at the second), just as the words of Lomaharṣaṇa (at the first level) paraphrase those of the Tortoise (at the second). As one might expect, the question *directly formulated* by Indradyumna leads to *mokṣa*, the final release. Inevitably, a transcendental question – *What happens at the end of time?* – lies at the very core of the hyper-narrative, the last of the inserted stories.

* * *

Let us now face an inescapable problem. Indradyumna is the name of a character found in different narratives. But, apart from homonymy, is there any convincing relationship between the old Sovereign who turned himself into a horse in search of his forgotten past (*Mbh*), the King reborn as a Brahmin (*KP*), and the founder of the Jagannātha Temple (*SkP*, *BrP*, etc.)? In the tales included in the third book of the *Mbh* and the first chapter of the *KP* there is no reference whatsoever to Jagannātha (or to the Puruṣottama kṣetra). Neither do these texts suggest any *explicit* relationship with the socio-religious context of Orissa. Although the lake of Indradyumna is mentioned in the *Mbh*, there is no reason to assume that it corresponds to the homonymous *tīrtha* in Puri.

Sustaining the Vaiṣṇava origin of the *KP*, Hazra claimed that the original content of its introductory chapters had been deeply modified "by the worshippers of Śiva and Brahmā" (1940: 59).[12] To support

[12] In Hazra's opinion, "the upper limit of the date of composition of the Viṣṇuite Kūrma-p[urāṇa] cannot possibly be earlier than 500 A.D.... If a period of at least fifty years be allowed to intervene between the date of composition of the Viṣṇuite Kūrma-p[urāṇa] and that of its recasting, then *the date of composition of the Visnuite Kūrma-p[urāṇa] falls between 550 and 650 A.D. and that of its recasting between 700 and 800 A.D.*" (1940: 71).

this thesis, the author refers to the passage (I, 107-121) in which "Indradyumna is made quite irrelevantly to go to see Brahmā, obviously with a view to adding to the glory of the latter" (*ibid.*). Is this a reasonable perspective? The King's visit to Brahmā is not a mere interpolation, an episode extraneous to the plot. The description of the event in the *KP* is similar, after all, to the one included in Oriya (or Orissa-related) versions: in the *SkP*, the Sovereign's journey to the abode of Brahmā determines the occasion for the consecration of the Jagannātha Temple, a crucial performance after which, according to the *BrP*, Indradyumna relinquishes his immense power and finally achieves liberation. Should one infer that these references to the demiurge (alluded to by the *SkP* and by several Oriya versions) are misplaced in the context of the Jagannātha cult? This would prove unacceptable (see below, Chapters 5 and 6).

Despite some obvious differences, the versions of the story presented so far are related by a common substratum. In this connection, a formal argument may also be adduced. The last phase of Indradyumna's mystical journey – the decisive moment leading to deliverance, to Brahmā's presence or simply to heaven – always lies at the deepest level of a complex, nested narrative structure. As we have seen, the *Mbh* and *KP* place, at the core of a hyper-narrative, a tale of Indradyumna directly or indirectly connected with the churning of the Milky Ocean. In both cases, the story is told by the Tortoise – Akūpāra or Kūrma (Fig. 24, 27). The churning-of-the-Milky-Ocean motif, which depicts "creation" through a *soma* sacrifice, and the image of the Tortoise under Mount Mandara, which evokes the *agnicayana*, are common features in Orissan traditions concerning the great temple of Puri. The short Indradyumna's stories from the *Mbh* and *KP* clearly anticipate later narratives: they capture, in a nutshell, the main aspects of the Jagannātha myths and rituals.

IV

Given the Vaiṣṇava character of the *KP*, the role of Brahmā in the story of Indradyumna appeared displaced, and hence, suspect to Hazra.[13] The author's implicit assumption is that clear borderlines separate Viṣṇu, Śiva and Brahmā. But, in this text as elsewhere, the "true" identity of the demiurge is an eternally undecided question... This unsolvable problem is graphically portrayed by an episode of the *KP* (I, 9) in which both Viṣṇu and Brahmā insist they are the origin of the Universe. Viṣṇu enters Brahmā's body, where he confirms the existence of the three worlds; coming out, he invites Brahmā to inspect the interior of his own body – where the same reality is found. Whilst asserting the progenitor role, each of them enters his rival's body and, significantly, emerges from it newly born. We are thus entitled to assume that every 'paternity' (or 'maternity') claim leads to reversibility. In O'Flaherty's words, the divergence between Viṣṇu and Brahmā "takes on interesting iconic aspects because of the ambiguity of the image of the lotus growing from Viṣṇu's navel":

> Since in Indian mythology the lotus is a symbol of the womb, Viṣṇu acts as the mother of Brahmā, which is what Viṣṇu insists is the case; but if one interprets the image anthropomorphically, it is apparent that the lotus stalk is a cord that connects the navel of Viṣṇu to a womb-lotus that is part of the body of Brahmā, and this, in human terms, would make Viṣṇu the child of Brahmā, which Brahmā insists is the case.... The navel is often a symbol of the center or womb of the world, the place of origin. If Viṣṇu's navel is a womb-symbol and Brahmā's lotus is a womb-symbol, the two gods are at a standoff (1984a: 256).

[13] Generally speaking, Hazra adds, the position occupied by Śiva and Brahmā "in the earlier portions of the extant Kūrma-p[urāṇa], is certainly inferior to that of Viṣṇu" (*ibid.*: 60).

FIG. 28. Brahmā and Viṣṇu.

Like the *Kūrma*, the *Śiva Purāṇa* (*ŚP*) deals with the ambiguous identity of the demiurge. Here again, several narrative levels become entangled, as if to underlie the gods' inward ambivalence. The *ŚP* reasserts that a lotus stem emerged from Viṣṇu's navel, Brahmā being born from its corolla. The latter slides down the stem in order to discover his origins. To no avail. Trying the opposite direction, in search of the very top, he fares no better: the stem has neither beginning nor end. In his wanderings, he meets Viṣṇu, who greets him: "Welcome, my son. Don't be afraid". Brahmā feels insulted and there is a bitter quarrel between the gods when, suddenly, they see a mysterious column of fire. To discover its origins, they decide to separate. Viṣṇu goes to the lower regions, Brahmā to the heavens. But the column, like the stem, has neither beginning nor end. This time, however, both recognise it as a manifestation of Śiva.

The story is organised as a set of overlapping frames: under a first enigma (Brahmā's origin) lies a second (the common origin of Brahmā and Viṣṇu) which, in turn, leads to a third (the fire column's origin). Although these relationships seem rooted in antinomy (above/below; water/fire, etc.), the episodes reflect each other. Emerging from Viṣṇu's navel, the stem of the *aquatic plant* is, in fact, a multiform version of Śiva's *column of fire.*

The great divinities of Hinduism - Brahmā (a personification of the *brahman*), Viṣṇu and Śiva - are commonly seen as Creator, Preserver and Destroyer. However, the Vedic Supreme Being (Puruṣa-Prajāpati) reflects holographically on each of them. Hence, each god "may appear in any or in all of the roles... [I]n substance [they] are identical" (Zimmer 1955, I: 12). In the *Puruṣottama Māhātmya* of the *SkP*, Brahmā is an exhausted demiurge, worn out by countless creations - an obvious allusion to Prajāpati's extreme fatigue after the primordial self-sacrifice. Even so, he is here subservient to Viṣṇu, who plays - or seems to play - the role of the supreme divinity.

Stories about "mutual creation" or "mutual parenthood" are strikingly recurrent and often evoked apropos of the relationship between the main Hindu deities. However, such ambiguity does not characterise exclusively the gods' interplay. The erratic trajectories of Brahmā

SkP:	*EzV:*
Inbreathing,	Outbreathing,
Viṣṇu "interiorises" Mārkaṇḍeya.	Mārkaṇḍeya "exteriorises" himself from Viṣṇu.
The god protects the sage from the waters of dissolution.	The sage aggresses the god: his flaming breath partially reduces to ashes the banyan tree representing Viṣṇu.
This story is presented as an introduction to the myth of Indradyumna.	These events announce the first intervention of Indradyumna, collecting from the shore the half-burnt trunk.

FIG. 29

inside Viṣṇu and Viṣṇu inside Brahmā are obviously replicated by those of Mārkaṇḍeya within Viṣṇu's body.[14]

In the Purāṇic accounts concerning Viṣṇu and Mārkaṇḍeya, the god's inbreathing "interiorises" the sage, preserving him from the devastation of cosmic waters. Their respective roles are reversed in the *EzV*. Here, Mārkaṇḍeya "exteriorises" himself from Viṣṇu by means of a flaming breath endowed with the power of fiery destruction (Fig. 29).

The banyan (representing Viṣṇu) appears in the Purāṇic account as an *instrument of protection*, allowing the Brahmin to escape from the waters. The same tree, set ablaze by Mārkaṇḍeya, becomes an *unprotected* object in the *EzV*. As he learns, the sage is part of the god. He is thus bound to suffer the consequences of his own act: striking with fire, the very element from which he tries to protect himself, he is a paradigmatic example of the *offender offended*.

Viṣṇu (in the *SkP*) and Mārkaṇḍeya (in the *EzV*) are mirror images of one another: in this symbolic representation of cosmic breathing, "interior" and "exterior", "fire" and "water", "aggression" and "protection" are ultimately interchangeable.[15]

---

[14] *Cf.* O'Flaherty 1984a: 255. We have seen also that, according to Goldman, the theme of a swallowed and disgorged (or otherwise expelled) figure is typical of the Bhārgava mythology, deeply concerned with death and return from death. This motif, the author remarks, is "flexible enough" so that the same character may assume "the roles of both swallower and swallowed" (1971: 90).

[15] The shadowless tree in the *EzV* motivates Mārkaṇḍeya's bad temper. The sage's irritable humour is otherwise explained by Purāṇic accounts. Having lived through so many aeons, the old man is outraged by Viṣṇu's indulgent, childlike tone of voice: "Mārkaṇḍeya, my son, come and shelter under my protection". The wrath of the Brahmin – feeling *insulted* by the god who *does protect him* – might be understood as a sign of ignorance (*avidyā*). It should also be noted here that the Bhārgavas are often credited with unexpected attitudes, "a pattern of behavior that is aberrant with respect to the norms of brahmanical activities set forth in the dharma literature" (Goldman 1971: 5). This includes "open hostility to the gods themselves" (*ibid.*) and, from this point of view, the *EzV* version appears again remarkably consistent with the main trends of Hindu traditions. But in the holistic perspective of the texts, the seeming paradox of *being threatened by a protective gesture* is just a new expression of the *offender-offended* motif. The recursive nature of cosmic transformation is thus persistently underlined.

CHAPTER FIVE

NON-DUAL CONCEPTS, DUALISTIC INTERPRETATIONS

[W]hen someone asks, "Who are you? A goddess, an Asurī, a Yakṣī, a Rākṣasī, or a Mānuṣī?" it is a cat-and-mouse game for all concerned, whether they are inside the [story] as characters, or into it as performers, audience, or readers.

A. Hiltebeitel

I

How should we read a hyper-narrative? The main purpose is not to bring into focus the several levels of a nested structure in succession, but rather to illuminate its different strata simultaneously. Let us concentrate on the *SkP* version of Indrayumna's story.

The story of Indradyumna
***(SkP, II, Puruṣottama māhātmya,* 6-29)**

I. Vidyāpati leaves Malwa

Once, in the court of Indradyumna (King of Malwa during the *kṛta yuga*), somebody described the beautiful Puruṣottama kṣetra. On the top of Nīlagiri, not far from the Rohiṇī Kuṇḍa (a basin of holy waters) stood a huge banyan tree whose branches protected a blue stone image of Viṣṇu. An ancient tradition stressed the sanctity of this place:

> Long ago, as the narrative goes, a thirsty crow came to drink in the Rohiṇī Kuṇḍa. The bird achieved instantaneous liberation, becoming one with Viṣṇu.

Vidyāpati, a Brahmin of the King's circle, promptly sets off for the region. Well received by Viśvāvasu, the chief of the Śabaras who inhabit the forests around the Blue Mountain, he discloses the reason for his journey. The Śabara chief foresees the events that will shortly occur. He feels worried but agrees to honour his guest, helping in every way. He guides him along the narrow, dark and thorny paths of the Blue Mountain. When they finally reach the banyan, Vidyāpati requests that Indradyumna should be granted the right to perform a thousand *aśvamedhas* there, and to build a great temple to house the sapphire. Viśvāvasu then narrates the following Śabara story:

> It has been said since time immemorial that Indradyumna, King of Malwa, would one day come to the Puruṣottama kṣetra. According to Viṣṇu's promise to Yama, the sapphire would have disappeared by that time. The Sovereign, however, should be granted the privilege of founding a new cult, dedicated to wooden images.

[Viśvāvasu makes clear that this story is never to be told in Indradyumna's presence.]

II. Back to Malwa

Vidyāpati leaves Orissa. On the same day, the sapphire disappears, swallowed up during a sand storm. Arriving in Malwa, the Brahmin tells Indradyumna the details of his expedition, leaving out any mention of the Śabara tale and its prediction.

III. Indradyumna leaves Malwa

Indradyumna prepares himself for the journey that is to begin in *jyeṣṭha* (May-June). Led by Nārada (Brahmā's son) and escorted by his army and all his subjects, he reaches the banks of the Citrotpalā (the Mahānadī), where he rests. A local Sovereign comes to meet him and tell him about the disappearance of the sapphire: since that time, the country has been devastated by innumerable calamities, and ravaged by drought and hunger. Notwithstanding this information, Indradyumna occupies the region and orders an *aśvamedha* to be performed. At the high point of the ceremonies - the extraction of the *soma* - a tree bearing the emblems of Viṣṇu rises from the ocean. Its upper branches plunge into the water, its roots float on the waves. Picked up and carried into the *mahāvedi*, the trunk is entrusted to an old craftsman - Viṣṇu himself, under disguise.

The Brahmins who performed the rituals are generously rewarded by the King. The vast herd of cows he offers them is gathered together in one place and held there for some time. Gradually, they wear away a large depression in the ground, creating a basin - the tank of Indradyumna (*Indradyumna saras*). Feeling, however, that his merits have diminished, the Sovereign orders a great temple built at the peak of the Blue Mountain.

IV. Ascension into Brahmaloka

Once the temple has been built, Indradyumna ascends to Brahmaloka (the highest celestial abode) to ask the demiurge to consecrate his work. The god agrees but invites the King to go to Orissa ahead of him, to speed up the preparations for the ceremony.

V. Back to Orissa

The moment Indradyumna returns, the gods chant a recitation to Viṣṇu (with whom Puruṣa is identified here):

> *... The Vedas were born from your body; from your body the primordial sacrifice was born... The Brahmins were born from your mouth; the Kṣatriyas from your arms; the Vaiśyas from your thighs; the Śūdras from your feet...*

Divine time is incomparably longer than human time: during the absence of the Sovereign in the Brahmaloka, an incalculable period of time passed in the human world. The kingdom was now ruled by Gāla Mādhaba, who had placed a stone image of Viṣṇu in the temple. Indradyumna orders it moved to another place. Gāla Mādhaba is indignant but, recognising Indradyumna's prerogative, finally bows to his authority. Brahmā appears and the wooden images are set in the temple.

The King of Malwa is introduced to the sacredness of the Puruṣottama kṣetra through the short tale of the thirsty crow. The motif revolves around important features in Indradyumna's myth: spiritual thirst; mystical quest; the Cosmic Tree as means of transition between earth and sky; ascent into and descent from the sky.

We met some of theses themes in Jaimini's prologue. A first narrative states that, falling from the branches of the banyan and diving into the waters of a pool nearby, a crow – with Brahmā as witness – achieved instantaneous liberation. Leaving her physical body, the bird identified herself with Viṣṇu. "This crow", G. V. Tagare observes, "was named Bhuṣaṇḍa Kāka and is installed... inside Jagannātha Temple". Her image "has four hands holding a disc, a conch-shell, a club, and a lotus-like Lord Viṣṇu".[1]

[1] *SkP* (*AITMS*), V: 5, note 2.

The thirsty-crow motif is found in vernacular versions, related this time to Vidyāpati. The *Deula Tolā* [*DT*] by Kṛṣṇa Dāsa[2] and an oral variant recorded by Hunter[3] remark that on his arrival at the top of the Blue Mountain, the Brahmin noticed a crow perching on a branch of the banyan. The bird, Kṛṣṇa Dāsa writes, fell into the nearby basin and, gifted with four arms (*caturbhuja*), went straight to the paradise of Viṣṇu (*kāka baikuṇṭhaku galā*). Realising that liberation was easily obtained here, Vidyāpati climbed the tree. He was about to precipitate himself from the top of the banyan when a celestial voice reminded him that Indradyumna was still unaware of the outcome of the mission with which he had been entrusted. The priest abandoned his premature project and returned to the ground.[4]

Achieving liberation before Brahmā or showing Vidyāpati the path to Viṣṇu's paradise, the crow performs, in this episode, the role of a psychopomp.[5] The tree-climbing motif plays a similar function in the story. As noted by Coomaraswamy, Vedic literature often represented the ascension of the spirit in terms of tree climbing, and some sacrificial performances included a variety of explicit climbing rites.[6] The sacrificer, to whom a glimpse of imminent release was thus granted, was nonetheless invited to invert the ascending path, under the threat of death or madness.[7] He certainly approached the thresh-

[2] Dating from the 18th century, the *Deula Tolā* ("The Building of the Temple") by Kṛṣṇa Dāsa is the recasting of an earlier homonymous work by Nīlambara Dāsa (written between the end of the 17th and the beginning of the 18th century).

[3] Hunter 1872, I: 89-93.

[4] See Chapter 7: Indradyumna's story (Kṛṣṇa Dāsa, *DT*, fragment 1).

[5] Eliade stressed "the mythical image of the soul in the form of a bird and the idea of birds as psychopomps" (1964: 479).

[6] Coomaraswamy, "*svayamātṛṇṇa*: Janua Coeli" [1939], in Coomaraswamy 1977, I: 470.

[7] "The initiated Sacrificer", Coomaraswamy observes, "is ritually dead, no longer a man but a Deva; 'if he did not descend again to this world, he would either have gone to the suprahuman world, or he would go mad' (*PB, xviii.10.10*), 'would either go mad or perish' (*TS vii.3.10.4*); 'if he did not relinquish the operation, the sacrificial fire [in which he has symbolically immolated himself] would be apt to consume him' (*TS 1.7.6.6*)" (*ibid.*: 472).

old of immortality but, before the last step, it was demanded that he live out his terrestrial existence. Furthermore, the Cosmic Tree evokes the arrangement of the "naturally perforated" bricks (*svayamātṛṇṇa*) which allowed the passage of the *hiraṇyapuruṣa*'s vital breath through the Vedic "fire altar".[8] We understand therefore that the "thirsty-crow" and "tree-climbing" motifs appear side by side, both conveying the same meaning: the transition between earth and sky.[9]

Though interwoven at the end of Vidyāpati's travel (according to vernacular accounts), the two motifs may also be separated. Let us recall the prologue to the story of Indradyumna in the *SkP* (see Chapter 2). When Brahmā reaches the Puruṣottama kṣetra, he sees a bird falling from the banyan and diving into the basin (1st level of discourse). The perfect union with Viṣṇu is here presented through the "thirsty crow", the "tree-climbing" theme being neglected. The opposite happens in Śrī-Lakṣmī's account (2nd level). On one occasion, as the goddess related in her sub-narrative, Mārkaṇḍeya climbed to the top of the same banyan tree, from where he penetrated into Viṣṇu's body. The passage from "outside" to "inside" Viṣṇu's body is here symbolised by "tree climbing", not by the "thirsty-crow" motif.

* * *

[8] Coomaraswamy, *ibid.*: 465 ff. See also Staal 1983, I: 140.

[9] Eliade emphasised the ornithological symbolism inherent in ritual tree climbing: "Along [the] cosmic pillar [i.e. the *yūpa*] the sacrificer goes up to heaven, alone or with his wife. Setting a ladder against it, he addresses her: 'Come, wife, ascend we the sky!' She answers: 'Ascend we!' And they exchange these ritual words three times [*Śatapatha Brāhmaṇa*, V, 2, 1, 10, etc. (tr. Eggeling)]. Reaching the top, the sacrificer touches the capital and, spreading his arms (like a bird its wings!), cries: 'We have come to the heaven, to the gods; we have become immortal!' [*Taittirīya Saṃhitā*, *I, 7, 9, e*; etc. (tr. Keith, p. 550)] (1964: 404).

The role of Vidyāpati before the Cosmic Tree (Kṛṣṇa Dāsa; Hunter) is a wonderful illustration of mythical implicate order. The figure below reassembles some of the elements scattered through different versions of the story:

Indradyumna's story (*DT*; Hunter):
Vidyāpati sees a crow perching on a branch of the banyan tree (on the top of the Blue Mountain). The bird falls from the branch and reaches Viṣṇu's paradise. Vidyāpati climbs the tree and returns to the ground.

> **Prologue to the story of Indradyumna (*SkP*) - 1st level:**
> Brahmā sees a crow perching on a branch of the banyan tree (on the top of the Blue Mountain). The bird falls from the branch and obtains liberation.
>
> > **Prologue to the story of Indradyumna (*SkP*) - 2nd level:** Mārkaṇḍeya climbs the banyan tree (on the top of the Blue Mountain) and enters into Viṣṇu's body.

FIG. 30

Seeing the Crow perching on a branch of the Cosmic Tree, the Brahmin Vidyāpati (vernacular versions) replicates Brahmā (*SkP*, Jaimini's prologue, 1st level). Moreover, climbing the banyan to obtain liberation, he identifies with the Crow - who had reached Viṣṇu's paradise from there (*SkP*, Jaimini's prologue, 1st level) - and with Mārkaṇḍeya - swollen by the god at the top of the tree (*SkP*, Jaimini's prologue, 2nd level).

The same yearning for deliverance unites the Crow, Brahmā, Mārkaṇḍeya, and Vidyāpati. Their trajectories are intimately entangled. As a psychopomp, the Crow is an epitome of the mystical quest. While observing her, Brahmā recognises the Puruṣottama kṣetra as the ideal location for final release. But the bird's spiritual thirst, appeased in the presence of Viṣṇu, also calls to mind Mārkaṇḍeya's distress, afflicted as he was with heat and thirst in the course of a *pralaya* (*EzV*). The fire that consumes the sage, and by which the sage consumes the shadeless banyan tree, is, after all, a mystic flame, responsible for the reappearance of Viṣṇu. The Crow, Brahmā and Mārkaṇḍeya converge into Vidyāpati as if they were somehow implicated in his role.

II

Having found the precise emplacement of the banyan, Vidyāpati – like Brahmā and Mārkaṇḍeya in previous narratives – acknowledges the entrance into a superior world. The Cosmic Tree, a privileged place for ultimate liberation, marks the point where the Jagannātha Temple will later be located.

The double movement of the Brahmin along the banyan's trunk – in a sense, the sketch of a Vedic "fire altar" – is also the implicit blueprint of the temple itself. Vidyāpati's trajectory – climbing the tree and returning to the ground (according to vernacular accounts) – is a paradigm of the future intervention of Indradyumna, building the monument, ascending into Brahmaloka, and returning to Orissa for the consecration ceremonies.

Construction of the temple is also anticipated by the remarkable interplay between Vidyāpati and his host, Viśvāvasu. The Śabara plays a key role in the *SkP* story. He welcomes the King's emissary and becomes his friend; he guides him in the Blue Mountain through a dark landscape (in many versions the Brahmin even walks blindfolded). The unilluminated path leading to Viṣṇu's image prefigures, of course, the worshipper's movement towards the gloomy atmosphere of the *garbhagṛha* (the sanctum sanctorum). But climbing to the Mountain peak along difficult and narrow tracks has also initiatic hints. Narrowness (or exiguity) and ascent are characteristic of initiatory mythologies (Eliade 1964: 121; 485).

Let us consider particularly the puzzling dialogue between Vidyāpati and Viśvāvasu, near the Cosmic Tree. The question put by the former – *Could Indradyumna settle here, perform his* aśvamedhas *and build a temple for Viṣṇu's image?* – is again the pretext for another story, a traditional Śabara tale which, however, *should not* be retold.

Given the homology (already acknowledged) between *what* is said and the *way* it is said, *secret* words are particularly appropriate to announce the *hiding* of the sapphire. This is congruent, after all, with the secrecy surrounding not only the dissimulation of the blue stone but the blue stone itself as an object of worship. Only silence can express the unnameable reality of the Supreme Being. Accordingly, as far as the hyper-narrative is concerned, Viśvāvasu's secret account occupies the centre of the structure, the inviolable space of the inserted stories, just as the sacred image is the centre, the inviolable space of the temple.

Playing for a moment the narrator's role, Viśvāvasu makes it clear that Indradyumna will never find what he is looking for. From his words one could infer a firm dismissal of Indradyumna's project. But Viśvāvasu is a quibbler. As we know, the concealment of the image prefigures the revelation of the god in the form of his temple. Indeed, in *revealing* to the Brahmin the *concealment* of the blue stone whilst demanding from him total discretion on the matter, Viśvāvasu is far from opposing Indradyumna's journey. Behind the apparent objection, there is actually assent and even encouragement to action. Because he announces the disappearance of the blue stone but keeps Indradyumna in ignorance of this fact, the Śabara ultimately guarantees the presence of the King in the region and his participation in the process of socio-cosmic reorganisation. His answer is presented as a riddle: Indradyumna's apparent failure is the very expression of his complete success and good fortune.

Viśvāvasu's answer to Vidyāpati takes the form of an inserted short narrative which matches the frame-story in the most conspicuous way:

The King of Malwa sends Vidyāpati in search of the sapphire; the Brahmin meets Viśvāvasu and tells him that the Sovereign intends to come to the Puruṣottama kṣetra, perform his *aśvamedhas*, and build a temple to house the sapphire...

> Viśvāvasu tells Vidyāpati the Śabara version of Indradyumna's story: the King of Malwa will soon arrive at the Puruṣottama kṣetra, to witness the disappearance of the sapphire.

... Vidyāpati returns to Malwa; Indradyumna sets off for the Puruṣottama kṣetra and witnesses the disappearance of the sapphire.

FIG. 31

Just like the "exterior" and "interior" of a temple (or the *blue stone* in the *Blue Mountain*), the core and periphery of the hyper-narrative are one and the same reality. Even so, the ("interior") version of Viśvāvasu sheds light on Jaimini's ("exterior") version. Again, the sub-story relates to a higher form of knowledge and, therefore, demands replacement of the narrator. But who, this time, is the narrator of the sub-narrative?

As for other figures we have met, Viśvāvasu has the double role of narrator and actor in the drama, where he performs with Indradyumna (about whom he speaks), and with Vidyāpati (to whom he talks). His vision of the whole holds the key to the plot. Endowed with supreme knowledge – knowing the past and foreseeing the future –, he leads the Brahmin along obscure paths, into the sapphire's presence. The very term Vidyāpati, "Lord of Knowledge", may be a reference to the Hindu priest's enlightenment by Viśvāvasu's higher consciousness.[10] As narrator, the Śabara's role is complementary to that of Śrī-Lakṣmī, who presented the prologue's sub-story. Significantly, in another version of the myth (Sāraḷā Dāsa), he reappears as the craftsman who carves the sacred images, a task often undertaken by Viṣṇu.[11] In this context, the narrative performance of Viśvāsu, the quibbler, is also highly meaningful. Disclosing what he pretends to hide, the Śabara evokes the illusory proceedings of Viṣṇu himself who, burying the sapphire in the sand, brings about the building of the temple.

An implicit homology is thus posited between Viśvāvasu and the Supreme Being. In fact, the omniscience attributed to him transforms his complicity with the Brahmin (whom he leads up to the sapphire, but by whom he will be, indirectly, ostracised) into a metaphor for the primordial self-sacrifice.[12]

---

[10] From this perspective, an asymmetric link is established between the Brahmin and Śabara. To be sure, it partially reflects the ambiguous nature of the guest/host relationship (such as is known from Vedic and Hindu sources). Accepting Viśvāvasu's hospitality and relying on it to find the blue stone, Vidyāpati implicitly admits the superiority of his host. As Stephanie Jamison points out, "the beggar in some sense puts himself into the power of the giver and acknowledges his superiority" (1996: 202). But this is not the whole story. See below, note 12.

[11] The craftsman is also identified with Viśvakarmā, another manifestation of the Supreme Being.

[12] Now it is the host who finds himself depending on his guest. "I would suggest" – writes Jamison – "that behind the hospitality relation in general was the unsettling notion that a host might *have to give* whatever a guest demanded..." (1996: 162). And she concludes: "Hospitality can hardly exact any higher price than self-immolation" (*ibid*.: 163). We will come back, in Chapter 8, to the ambiguity inherent in the relationship between Vidyāpati and his host.

Viśvāvasu is an epithet used for Viṣṇu. As noted by Hunter,

> [Vāsu or Viśvāvasu], the name of the [Śabara] fowler in my legend, etymologically means 'the dweller'. It has probably been given to him by the Sanskrit writer of the legend, by a reflex process from the name of his god [Vāsudeva], or because he is the typical aboriginal dweller in the land throughout the story. The word is also used as a name for Vishnu, and the writer of the legend may mean that the aboriginal fowler was himself Vishnu in an earlier form (1872, I: 96, note 25).

We shall shortly find other resonances in this relationship – not to be understood, of course, in terms of the "tribal thesis". But let us focus for now on Viśvāvasu as an "ancestor" of the Daitās, the Śūdra ritualists of the Puri temple. The term *daitā* is locally interpreted as a derivative of the Sanskrit *daitya*, "demon".[13] In spite of this, and notwithstanding their partial untouchability, the Daitās are, as mentioned earlier, blood relatives of Viṣṇu-Jagannātha. "Undervaluation" (in social terms) and "overvaluation" (in ritual and religious terms) thus converge in the "double" identity ("demoniacal" and "divine") of the Daitās. For many authors, this is paradoxical. But what really is a "god" (*deva*) or a "demon" (an *asura* or a *daitya*)? This question entails a new digression.

III

> Devas and Asuras, Angels and Titans, powers of Light and powers of Darkness in RV., although distinct and opposite in operation, are in essence consubstantial... The Titan is potentially an Angel, the Angel still by nature a Titan; the Darkness in actu is Light, the Light in potentia

[13] Daitya (instead of Daitā) is actually the term used by R. Mitra (1875). On symbolic associations between "demons" and 'low status' social groups in general, *cf.* Kuiper 1960: 221.

> Darkness; whence the designations Asura and Deva may be applied to one and the same "Person" according to the mode of operation... (Coomarasway 1935: 373-374).

These words, often quoted, express a view which hardly fits western analysis of Hinduism[14] (dominated by an insuperable tension between good and evil, order and chaos, etc.) The non-dual character of Hindu concepts tends to be avoided rather than readily admitted. Dealing with the *Mbh*, in a text contemporary to that of Coomaraswamy, Held acknowledges that epic narrative can be defined as "[an] attempt at bringing about a unity of opposites" (1935: 171):

> Śiva is not Viṣṇu, nor is Viṣṇu Śiva. We are not here concerned with the question of a logical similarity and equality of the nature of: A = B, therefore B = A; it is a religious identity that has our concern. Vi ṣṇu is Śiva, but that does not imply, reasoning upon a religious basis, that Viṣṇu is one and coincident with Śiva; he is neither more nor less than Śiva; the fact is, he is a different being. It all sounds very strange, but we must simply take things as they are (*ibid.*: 168).

There is a feeling of awkwardness in these words. Confronted with "seeming oddities,... things we are at a loss what to make of or what to do with", Held is puzzled by the "illogical logic of A being the same as but not identical with B" (*ibid.*: 171). His bewilderment ("it all sounds very strange"), however, turns into down-to-earth compliance: "we must simply take things as they are"...

The idea of the unity of opposites – "a fantastic whim of the Indian mind" (*ibid.*) – has been ignored by countless scholars before and after Held. Jan Gonda postulates a split between Śaivism and Vaiṣṇavism, conceived of as "distinct religions" (1976). Vedic literature would have made of Viṣṇu a benevolent divinity,[15] as opposed to

---

[14] Cf. Marriott 1989.

[15] "Viṣṇu is benevolent, never inimical" (Gonda 1970: 3).

Rudra-Śiva, a malevolent, cruel god.[16] In certain passages, Gonda seems to endorse a less rigid perspective: "The benevolent or rather merciful aspects of [Rudra's] ambivalent nature find... expression in some epithets such as Śambhu 'the beneficent or kind one' and Śiva" (*ibid.*: 4). Shortly afterwards, however, he insists that the essence of Rudra "was, in the minds of Vedic men, the power of the uncultivated and unconquered, dangerous, unreliable, unpredictable, hence much to be feared nature, experienced as a divinity" (*ibid.*: 5). Accordingly, the *Mbh* would be a manifestation of the antithesis between Śaivism and Vaiṣṇavism: "[T]he epic combatants, generally speaking, appear to have different faiths" (*ibid.*: 90).

Dumézil also saw in the epic the expression of a conflict "*entre les 'bons' et les 'méchants'*" – between the 'good' Pāṇḍavas and the 'bad' Kauravas. He recognised nevertheless that this relationship did not express a perfect dichotomy. Dhṛtarāṣṭra and Vidura (brothers of Pāṇḍu) are defined as "good" even though, paradoxically, they join the "bad" side (1968: 171). A number of other characters behave in the same way: "In this confrontation between 'Evil' and 'Good', in this rivalry for power between Kali-Duryodhana and Dharma-Yudhiṣṭhira, why is it that so many 'good' characters are found on the side of Evil?" (*ibid.*: 253, *author's translation*). Dumézil had no explanation at all ("aucune explication n'est prête"; "la difficulté est, *hic et nunc*, sans solution") (*ibid.* : 254, 255).

The general tendency to oppose Śiva and Viṣṇu, "as if they were mutually exclusive or had only hostile relations" (1976 a: 102), was critically discussed by Madeleine Biardeau. She states however that the two figures symbolise the "bipolarity that is drawn between the world of sacrifice – the organised and pacifying human world – and the exterior world, savage, impure, or simply dangerous" (*ibid.*: 96). And she concludes: "the character of Rudra... is... clearly antinomic

---

[16] "He houses in forests and jungles, in places where man falls a victim to fright and terror. He is the lord of the wild animals, which are said to be a manifestation of his cruel nature" (*ibid*: 4).

to that of Viṣṇu" (*ibid.*) In the same way, the Pāṇḍavas and Kauravas are set in "two opposing camps"; the *Mbh* is basically the story of "the good triumphing over the bad" ("la victoire des bons au détriment des méchants") (1976 b: 142, *author's translation*).[17]

J. Scheuer claimed that the *Mbh* is a "unified and coherent whole", a myth expressing "a vision of the world in which Viṣṇu and Śiva – or Kṛṣṇa and Rudra – have complementary positions, more than exclusive ones" (1982: 16, *author's translation*). He concedes that the two divinities, opposite in certain circumstances, are assimilated in many others (*ibid.*). It could therefore be said that Śiva "is" Viṣṇu ("Śiva 'est' Viṣṇu"). But then, how are we to understand that his interpretation is intended to show that they play "distinct roles", presenting "particular" and irreducible "personalities"? (*ibid.*: 28).[18]

The persistence of this kind of argument appears all the more surprising since, after all, the strict duality adduced by so many scholars has never been clear to themselves. Śiva is not only considered a god of "destruction"; as is often maintained, he also destroys with the recreation of the universe in mind. Symmetrically, Viṣṇu is not con-

---

[17] Biardeau acknowleges that "the avatāra is undoubtedly Viṣṇu, but with a 'terrible' component" (*ibid.*: 183). Seen, however, as a "strange combination", this blend of "destruction" and "creation" (*ibid.*) does not modify the dominant dichotomic view.

[18] Viṣṇu is thus exclusively associated with order (*ce qui est dharmique*), Śiva exclusively associated with destruction, violence and danger (*ibid.*: 107-108). But Viṣṇu – Kṛṣṇa in particular – often appears in the role of an illusionist, "a shameless deceiver", to use Held's expression (1935), a "devious divinity" in Matilal's words (1991). The condemnable attitudes sometimes attributed to him as a helper of the "good heroes" of the *Mbh* led, in the past, to the origin of the famous "inversion theory": the Pāṇḍavas would have usurped the place formerly belonging to the Kauravas. Unacceptable in Holtzmann's simplistic terms, this theory acknowledged an element of ambiguity that appears, in multiple forms, not only in the classical epic but also in its vernacular transformations. According to the oral Hindi epic of northern India (Ālhā), "at the end of the *Mahābhārata* war the Pāṇḍavas had not yet had their fill of fighting and approached Kṛṣṇa on this matter. He granted them the chance to fight some more by reincarnating them [and the Kaurava] in the Kali yuga... This time, however, the roles would be reversed: the Kaurava would win and the Pāṇḍavas lose" (Sitaramji, according to Schomer 1989: 148).

sidered as purely a god of "creation" or "preservation." In Hopkins' words, he "is not especially preserver, but as the All he is also destroyer" (1915: 207).

The relationship between the gods takes multiple forms. From one first myth (or from a myth's first episode) to a second, close friendship (or even a merged identity) often turns into acrimonious hostility. In spite of their "mutual parenthood", Brahmā and Viṣṇu behave sometimes as enemies. Śiva beheads his own son, Gaṇeśa, before bringing him back to life in a restored, renewed body. In these examples, it is the process of ever-evolving relationships that must be stressed: conflict, an essential aspect of cosmic transformation, should not be taken literally in mythical narratives. Sometimes, it merely expresses the Supreme Being's self-division, thus reenacting the primordial sacrifice.

The *opposition* of Good and Evil is likewise inadequate to describe the ties between "gods" and "demons". Observing, a century ago, that by their *generosity* and *valour*, "demons" are sometimes comparable to the "gods" (*ibid.*: 47), Hopkins stressed that "no great difference" had been established between them by the earliest texts in Indian literature (*ibid.*: 52). But he immediately resorted to a commonsensical, if unexpected formula – "When good, a god; when destructive, a demon" (*ibid.*) – which dismisses his initial scepticism.

O'Flaherty remarked that "the demons do not always represent... misfortunes, which are often attributed to the gods; nor by any means do the gods always represent unmitigated 'good'" (1976: 58).[19] She

[19] "Though the Gods and the demons were perpetually at war", Kramrisch writes, "the gods, the Devas, the shining ones, had many traits in common with the demons.... The character of the gods and the demons did not coincide with the dichotomy of good and evil" (1988: 394). Normally seen as a human manifestation of the goddess Lakṣmī, Sītā, the daughter of King Janaka according to the classical *Rāmāyaṇa*, plays an important role in the destruction of Rāvaṇa, the "demonic" king of Laṅkā. But here antagonism and identification are not mutually exclusive: in certain South Indian oral versions, Sītā *is* the daughter of Rāvaṇa himself (Ramanujan 1999: 148). P. B. Courtright also observed that "in many respects Gaṇeśa is one with the demons in Hindu mythology" (1985: 129). And he added: "coming from demon stock is not particularly disadvantageous in the context of Hindu

"assumes that the reader will assume that the Hindus assume their gods to be good, their demons evil (...)"; and she adds:

> [P]roceeding from this chain of half-truths, I have set out to rectify the imbalance by setting forth the less obvious corollary – that the gods are not good, nor the demons evil, in any consistent or significant sense of these important words (*ibid.*: 12).

But the problem re-emerges. In certain passages from the *ŚB*, Prajāpati seems "to reverse the creative process" and, according to O'Flaherty, he then "behaves not only like a demon but like Death himself" (*ibid.*: 218). We are not far from Hopkins' definition: "When good, a god; when destructive, a demon".

Stressing that Brahmanic India is not Manichean, Biardeau proposed the adjective "démonique" in place of "démoniaque" so as to eliminate associations "over-familiar to Western mentality" (2002, I: 47). It is doubtful, however, that the difficulties inherent in the current conception would be overcome by a simple terminological inflection.

* * *

In the myth of Indradyumna, Viśvāvasu's apparent ambiguity is similar to that of the characters we have met so far. Let us recall the episode where Mārkaṇḍeya reduces Viṣṇu's banyan tree to ashes. Is this a "destructive" behaviour, causing the god's *disappearance*? Or is it a "creative" action, determining the *appearance* of the trunk from which the new image is carved? And how should we characterise Indradyumna's endeavours in search of the sapphire? Did we not see that the very prediction of his "failure" is expressed in terms conveying auspiciousness? In this unremitting play of light and shadow, reality is more than meets the eye.

---

mythology... [Demons] perform mighty acts of asceticism to win boons from the gods, which enable them to destroy the universe and undermine *dharma*. But they also sacrifice themselves as model devotees and become transformed thereby into beings of divine stature" (*ibid.*: 130). On "demon devotees" *cf.* Shulman 1980, Chapter V; Hiltebeitel (ed.) 1989.

CHAPTER SIX

THE *AŚVAMEDHA* IN THE *AŚVAMEDHA*

I

The Brahmin's itinerary from Orissa to Malwa and the King's journey from Malwa to Orissa produce "opposite" results. According to the *SkP*, a cyclone devastated the country when Vidyāpati left the Blue Mountain. Strong winds whipped up a severe sandstorm that engulfed the sapphire. The King's journey in turn, having begun in *jyeṣṭha* (May-June), the last month of summer, ends at the high point of the crisis. Before entering the Puruṣottama kṣetra, Indradyumna decides to rest on the banks of the Mahānadī. Here, he meets a local Sovereign who informs him of the chaotic state into which the region has plunged. The sandy banks of the Mahānadī and the last month of summer define the spatial-temporal "frontier" that Indradyumna will have to transpose in order to build the Jagannātha Temple and reorganise the country:

Brahmin: Orissa → Malwa: sand storm; the sapphire disappears
King: Malwa → Orissa: reorganisation; building of the Jagannātha Temple.

Vidyāpati's *departure from*, and Indradyumna's *arrival in* Orissa announce, respectively, the "opening" and "closing" of a long period of time (conceived of as a *pralaya*):

Vidyāpati leaves Orissa when the sapphire disappears, buried by the sand.

Intermediary period symbolically associated with a *pralaya*: calamities; disorder.

Indradyumna arrives at Orissa to build the temple and put in place the images replacing the sapphire.

FIG. 32

The turmoil provoked by the disappearance of the blue stone only comes to an end with the consecration of the temple. But there is no real opposition between these two events: the sapphire is a metonymic substitute for the Blue Mountain, just as the temple is its metaphoric replica.

In most versions, Indradyumna leaves Malwa in the course of the *kṛta yuga*[1] and establishes in Orissa the worship of Jagannātha – Kṛṣṇa's manifestation during the *kali yuga*. The *tretā* and the *dvāpara yuga* seem to have been sidestepped:

I.

Indradyumna leaves Malwa
during the *kṛta yuga*;

II.

Elision of the *tretā* and the *dvāpara yuga*

III.

Indradyumna establishes his power in Orissa at the beginning of the *kali yuga*:

a) construction of the temple;

b) installation of the wooden images.

FIG. 33

[1] The different moments of the daily routine of an exemplary Sovereign were symbolically associated with the four *yuga*. The Laws of Manu state that the King is the *kali yuga* during his sleep; the *dvāpara* the moment he wakes up; the *tretā* when preparing to act; the *kṛta yuga* when fully committed to action (*Manu Smṛti*, IX, 301-302).

Between (*a*) the construction of the temple and (*b*) the installation of the images, Indradyumna undertakes a second ascending journey, leading this time to Brahmaloka. The texts mention, in connection with this episode, that the time of the demiurge is infinitely longer than that which governs human existence (a *kalpa* – a thousand cycles of 12,000 divine years – is no longer than a day and night of Brahmā). Therefore, the short stay of the King in the god's presence corresponds, on earth, to an immense temporal period, during which millions of sovereigns ruled the country:

X.

Indradyumna orders the building of the Puri temple.

Y.

Journey to Brahmaloka: abrupt temporal discontinuity.

Z.

Return to earth and installation of the images: beginning of the *kali yuga*.

FIG. 34

It is obvious that the journey to Brahmaloka (Fig. 34) reproduces the one Indradyumna himself had undertaken between Malwa and the peak of the Blue Mountain (Fig. 33). The homology is confirmed by an episode which, ignored by the *SkP*, figures in Kṛṣṇa Dāsa's *DT* and Hunter's oral version: during the Sovereign's sojourn in the sky, the temple was hidden under the sand, reappearing only at the moment of its inauguration. The texts thus reaffirm a correspondence between the temple and the sapphire. Here, as in many other instances, the different versions are inextricably interwoven.

Let us consider the figure below:

I. During the *kṛta yuga*, Indradyumna
leaves Malwa to find the sapphire;

II. The regular succession of cosmic periods is suspended.
The sapphire disappears under the sand.

III. a) X.
Indradyumna establishes his power in Orissa.
He orders the Puri temple built...

Y.

Journey to heaven; abrupt temporal discontinuity. Disappearance of the temple under the sand.

Z / b.
... and places the wooden images inside the temple
(beginning of the *kali yuga*).

FIG. 35

The set formed by elements X, Y, Z in Fig. 34 is but a *fragment* of a larger canvas represented by sequence I, II, III in Fig. 35. Level III in Fig. 35 splits into two segments [a) and b): Fig. 33], encompassing X, Y, Z (Fig. 34).

It is clear by now that the different configurations under scrutiny reveal a strikingly persistent pattern. An expression of the Void – unbound exiguity, "superluminous darkness", eloquent silence... – is always found in the innermost part of these symbolic structures. It lies at the core of the "fire altar", the plan of the temple, the sacred topography of Puri, as well as in the concentric arrangements of encapsulated narratives, sets of questions and answers, cosmic cycles, and successive moments of mystical itineraries. But there is more. Organised around its own empty centre, each image of totality splits, reverberating indefinitely. The elements in Fig. 35 are part of a still larger picture that includes the Brahmin's initial journey. This new whole (Fig. 36) irradiates itself from an empty centre (level 4: elision of the *tretā* and *dvāpara yuga*). The two halves into which the whole splits are also organised around an empty centre (levels 2 and 6, respectively).

1.

Vidyāpati leaves Orissa and returns to Malwa. The blue stone vanishes.

2.

Spatial and temporal disruption. The concealment of the blue stone provokes a succession of calamities. This period is conceived as a *pralaya*.

3.

Indradyumna leaves Malwa during the *kṛta yuga* in order to find Viṣṇu's stone image.

4.

Spatial and temporal disruption: elision of the *tretā* and *dvāpara yuga*.

5.

Indradyumna arrives in Orissa. He orders the performance of a horse sacrifice and the construction of a temple. The cult of Jagannātha inaugurates the *kali yuga*.

6.

Spatial and temporal disruption: Indradyumna ascends to the abode of Brahmā and penetrates into the quasi-eternal realm of the god.

7.

Indradyumna returns to the Blue Mountain. The wooden images are installed and the temple is consecrated at the outset of the *kali yuga*.

FIG. 36

The terminal levels in Fig. 36 (1 and 7) encompass the events leading, step by step, from the concealment of the blue stone to the temple consecration through an alternation of hesitant beginnings (the King's departure; the *aśvamedha* and the temple building; the installation of the wooden images) and sudden, unexpected moments, of spatial and temporal disruption.

Couched in the form of a specific narrative structure, this remarkable blend of "destruction" and "recreation", "void" and "plenum" seems to be an allusion to the subtle implication of the Vedic "fire altar" in the architecture of a Hindu temple. Like a *yantra* – whose intricacy captures the essence of the sacred building –, the myth of Indradyumna invites the reader (or listener) to visualise the inner structure of the object to which it refers. At the outset of the process described in Fig. 36, the concealment of the sapphire under the sand is the replica of the burying of the "golden *puruṣa*" (during the foundation rituals of the "fire altar"); at the end, the monument is inaugurated in the presence of Brahmā. But the narrative structure highlights the never-ending sucession of "retraction" and "manifestation" – *nivṛtti* and *pravṛtti* – and this recalls the alternation between "death" and "life", that is, the "perishable" and "imperishable" parts of the demiurge's body represented by the layers of arable land and the strata of clay bricks in the Vedic "fire altar". On the other hand, the void brought about by the three phases of *spatial and temporal disruption* is reminiscent of the three empty spaces formed by the superposition of *svayamātṛṇṇa* (the "naturally perforated" bricks) at the centre of the first, third and fifth strata of the bird-shaped altar.

Different levels of meaning thus cohere in the myth, from the "prologue" to the main plot of the story. Episodes and characters interplay as mirror images: the apparently double trip of the Sovereign (first to the summit of Nīlagiri, then to the abode of Brahmā) is a replica of the apparently double journey of Vidyāpati (first to the peak of the Blue Mountain, then to the top of the Cosmic Tree) – and this, in turn, seems to take as a model the apparently double roaming of Mārkaṇḍeya ("inside" and "outside" Viṣṇu's body).

As seen, the Brahmin's departure from Orissa "closes" a temporal cycle; the King's arrival "opens" a new one. Carried out, respectively, at the "end" and the "beginning" of a period, the itineraries of Vidyāpati and Indradyumna are strictly equivalent. Climbing the Cosmic Tree and returning to the ground (actions predating the "disappearance" of the sapphire), ascending to Brahmā's abode and going back to Orissa (actions predating the inauguration of the temple and, in some versions, its "reappearance" from the sand) are mutually reflective occurrences.

II

In the *SkP*, the recursive structure of Indradyumna's myth reflects the recursive structure of the "prologue", and both replicate the recursive structure of the Puri temple. These nested designs also reproduce the mutually embedded rituals of an *aśvamedha*.

A horse sacrifice is performed upon Indradyumna's arrival in Orissa. But, according to the *SkP*, the wanderings of the stallion can only begin when permission from the divinities associated with the *four directions* has been obtained. The reason of this is rather obvious: the horse sacrifice (and the confirmation of sovereignty it ensures) is the appropriation of space itself, the symbolic subduing of the *four cardinal points*. Similarly, the *BrP* states that the power of Indradyumna is acknowledged by the invited sovereigns, proceeding from the *four directions* of space. We find the same idea in the vernacular versions. But now the action begins in Malwa: the King entrusts the search for the sapphire to *four of his priests* who set off, one in each of the *four directions*. Some time later, those who went North, South and West return; he who went East enters the dense forests of Orissa. On hearing that the image has been found in the Blue Mountain, the King leaves and occupies the region by force.

The expansion of Indradyumna's sovereignty – an event whose epicentre usually lies in Orissa – is, this time, part of a more widespread movement unfolding from Malwa:

N	N
|	|
W — ORISSA — E	W — MALWA — E (Orissa)
|	|
S	S
(Purāṇic versions)	(Kṛṣṇa Dāsa; Hunter)

FIG. 37

Behind a landscape one discovers another, as behind a first *aśvamedha* a second may be envisioned.

The *SkP* places Indradyumna's *aśvamedha* between the military appropriation of Orissa and the consecration of the temple. Hence the horse sacrifice literally splits the text:

1. The land of Orissa is annexed to Indradyumna's dominions.

> Indradyumna performs an *aśvamedha*, a ceremony including two fundamental moments:
>
> I. The territories crossed by the horse are annexed to the King's dominions;
>
> II. The building of the "fire altar" guarantees the ascension of the sacrificer.

2. The building of the temple (the transformation of the "fire altar") guarantees the ascension of Indradyumna.

FIG. 38

Episodes 1 and 2 of the frame-narrative *reflect* episodes I and II of the ritual sequence –, conceived of as an inserted story.

The insertion of a ritual description in the middle of the story is more than a literary device creating an *aśvamedha* within an *aśvamedha* or a process that merely enlightens the "exterior" from an "interior" viewpoint. The authors insert part of the outer frame-story in the web of the inner sub-story (the account of the *aśvaṁedha*) but the relationship of the horse sacrifice to the narrative as a whole changes from one text to another. In the *SkP*, as we have just seen, the building of the temple *follows* the performing of the horse sacrifice:

Conquest of Orissa...

> *Aśvamedha*: In the course of the *soma* sacrifice, an inverted tree emerges from the ocean. Its trunk is carried to the *mahāvedi* and entrusted to a craftsman (Viṣṇu) who carves the images.

... and building of the temple.

FIG. 39. *Aśvamedha*'s place in the story, according to the *SkP*

The building of the temple is here *excluded* from the *aśvamedha* in which the carving of the wooden images is *included*. A ritual action (the *soma* pressing, part of the horse sacrifice) seems to be suspended for a moment so as to include and absorb another one (the carving of the wooden images), just as the sacrificial arena receives the trunk of the banyan. Myth and ritual are mutually embedded: the *aśvamedha* is part of the narrative structure, the latter being, in turn, integrated in the former.

Let us now consider the corresponding episodes of the *BrP*:

The story of Indradyumna
(*BrP, Puruṣottama māhātmya,* 44-53)

After the occupation of Orissa, Indradyumna orders the performance of an *aśvamedha* to which he invites sovereigns from the four corners of the world; simultaneously, he commands a great temple to be built. At the conclusion of the *aśvamedha* ceremonies (and the building of the temple), a deep restlessness comes over him: how can he obtain the god's image? One night, he receives the answer in a dream: he should seek the sacred tree at the place where the land meets the sea, cut it down and carve a new representation of the divinity. He immediately performs the first part of his mission, but it is Viśvakarmā, the divine architect, who is finally charged with producing the wooden icons. When the images are placed inside the temple, Indradyumna gives up all his worldly goods and ascends to heaven.

The horse sacrifice is now located between the conquest of Orissa and the felling of the sacred tree:

Conquest of Orissa...

> *Aśvamedha*: the building of the Jagannātha temple is here the replica of an *agnicayana* (the piling up of the "fire altar" clay bricks).

... and felling of the sacred tree.

FIG. 40. *Aśvamedha*'s place in the story, according to the *BrP*.

Being this time coterminous with the *aśvamedha*, the building of the temple is seen as a typical *agnicayana*. Conversely, the felling of the tree and the carving of the icons occur after the conclusion of the horse sacrifice.

Located on the Puri shore, the banyan reappears as a multiform of the Vedic *yūpa* whose base, resting on regularly watered ground, stands out on the eastern edge of the *mahāvedi*, half inside and half outside. Cutting down the tree-post (the *yūpa* which represents the *yajamāna*), the Sovereign reenacts Prajāpati's self-immolation. But, since the *aśvamedha* (just performed) evokes Prajāpati's sacrifice, the immolation of the demiurge is reenacted yet again: when Indradyumna fells the banyan, the ritual performance of the horse sacrifice is both extended and replicated.

III

The felling of the banyan tree by Indradyumna is not found in the *SkP*. This motif – which plays such a crucial role in the *BrP* – is here replaced by the description of a mysterious event. At the high point of the horse sacrifice, right at the moment of the *soma* pressing, an upside-down tree uncannily emerged from the ocean: its branches plunged into the depths of the ocean, its roots floated upon the waves. The *nyagrodha* – the banyan –, with its aerial roots extending downward, is frequently seen as an "inverted tree".[2] It also presents strong metaphysical connections with the *soma* (or with King Soma, as stated by the *Aitareya Brāhmaṇa*).

We know that a *nīm* (not a banyan) is currently used in the carving of the sacred images. Yet, before the felling, the *nīm* is associated with the *nyagrodha*. At that moment, an inverted human figure is drawn

---

[2] In India, the *aśvatta* (*ficus religiosa*) is also an "inverted tree". According to *RV*, I, 24, 7, Varuṇa upholds an *aśvatta* whose roots point upwards, and whose branches point downwards. Similar statements are found in the *Mbh*. But "There appears to have been some confusion... regarding the identity of the *Ashvattha*. *Ashvattha* tree does not grow any 'roots above', but the *Nyagrodha* tree does" (Gupta 1996: 79).

on the tree (Tripathi 1978 b: 247), and this, Starza argues, "seems to reflect the symbolism of the inverted cosmic fig-tree with 'roots above and boughs beneath' described in the *Rgveda* (1.24.7) and the *Katha Upanisad* (6.1-4)" (1993: 120-121). Furthermore, the representation of Jagannātha

> ... is called *cakrakrti* (having a round shape like the *cakra*) because the length of his figure should be the same as the breadth of his arms. This no doubt is ultimately based on the idea that Jagannatha like the *cakravartin* (emperor)... is represented by the *Nyagrodha-parimandala* or a figure resembling the rounded trunk of a *nyagrodha* (*ficus indica*) tree (*ibid.*: 120).

As an "inverted tree", the Cosmic Pillar projects itself towards the zenith and nadir. This double movement is captured by the Hindu temple. Bruno Dagens emphasises the perspective effects created by religious architectonic structures and the use of a mirror of water as a reflective surface. This is the case with some of the most famous Bhubaneshwar temples – the Mukteśvara, from the mid 10th century, and the Brahmeśvara, from the mid 11th (2005: 185). The procedure explores the analogy between the temple-mountain and Mount Meru, the *axis mundi* which, as certain texts state, goes as deeply into the ground as it rises heavenwards (*ibid.*: 184-185).[3]

But the Hindu temple, a mirrored object, is also the mirror (*ibid.*: 195) through which the deepest meaning of mythic and social relationships may be revealed.

---

[3] In the *EzV*, as we have seen, a golden Jagannātha temple is buried in the very place where the current monument stands. The story illustrates the mirroring effects attributed by mythic narratives to religious architectonic structures.

IV

Indradyumna reappears in the *SkP* as a human representative of the demiurge – a new reverberation produced by the Temple of Jagannātha. In this respect, the episode of the King's return from Brahmaloka is particularly meaningful.

In symbolic terms, it is highly significant that, having guaranteed Brahmā's collaboration, the Sovereign *precedes* the god on the journey to Orissa. Just as important is the fact that his arrival at the Puruṣottama kṣetra is welcomed by a recitation of the *Puruṣa sūkta*, the Vedic hymn celebrating the "creation" of the Universe.

Although Brahmā, Viṣṇu and Puruṣa are successively evoked on this occasion, it is Indradyumna who marks the crucial stages of the socio-cosmic "reorganisation". But to fully understand the episode of the temple's consecration, we also have to focus on the mirror relationship between Indradyumna, just returned from heaven, and the ruling Sovereign, Gāla Mādhaba.

Let us first stress Gāla Mādhaba's affinities with the god, Mādhaba and Nīlamādhaba being names attributed to the original representation of Viṣṇu.[4] The myth portrays the new King of Orissa as a Vaiṣṇava devotee who had ordered the installation of a (Mādhaba's) stone image in the sanctuary. Why is this unacceptable for Indradyumna?

It should be observed, following J.-M. Verpoorten, that Vedic rituals were dominated by the concern to prevent (or eliminate) two symmetrical excesses – that of similarity (*jāmi*) and that of difference (*pṛthak*). The first, making things indiscernible, is a cause of "confusion and conflict"; the second, introducing undue cleavages, provokes irremediable ruptures (1977: 84). B. Smith has noted, referring to

[4] Tripathi underlines that "around the 10th century, the Mādhava aspect of Viṣṇu... was very popular in coastal Orissa... [S]cores of such Mādhava images carved of black chlorite have been discovered and excavated in the Prācī valley" (2004: 13).

Verpoorten's text, that the immediate result of Prajāpati's self-sacrifice is an "imperfect Universe", threatened by one of these two tendencies:

> When the story of Prajāpati's emission has the emitted creatures indistinct or overly similar, the principle of *jāmi* or excessive resemblance is recalled. When, on the other hand, the creatures are said to be dispersed and overly distinct one from another, the equally dangerous metaphysical excess of extreme differentiation, *pṛthak*, is represented (1989: 59).

Similar ideas apply to the myth of Indradyumna. Under Viṣṇu's supervision, the concealment of the blue stone inside the Blue Mountain is a manifestation of transcendent oneness. But in the human sphere, the installation of a *stone image* in a *stone temple* expresses a critical *conjunction* of identical elements, an unacceptable lack of differentiation. In replacing the *stone icon* with the *wooden icon*, Indradyumna, on the contrary, suppresses chaos and reintroduces a balanced relationship between *stone* and *wood* – that is, between the temple (the *ersatz* mountain) and the image (the *ersatz* banyan tree).

The "divergence" between Indradyumna and Gāla Mādhaba was interpreted by Geib as a mythical survival of historical occurrences. Tripathi distances himself from this view: "One should be rather reserved in drawing historical conclusions from a temple legend contained in a Māhātmya, especially when the conclusion drawn from such a legend is of an extraordinary nature" (2004: 11). Yet, he believes that the introduction of Gāla Mādhaba into the story of Indradyumna is "an invention of the priestly class" in order "to explain the queer and unusual iconography of Jagannātha and the substance (wood) which it is made of" (*ibid.*: 13).

A problematic historical interpretation is thus replaced by another. The quarrel between Indradyumna and Gāla Mādhaba *is not intended to specify* either the material the icons are made of or their particular features. It rather underlines a socio-cosmic transformation, symbolised by a new relationship between *stone* and *wood*:

1. The Cosmic Tree which formerly carried out the function of a "wooden" temple – protecting under its branches the first representation of Viṣṇu – is replaced by the "true" stone temple (which Indradyumna ordered built). It is, however, the very Cosmic Tree which reappears inside the monument, now as a carved image;

2. Symmetrically, the sapphire "resurges" in the temple. Both are, as noted, transformations of the Blue Mountain.

However, when Indradyumna places the wooden icons in the stone temple, avoidance of excessive similitude is not his sole concern. According to Kṛṣṇa Dāsa's *DT* and Hunter's oral version, he orders the images carved *after returning from heaven* (that is, after the construction of the temple). The craftsman (Viṣṇu) wants to be alone within the sanctuary during the twenty-one days required to perform the task. But the queen, impatiently awaiting the moment when she can look upon the representation of Jagannātha (which should cure the sterility that afflicts her), persuades the Sovereign to open the temple doors prematurely. Her anxiety is fatal: the craftsman disappears, leaving his work unfinished.

The *vast period* spent by Indradyumna in Brahmaloka is followed by a *brief interim* which he was unable to respect. In other words, the *stone* temple (the cause of his journey to heaven) is associated with *long cycles*, *wooden* images with *short* ones. Indradyumna thus reaffirms the essential unity of the perishable[5] and imperishable. Indispensable for the consecration of the monument, his action is again reminiscent of Vedic conceptions: the "fire altar" expressed the alter-

[5] The banyan (out of which, according to the myth, the images are carved) is now a *vulnerable* object. We have seen that the *EzV* variant presents the Cosmic Tree as an unprotected object, exposed to Mārkaṇḍeya's fury. The *SkP* itself had announced that the banyan would soon be divided up. The fragmentation of the trunk and the partial reduction to ashes of the tree identified with Viṣṇu (and with *brahman*) once again symbolise Prajāpati's sacrifice and the dispersal of cosmic energy. The banyan tree's infinite capacity for renewal comes about through the weakening to which it is cyclically subjected. The *nīm* (used in current rituals) goes of course through the same process.

nation between the perishable and imperishable parts of the demiurge's body. The former (skin, hair, bones...) were represented by the layers of arable land between the strata of bricks; the latter (spirit, voice, flows of energy...), by the brick strata themselves. They were both compressed in the building process and it was precisely in this way that the altar, as a whole, became *immortal* (cf. Malamoud 1989: 78).[6]

According to the myth, the subtle reality of the *brahman* (symbolised by the banyan)[7] is protected by the stone construction. But let us now consider the rituals of renewal and consecration of the wooden images (*naba kalebara*). Here, the crucial moment is the transference of the *brahmapadārtha* (the god's "vital substance") from the old to the new icons. Tripathi describes this ritual sequence as follows:

> When the newly constructed images... are placed in front of their old prototypes, all the lights of the Temple are put out. The Daita entrusted with the job opens the belly of the old image in the dead of night with his eyes blindfolded and the hands wrapped up to elbows so that he may neither see nor feel the *brahmapadārtha* of the image. The casket containing the Brahmapadārtha is then taken out of the old *mūrti* and placed in the new one (1978 b: 260).

In Jagannātha temples outside Puri, the *brahmapadārtha* is a *śālagrāma*[8] – a black stone (with ammonite shell fossils), impregnated, it is believed, with the essence of Viṣṇu. But as for the images of the great temple of Puri itself, Tripathi adds, nobody knows what the *brahmapadārtha* really is. In the opinion of the priests, it might be also a *śālagrāma*, its black colour evoking the original dark chlorite (Nīla)mādhaba (*ibid.*) This view, even if considered a mere hypoth-

---

[6] The *ŚB* affirms that Prajāpati is a subtle combination of immanence and transcendence: he is mortal and immortal (XIV, 1, 2, 18), finite and infinite, limited and unlimited (VII, 2, 4, 30).

[7] The relationship between the "body" (as protective element) and the "soul" (as protected element) is also a recurrent idea in āgamic Śaivism: "it is said that the body is the temple and that the soul is the *liṅga* (*dehaṃ prāsādam ity uktaṃ dehī liṅgam iti smṛtam*)" (Dagens 2005: 134-135).

[8] *Cf.* Gonda 1954: 94-95.

esis, reinforces the idea that the consecration of the temple and that of the images reflect each other. In one case, the *perishable wood of the image* goes into the *imperishable stone of the temple*; in the other, conversely, the *imperishable substance* of the *brahmapadārtha* (a *śālagrāma*, according to the Brahmins) is inserted in the *perishable wood of the image*. The symbolic geography of old

Blue Mountain
Banyan tree
Nīlamādhava (blue or black chlorite stone)

reappears in the new structure

Jagannātha Temple (≈ Blue Mountain)
Nīm wooden images (ritual surrogate of the mythic *nyagrodha*)
Brahmapadārtha (black stone: *śālagrāma?*).

The terms of the two series correspond. But it is, of course, the last tripartite sequence, the visible outcome of sacrificial activity that displays the recursive nature of Vedic rituals: the *brahmapadārtha* is encapsulated in the images which are encapsulated in the temple (*stones* nested in *wooden* structures, nested themselves in a *stone* protection).

* * *

The central sequence of the *naba kalebara* – in which a Daitā (or Pati Mahāpātra[9]) presents himself blindfolded and with his hands bound – takes us back to Indradyumna's story. According to certain versions (see next chapter), the Brahmin meets the firm opposition of his host, who has decided not to reveal the access to the sacred image. The Śabara, it is true, finally accepts to lead the King's emissary to the sapphire but carefully blindfolds him. The latter, however, receives a

[9] Pati Mahāpātra, a functionary of the temple, is seen as half-Brahmin, half-Śabara. He is supposed to descend from Lalitā (a Śabaruṇī) and Vidyāpati.

provision of seeds which he drops fortuitously, one by one, along the way. What is "hidden" from his *eyes* is therefore "revealed" by his *hand*. The symbolism of these solidary gestures is reflected in the ceremony of transferring the *brahmapadārtha*. Invisible to the ritualists, the "death" of the gods cannot be detached from their "rebirth", which is enabled by the hand introducing the vital substance into the new images. A strong connection should thus be recognised between the Hindu priest of the mythical narrative and the Daitā in the ritual (see Chapter 7):

Myth of Indradyumna	Ritual (*naba kalebara*)
A blindfolded Brahmin, dropping seeds on his way to the sapphire, anticipates the inauguration of the new wooden images.	A blindfolded Daitā introduces the *brahmapadārtha* into the new wooden images.

FIG. 41

But there is also a striking analogy between the consecration of the wooden image by a Daitā and that of the temple by King Indradyumna (according to the *SkP*):

Myth *(SkP)*	Ritual (*naba kalebara*)
Indradyumna sets the wooden icons within the stone temple.	A Daitā sets the *brahmapadārtha* (a *śālagrāma* stone?) in the new wooden images.

FIG. 42

The Daitā mirrors here the inaugural action of the Sovereign. The implicit homologies in the above Figures (41, 42) are, of course, hardly compatible with common perspectives which tend to emphasise asymmetrical statuses. In Tripathi's opinion, the Brahmins are "marginalised" during the *naba kalebara*:

> [T]hey are kept away from knowing the 'life-substance' of the Deities and it seems that they have had to struggle hard to get hold of the statues at least on the last day, just before the end of the whole ceremony, in order to make a small stroke in the eyes of Jagannātha and others (1978 b: 264).

The underlying idea is that the *naba kalebara* is a "nice example of the superimposition of the Brahmanic Hinduism on a cult which was purely tribal in origin". Accordingly, "the presence of the Daitas... everywhere in the ceremony" would be "an irrefutable proof to this effect" (*ibid.*). Insisting on the relative invisibility of the Brahmins as evidence of a tribal past, the author indulges in the usual practice of declaring "irregular" (i.e. not genuinely Hindu) any context where the role of "subordinated" groups appears conspicuous. Starza also stresses the contrast between Daitās and Brahmins, devaluing this time the ritual function of the former:

> [T]here is really nothing unusual in *sudras* repairing and painting the processional icons in the Gundica festival. Actually they are not allowed to colour the pupils of the eyes of the deities..., and once their work is over, the images and the temple are purified. The *daitas* are of course the "body servants" whose duties include the carrying of the heavy icons to and from the cars. They are associated with the left just as the brahmins are with the right, their work is usually inauspicious (connected with the illness of the gods and repair of their bodies) (1993: 116).

The divergence between the two perspectives is significant: Starza favours the aspects he believes congruent with the Daitās' low position; Tripathi acknowledges their prerogatives in order to emphasise that they are incompatible with a Śūdra condition. But, as we will see, far from being linearly inferred from sociat status, the roles played by ritualists and mythical characters reflect each other. They are facets of a symbolic context dominated by the Jagannātha Temple – the great mirror.

PART III

REFLECTED FIGURES

CHAPTER SEVEN

THE VĀMANA'S THREE STRIDES AND THE ROLE OF THE *GRĀVASTUT*

I

A passage from the *ŚB* (XI, 1, 6, 1-3) states that, in the beginning, the primordial waters wished to reproduce themselves, and that a golden egg was born of this desire. The egg floated on the waves and hatched after twelve months. When appearing from this egg, Prajāpati uttered the first words: *bhūḥ, bhuvaḥ, svar* (Earth, Air, Heaven).[1]

The golden egg's wanderings lasted as long as those of the Horse before its sacrifice in the *aśvamedha*. The twelve-month gestation evokes, on the other hand, the twelve-day initiation of the sacrificer. Returning to the embryonic state, he is reborn identified with Prajāpati, whose words he reproduces: *bhūḥ, bhuvaḥ, svar*.

During the initiation, the *yajamāna* simulates the "three strides" thanks to which, according to another etiological narrative, Viṣṇu had once conquered the Universe – Earth, Air and Heaven. Before the dawn of time, the Cosmos was undifferentiated. Vṛtra, the Vedic Serpent-Dragon – a "demon" representing the "power of obstruction" – covered all the space between earth and sky (*ŚB* I, 1,3,4) and, couched on the primordial mountain, prevented the waters from flowing. Indra turned to Viṣṇu, seeking his help (*RV* IV, 18, 11; VIII, 100, 12). With three "great strides", the latter covered the Universe, opening up space. "His first step", Kuiper wrote, "corresponds to the netherworld (which includes the earth), his second step to the upper world, but his third step is a mystery, not perceptible to the human eye" (1962: 149).

Indra could then throw his weapon, the thunderbolt (*vajra*), to prop up the sky and slay the "demon". Immediately, the waters imprisoned by the mountain began to flow, dawn broke, the sun started its daily course (*RV* X, 104, 9-10).

---

1 A similar narrative is presented by the *Chāndogya Upaniṣad* (3, 19, 1-2): the egg hatches after a year and the two halves of the shell, made of gold and silver respectively, form the earth and the sky.

The collaboration between Viṣṇu and Indra summarises the spirit of sacrifice: the latter's destructive act "is needed for the birth of the world, but it is the sacrifice which transforms it into an organised cosmos" (Biardeau 1976: 90, *author's translation*).

The motif of Viṣṇu's "three strides" reappears in the Purāṇic literature.

The three strides of Vāmana
(*Bhāgavata Purāṇa*, 8, 15-23)

> A demon called Bali attacks the city where the gods had gathered together. Indra cannot defeat him but Viṣṇu, in the form of a dwarf (Vāmana), goes in search of the demon, whom he finds performing an *aśvamedha*. Knowing that, as a *yajamāna*, Bali could hardly refuse any request made to him at this time, Vāmana asks for an area equivalent to three of his small steps. Bali agrees. The first step covers the earth; the second, the whole of heaven. So as not to be accused of bad faith, Bali offers his own head as a support for the *avatāra*'s third step. The demon, henceforth, is consigned to the lower regions of the *sutala*.

The third step now sinks into the underworld. The vertical axis defining Vāmana's three strides is reminiscent of the Tree of Life, conceived of as "a ladder on which there is a perpetual going up and down" (Coomaraswamy 1977, I: 390). The same pattern applies to different episodes in the sory of Indradyumna – the double movement of the thirsty crow (from the banyan's summit into the waters of the Rohiṇī kuṇḍa and from these into the upper world) and, of course, the ascending and descending displacements undertaken by Vidyāpati. The tree-climbing motif can thus be understood as a transformation of Viṣṇu's three steps. Consider the following Oriya version, to which we alluded in Chapter 5.

The story of Indradyumna
(*Kṛṣṇa Dāsa*, *DT*, Fragment 1)

Eager to discover the blue stone, Indradyumna, King of Malwa, sent his messengers to the four quarters. In the Orissa forests, Vidyāpati finds a tribal hunter, Vasu, whose daughter, Lalitā, he is obliged (under severe threat) to accept as his wife. Seeing that Vasu is often away from the village, the Brahmin sinks into deep thought, apparently growing weaker and weaker (*brāhmaṇara deha kṣīṇa helā*). Lalitā believes this is due to the inadequate and insufficient food available in the forest. "No. That is not the reason", says Vidyāpati. "Tell me, where does your father go every night?"

Lalitā asks her father to guide Vidyāpati to the stone image on the Blue Mountain peak. Although he begins by refusing to grant her this request, he finally blindfolds the Brahmin and leads him to that place of worship. Before departure, however, the Śabaruṇī had given her husband a handful of mustard seeds which he secretly drops as he goes along.

On arrival, Vasu unbinds the Brahmin's eyes and, leaving him in the god's presence, goes off for a while. At that very moment, a crow swoops from a branch of the banyan, falls into the waters of the pool and immediately ascends to the paradise of Viṣṇu. Vidyāpati climbs to the top of the tree with the idea of following the crow's example. Realising the need to inform Indradyumna of the results of his mission, however, he climbs down and meets Vasu again, who meanwhile has gathered some tubers to offer the god. Viṣṇu refuses them and announces the imminent disappearance of the blue stone. A wooden image – to be set within a temple – will take its place.

This version differs on various important points from that of the *SkP*. Instead of the close friendship between the Brahmin and Śabara (now called Vasu), the Oriya text describes a matrimonial alliance between Vidyāpati and his host's daughter. Yet, a feeling of animosity pervades the relationship between the two men.

The conquest of the hostile country, the "foundation" of the new kingdom, and the establishement of the new cult are here the result of direct collaboration between the typical protagonists of a sacrifice – the Brahmin and the Sovereign, the ritualist and the quintessential sacrificer. Acting on the King's request, and preparing his triumphal journey, Vidyāpati evokes Viṣṇu as a "giver of space", whilst the King

– Indradyumna, "the one endowed with Indra's 'splendour' or 'majesty' (*dyumna*)" – is an obvious representative of the warrior god. The space stretching as far as the sacred tree (homologue of the *yūpa*) corresponds to the area of the *mahāvedi* – and the Brahmin's procedure, throwing the mustard seeds provided by Lalitā, is apparently inspired by the ritual sowing of the *agnikṣetra*. Scattering the grains on the soil, Vidyāpati masters the Universe (symbolised by the *mahāvedi*) and anticipates the King's victorious campaign.[2] But that is not all. Surreptitiously throwing the seeds, the Brahmin deceives his father-in-law, a trickery which calls to mind the Dwarf's attitude towards Bali. When Vāmana asked for an area corresponding to three of his small steps, he adopted indeed a fraudulent stratagem – a common, if puzzling attitude, as far as the god is concerned.[3]

The next episodes in the story of Indradyumna (Kṛṣṇa Dāsa) are no less revealing:

1. The Brahmin reaches the banyan (escaping Vasu's vigilance, whose help he had received).
2. Seduced by the possibility of immediate freedom, he climbs to the treetop.
3. Returning to the ground, he again meets Vasu, whom the god is about to abandon.

[2] As we saw in Chapter 5, the path of the priest towards the tree, the scaling of the trunk and the return to the ground foretell the building and consecration of the temple by Indradyumna (which determine successively the King's journey to the Blue Mountain's peak, the trip to Brahmaloka and the return to Orissa). Therefore, dropping seeds along the way, the Brahmin may also evoke the ritual of *aṅkurārpaṇa* ("the offering of the shoots") which precedes the building of a Hindu temple.

[3] The myth of the churning of the Milky Ocean includes a similar motif: that of Viṣṇu taking on the form of a beautiful woman in order to seduce the *asuras* and obtain the *amṛta* from them. See Dange, 1969.

The analogies with the Purāṇic scheme are remarkable:

Bhāgavata Purāṇa:
Vāmana covers the earth.
Vāmana covers heaven and aerial space.
Vāmana moves downwards. This third stride consecrates the *avatāra*'s supremacy over the "demon".

FIG. 43

Vidyāpati's metamorphosis further confirms the identification between the Brahmin and the *avatāra*. Kṛṣṇa Dāsa's words (*brāhmaṇara deha kṣīṇa helā*) seem here deliberately vague: *kṣīṇa helā* refers to a physical state interpreted by the Śabaruṇī as "emaciation" caused by an inappropriate diet. This is contradicted by the Brahmin's response. In fact, Vasu's nocturnal and mysterious roamings are the only cause of his sudden transformation. *Kṣīṇa*, "thin", "weak", "emaciated", also means "small", "diminutive". Therefore, *brāhmaṇara deha kṣīṇa helā* can be understood as "the Brahmin's stature had diminished", an allusion to the dwarfishness of the *avatāra* – as if Vidyāpati's metamorphosis were an initial reaction to the Śabara's challenge.

Vāmana's iconographic features generally comply with Purāṇic descriptions. The *Matsya Purāṇa*, for example, mentions the long hair of the *avatāra* who also wears the Brahmins' sacred thread. He carries the Veda, the water pot (*kamaṇḍala*), a bundle of *kuśa* herbs, the sceptre (*daṇḍa*) and the sacred umbrella.

FIG. 44. Vāmana

In a Sāraḷā Dāsa version, as we shall see, the description applies in almost the same terms to Indradyumna's envoy. He stands out by his long hair (*lambita juḍā*), the sacred thread, and a cloth (*uttarī*) whose folds conceal the Veda and other manuscripts. He possesses all the instruments needed by a priest: the water pot (*kamaṇḍala*), the ceremonial spoon, and a bundle of *kuśa* herbs. He also bears a sacred umbrella.

We have previously identified Vidyāpati, the protagonist of a tree-climbing ritual, with Mārkaṇḍeya, the Brahmin who undertook a decisive ascension along the *nyagrodha*. But it is clear that, preparing the way for Indradyumna, the human replica of Indra, he is *also* Viṣṇu-Vāmana. Now, according to this last reading of the story, only one role is left to the Śabara – that of Vṛtra-Bali, the "demon" whose "resistance" had to be overcome for a new socio-cosmic order to emerge. Unlike Viśvāvasu, the benevolent host of the *SkP*, Vasu appears in the *DT* as the embodiment of a "power of obstruction". From one version to another, the tribal hunter's features seem to change radically. Yet, the Śabara's unfriendly feelings towards the Brahmin do not prevent (in fact, they rather imply) the alliance between Vidyāpati and Lalitā. The Śabara's reality fades away whenever we try to capture it in a single image. The ultimate mystery of his identity – the *id* in everyone's *id-entity* – is the hidden nature of God himself.

II

In ancient times, according to the *ŚB* (III, 2, 4, 1-2), the *soma* was in the sky, and the gods were on earth. The goddess Gāyatrī obtained the plant in heaven. However, on her return journey, she was intercepted by a celestial genie, a *gandharva*[4] called Viśvāvasu, who took her precious merchandise. Knowing the *gandharvas* to be fond of women, the gods sent them goddess Vāc. Then, a deal was proposed by the former: "You will keep the *soma*; we will keep Vāc". The gods agreed and the *soma* was exchanged for the goddess (III, 2, 4, 3-4). But, after they had the plant in their possession, the gods tricked the *gandharvas*, seducing Vāc (through music and songs) and making her return to them.[5]

---

[4] The *gandharvas* are a group of celestial beings who play the role of mediators between gods and humans.

[5] This episode evokes the classical story of how the *devas* won the *amṛta* (through betraying the *asuras*). See Dange 1969: 267-268.

The bargain alluded to by the *ŚB* was ritually re-staged prior to any *soma* sacrifice. The ceremony included a dramatisation of the buying of the stalks. A "trader", represented by a Brahmin or a Śūdra, entered the *mahāvedi* area; then, the *adhvaryu* inquired about the provenance of the product and proposed purchasing it for a price that was invariably negotiated (1/16 of a cow, 1/12, 1/8, 1/4, until, finally, the whole animal). This negotiation symbolised the old conflict between *devas* and *gandharvas* (Malamoud 2005: 139-140).[6]

Like *soma*, the sapphire (kept under Viśvāvasu's control, in the story of Indradyumna) grants eternity. The localisation of the blue stone image also evokes that of the plant which, in Vedic tradition, grew on mountainous peaks, particularly on Muñjavant.

Conceived of as "mountains" (*parvata, adri, giri*), the millstones (*grāvan*) that grind the *soma* stalks are a metaphor for the primordial conjunction of the blue stone and the Blue Mountain (*nīlādri, nīlagiri,* etc.).[7] Being impregnated with the essence of *soma*,[8] they are, as the elixir itself, a symbol of immortality.

In Vedic India, when the *grāvans* ground the stalks, a hymn was chanted by a Brahmin, the *grāvastut* - "the praiser of *grāvans*". Blindfolded, he remained far from the operation.[9] The scene is probably at the root of the Śabara's intransigent demand: Vidyāpati should wear a blindfold during his journey to the sapphire.

---

[6] The cow given in payment is an allusion to goddess Vāc: "According to some texts..., Vāc and the cow with which the Soma is purchased are identical" (Gonda 1965: 68). It is also commonly assumed that the "*soma* trader" in the Vedic ritual is "the counterpart of the rivals of the gods who were in temporary possession of the elixir" (*ibid.*: 69).

[7] *Devas* and *asuras* produce the *amṛta* by spinning Mount Mandara on the back of the tortoise. Inspired, as we have seen, by the traditional technique of skimming milk, this episode also alludes to the movement of the *grāvans* in the extraction of the elixir. See Dange 1969.

[8] *Ibid.* 148-149.

[9] *Cf.* Staal 1983, I: 58.

The grinding of the stalks symbolises the sacrifice of king Soma and, Malamoud emphasises, it is the execution of the victim that the Brahmin is prevented from seeing. In the Vedic ritual, the *grāvastut* "displays his own dissimulation", proclaiming and denying simultaneously "the violence of which he is the non-spectator, the non-witness" (2005: 147).

Let us now return to the Oriya story. What is, in this context, the crucial event Vidyāpati should not see? The answer is clear. His journey is a preparation for the self-sacrifice of the god, whose stone image *will soon cease to be seen*. Viṣṇu's *invisibility* in the form of the sapphire is foretold by a Brahmin who is *forbidden to see*, and is himself a human replica of Viṣṇu (Vāmana). The subtle nexus introduced here between the god *who cannot be seen* and the priest *who cannot see* subsumes once more the perfect coincidence of the "creator" and "created being", of the "hidden" and "revealed" reality. As the *soma*, which *disappears* in the form of a stalk to *reappear* as an elixir - *dying* to become a *warrant of eternity* –, the Supreme Being sacrifices through the "self-dissimulation" by which he... "is revealed".

According to the *ŚB* (III, 6, 3, 19), Viṣṇu is *soma* itself. A strong connection is thus posited between the grinding of the *soma*'s stalks and the disappearance of the blue stone, a metaphor for the god's self-sacrifice. But this again is just a one-sided perspective. Since Vṛtra, the "demon", is also the victim of the *soma* sacrifice, we are entitled to assume that, in Kṛṣṇa Dāsa's *DT*, it is the very immolation of the Śabara that Vidyāpati, the Brahmin, is not allowed to see. The idea of the Śabara's immolation is likewise implied in the *SkP*. As mentioned before, Viśvāvasu knows every detail - past and future - of the story in which he is involved. He is granted the highest vision - the synthesis of syntheses - beyond the horizon of common awareness. Welcoming the Brahmin, becoming his friend, and leading him to the sapphire, he seems to renounce his own privileges - in some way, an expression of self-sacrifice.

Viśvāvasu, the Śabara, and Viśvāvasu, the *gandharva*, are therefore united by strong, if implicit, interconnections. This throws new light on the story of Indradyumna. The *gandharvas* are generally endowed with the ability to *stimulate* superior "knowledge", "intuition" or "vision" (*dhīḥ*) (Gonda 1963: 91). Such attributes are extolled by the *AV* (II, 1, 2): "May the gandharva, knower of the immortal, proclaim that highest abode that is in secret" (*ibid*). From this we can deduce that the momentary physical blindness the Śabara usually imposes on the priest favours – instead of hindering – the latter's vision. The *SkP* ignores this motif. But the *visual ban* normally inflicted on Vidyāpati is here transformed into *linguistic interdiction*, the Brahmin being forbidden to tell the story of the sapphire's disappearance. In any case, it is the Śabara who reveals the blue stone: as the *gandharva*, he is the "revealer of a secret".

* * *

There are also Tantric innuendos in the vernacular versions of the Oriya myth, where the feminine figure is particularly stressed. Lalitā (literally a "charming", "voluptuous", "lovely" woman) is a common designation for Tripura Sundarī, one of the ten Tantric Mahāvidyā. Śabarī, in turn, is one of the names of low or outcaste women representing the spiritual guide, the most valuable partner for Tantric practices.[10] Let us finally remark that Śabareśvarī (the "mistress of the Śabaras") is a goddess identified with Mātaṅgī, another Mahāvidyā (Kinsley 1997: 219).

Although Vidyāpati and Lalitā stay together for a very short period (he leaves the village not long after his arrival), their marriage plays an important role in the *DT* and in Hunter's version: overcoming her father's "resistance", the Sabaruṇī (or Sabarī) makes possible

[10] Tantrism celebrated the figure of the Ḍombī, the "washerwoman", a low caste or dissolute woman (Eliade 1958: 261, note 204): the greater the woman's depravity, the more appropriate she becomes for the purpose of the ritual. In the secret language of Tantrism, *ḍombī* means the final state of freedom: *nairātmya* – the state of nonego, or *śūnya*, "emptiness", is [sometimes] described as a girl of low caste or a courtesan (*ibid.*) *Cf.* Dimock Jr. 1966: 200; 217; O'Flaherty 1973: 52.

her husband's journey up to the Blue Mountain's peak, granting him a transcendental experience.

According to Tantrism, *soma* is produced through a return to Unity, symbolised by the *maithuna* (or sexual embrace) of the God and Goddess – a mystical convergence which seems to be realised, in our context, by the unexpected relationship between Lalitā and the Hindu priest. This is the final step of the Tantric process represented by the arousing and raising of feminine energy (*śakti*) in the form of a serpent (*kuṇḍalinī*). Now, on awakening, the *kuṇḍalinī* is supposed to move along the central channel of the subtle body identified with Mount Meru, the axis of both macrocosm and microcosm. Here, again, a deep symbolism is associated with rituals of *tree climbing*. By allowing her husband to *climb the Cosmic Tree* (the equivalent to the spinal column at a microcosmic level), Lalitā reappears as an embodiment of *śakti*, the divine feminine power.

The myth of Indradyumna allows for a plurality of readings. But the different roles played by the characters, and the interpretations they suggest, are subtly interwoven. They compose a synthetic unity.

CHAPTER EIGHT

THE OFFENDER OFFENDED

Crystallographers... speak of crystal growth in steps wherever there is a "dislocation", which makes for both order and growth, an open-ended system. When one compares the many *Mahābhāratas* or other works based on the epics, the way new incidents are added only in certain places where there seems to be a need for them, one thinks of such an analogy with crystal growth.

A. K. Ramanujan

I

Oriya literature, as is usually acknowledged, originates in the first half of the 15th century with Sāraḷā Dāsa, a Śūdra to whom we owe the written version of a vernacular *Mbh*.[1] According to Mansinha,

> It was a blessing to the nation and to Oriya literature that this great genius was born a peasant living close to Orissa's soil, absorbing into and displaying in his life the very essence of the national culture in all its aspects. It was indeed good also, that he grew up, it seems, completely ignorant of Sanskrit and was not highly educated in any sense (1962: 53).

In Mansinha's opinion, the Oriya *Mbh* is an uncommon work: "Sarala Dasa has painted real life ..., men and women of real flesh and blood, and not demi-gods and angels such as are found in the Sanskrit epics" (*ibid.*: 54).

This perspective is questionable. Studying the popular cult of Draupadī in southern India, Hiltebeitel compared the information gathered in the field with that contained in the Sanskrit epic about the same character. His findings led him to question many of the "oppositions that have enlivened Indological studies... over recent decades": folk/classical; Vedic/Hindu; popular/ Brahmanical; Aryan/Dravidian; Sanskritic/vernacular (1988: XIX). As he also remarked, the great Sanskrit epic "evokes, through its symbolism, certain cultural themes, myths, ritual practices, and social norms that are not fully attested historically until 'post-epic' times" (1980b: 151). It should, therefore, be interpreted from a double perspective – "not only retrospectively but, in a sense, prospectively" (*ibid.*)

---

[1] Written between 300 B.C.E. and A.D. 300, the classical *Mbh* is an immense work. Yet, in this vast array of material we find just a part of a still vaster mass of information, its critical edition being a provisional task: "There has never been a census of manuscripts of the *Mahābhārata*, and there is never likely to be. Such a census... could never pretend to complete comprehensiveness" (Dunham 1991: 1).

> [O]ne can pretty safely assume that the bards knew more about the main story, both in terms of variants and underlying symbolism, than they told. It is thus worth investigating whether what they left untold but implicit, or what they alluded to through symbols, is not still echoed in the vast oral and vernacular epic and epic-related traditions ... I have come to suspect that living traditions of and about the Mahābhārata are often in close touch with traditional epic meanings that have escaped the classically based literary scholars (*ibid.*: 152).

The same applies to Sāraḷā Dāsa, whose work develops – sometimes at length – episodes summarily presented by the classical text. The story of Indradyumna is given considerable space here, whilst the death of Kṛṣṇa is told in the light of generally ignored interpretations.

But before embarking on the study of Sāraḷā Dāsa's perspectives, we should recall some relevant aspects of the Sanskrit *Mbh.* Tradition credits Vyāsa with authorship of the epic. As pointed out by Bruce Sullivan, he is *doubly* the author of the poem, "for not only is he the reputed composer of the text, but is also the creator of the Bhārata family on which the story is centered" (1990: 2).[2]

Of the three characters he fathered (Dhṛtarāṣṭra, Pāṇḍu and Vidura), only the second was capable of ruling: the first was born blind; the last was conceived by a Śūdra servant. Condemned to sexual impotency, Pāṇḍu is a King without progeny. Fortunately, Kuntī, his first wife, possessed a magical *mantra* enabling her to summon the gods' physical presence and their aid. At her husband's bidding, she convokes Dharma, Vāyu and Indra, with whom she conceives Yudhiṣṭhira, Bhīma and Arjuna respectively. Using the same *mantra*, Mādrī, the King's second wife, calls upon the Aśvin twins and conceives Nakula and Sahadeva. These are the five Pāṇḍavas. They grow up with the Kauravas (the hundred sons of Dhṛtarāṣṭra) and together they are taught by the same preceptor, Droṇa, a Brahmin who mastered the science of arms. During this period, Arjuna stands out by his courage and skill in wielding weapons. There then follows a crucial episode:

---

2 See also Hiltebeitel 2001.

The story of Ekalavya
(*Mbh*, *Ādi parva*, 123)

One day, Droṇa is visited by a *niṣāda*, a tribesman, who wants to become one of his disciples. This request is refused but the *niṣāda* settles in the nearby forest, in a spot from where he can follow the lessons. His skill and dexterity are soon recognised; they even put Arjuna in the shade. Droṇa seeks him out. As the *niṣāda* insists on considering him his instructor, the Brahmin claims payment for the services unwillingly given. The young man is ready to pay whatever is requested and, when Dro ṇa demands his right-hand thumb, he pays his debt. Henceforth, he is known as Ekalavya, "an amputated (thumb)".

The Kauravas and the Pāṇḍavas complete their apprenticeship under Droṇa but the former feel jealous of Pāṇḍu's children, and, not accepting Yudhiṣṭhira as the future King, try to eliminate them. The Pāṇḍavas escape several persecutions and finally take refuge in the forest. It is during this period that Arjuna receives in a *svayṃvara*[3] the hand of princess Draupadī, who will be the five heroes' wife. On learning that the Pāṇḍavas have survived, the Kauravas agree to divide up the kingdom: they stay in Hāstinapura, whilst their cousins make Indraprastha their capital. Yudhiṣṭhira progressively consolidates his authority and performs a *rājasūya*, a ritual which turns him into a universal Sovereign. The Kauravas decide to put an end to his growing power. As part of a secret plan, they invite the Pāṇḍavas to a game of dice in Hāstinapura. The challenge is accepted; Yudhiṣṭhira, whose passion for the game is well-known, will play against Śakuni, the Kauravas' maternal uncle. Combining trickery with his unbeatable skill, Śakuni defeats his opponent throw after throw. Yudhiṣṭhira loses his vast riches, and next bets – and loses – each of his brothers. The game continues. He bets himself and loses; then he bets Draupadī who, in the midst of her menstruation, had remained secluded. Duryodhana, Dhṛtarāṣṭra's first born, orders a servant to bring her into their

[3] The *svayaṃvara* (or "self-choice") combines the abduction and choice of bridegroom by the girl (*cf.* Dumézil 1979: 33). See also Jamison 1996: 238; 246.

presence, but she refuses to appear at the *sabhā*, the assembly hall, where the players are gathered together. The description of what has just taken place raises a doubt in the princess' mind: did Yudhiṣṭhira bet her before or after betting himself? This is a delicate issue: can a player who has lost his own freedom still bet someone or something?[4]

Finally, Duḥśāsana (another of Dhṛtarāṣṭra's sons) is charged with bringing the princess to the assembly hall, and, ignoring her pleas, he brutally drags her by her disarrayed hair (a sign of the temporary state of feminine impurity). The humiliation of the Pāṇḍavas is condensed into the insults Draupadī suffers, displayed like a slave and treated like a prostitute. In the end, Duḥśāsana rips off her clothes but, as they are torn away, others appear and protect Draupadī until her exhausted aggressor admits his impotence.

Dhṛtarāṣṭra annuls the results of this first game. The Kauravas, however, convince him to allow a second one, the outcome of which depends, this time, on a single throw. Yudhiṣṭhira loses again. According to the rules laid down, the Pāṇḍavas and Draupadī must undergo a twelve-year exile in the forest, followed by a thirteenth year which they will spend, under strict secrecy, in a place of their own choosing. The court of Virāṭa, King of the Matsya (literally: the "Fish") is their

[4] As Hiltebeitel points out, "[W]hen the usher has explained the betting sequence, with Yudhiṣṭhira having bet himself before he bet her, [Draupadī] uses her wits: 'Go to the game. Having gone, ask in the sabhā, what did you lose first, yourself or me (*kiṃ nu pūrvam parājaiṣīrātmānam māṃ nu*)? Having learned that, then come to take me'. Draupadī formulates her question in a way that opens up two things that might work in her favor. She definitely wants the question raised 'in the sabhā', where she can expect it to be treated 'in court' as a case of 'law', dharma. And,... in asking Yudhiṣṭhira a question whose answer she has already obtained, she makes it clear at least to readers that her question is about more than it says.... For although one is forced to translate, 'What did you lose first, *your*self or me?' what she also says, literally, is, 'What did you lose first, self or me?' (2001: 242). The princess' words are also evidence of the tension between "interior" and "exterior", between the "hidden" and the "revealed". "It is clear that in all this talk about betting oneself, Draupadī's question is a philosophical one about the nature of self..." (*ibid.*: 260).

elected place. The end of this long banishment marks the beginning of the war between the two groups of cousins.

* * *

The exile is particularly revealing as regards the identity of the five brothers and their common wife. Let us start with the latter. Draupadī represents earth, as suggested by her dark complexion, to which the word 'Kṛṣṇā' – the "Black" one (another of her names) – seems to allude (Biardeau 1971-72: 41). In the classical *Mbh*, she is *explicitly* presented as a manifestation of Śrī-Lakṣmī, the goddess associated with sovereignty, power (*kṣatra*) and fecundity.[5] But the period spent in the forest and in the court of Virāṭa accentuates some new features. This is surprisingly clear in the popular cult of Draupadī, studied by Hiltebeitel in South India. "Street dramas" and regional folklore show a cruel, violent and "demonic" side to the princess – a fact dismissed by or even unknown to most scholars. She presents herself under a threatening form; she fights and kills flesh-eating, malignant beings:

> [W]hat is it that makes the forest Draupadī... such a certain match for these voracious and even cannibalistic demons? To put it simply, Draupadī is a cannibal herself. When I first heard this from a Telugu-speaking Brahman... in April 1975, I was stunned. ... How could the cannibalistic theme be adapted to the known mythology of Draupadī? (Hiltebeitel 1988: 290).

In the light of such ideas, the role she plays in the Sanskrit text deserves closer attention. She maintains, throughout the whole period of exile, "the state of menstrual impurity she underwent during the dice game" (Biardeau 1976: 153, *author's translation*); and, in Virāṭa's court, she passes herself off as a *sairandhrī* (an impure chambermaid

[5] *Cf.* Gonda 1954, chap. II.

and hairdresser), hiding her dishevelled hair under filthy clothes: "[H]er disguise... is the very antithesis of what one would expect from the incarnation of Śrī, whose other primary associations include good fortune and auspiciousness" (Hiltebeitel 1981: 192). Briefly, the author argues, she cannot be seen *only* as a human manifestation of Viṣṇu's wife; certain aspects of her personality call to mind also the goddess of "destruction" associated with Śiva – Kālī, "the exemplary Goddess of the dishevelled hair" (*ibid.*: 206).[6]

This change in perspective leads Hiltebeitel to a careful re-examination of the Pāṇḍavas' identity – that of Arjuna in particular. As a matter of fact, the "affinity of Arjuna and Draupadī with Śiva and the Goddess" is "an indispensible key to understanding the Draupadī cult", suggesting the need of "a fresh look at their portrayal in the Sanskrit epic" (Hiltebeitel 1980b: 153).[7]

Two examples will suffice to stress Arjuna's Śaivite nature.

1. One day, during the Pāṇḍavas' exile in the forest, Arjuna leaves his brothers and goes looking for the weapons which will be needed in the coming battle. Before he acquires them, Śiva appears to him as

[6] The author further points out that "Draupadī's dishevelled hair is... an image of Kālarātri, the Night of Time, the night of the dissolution (*pralaya*) of the universe" (1981: 207). His study completes – whilst modifying – the viewpoint of Dubuisson, who only saw in Draupadī's dishevelled hair a metaphor of the "Earth's vegetation" (1978). According to oral versions collected in southern India, "From the beginning of her life in the forest to the end of the *Mahābhārata* war, the period when she wears her hair dishevelled..., Draupadī nightly takes on the 'form of Kālī'..." (Hiltebeitel 1988: 291). *Cf.* also Kinsley 1975.

[7] It is true that Yudhiṣṭhira, the first born, holds the reigns of power and acquires, through the *rājasūya*, the title of universal Sovereign. But it is Arjuna who wins Draupadī's hand, the symbol of sovereignty (insofar as she *is* Śrī-Lakṣmī). Arjuna is the model of the Kṣatriya, the exemplary hero, guided and protected by Kṛṣṇa until the end of the war. He is, according to Biardeau, the *Mbh*'s "genuine sovereign", an "ideal king" presented in a coded manner (1978: 89). [See also Hiltebeitel 1980: 150, note 21; 1976: Chapters 9 and 10]. In Hiltebeitel's opinion, Biardeau exaggerates the importance of Arjuna's links with royalty. Obviously acknowledging the explicit ties between Arjuna and Kṛṣṇa (Hiltebeitel 1984; 1985), he also stresses the strong relationship between Arjuna and Śiva, of which there are many examples.

a Kirāta (a tribal hunter). At that moment, a wild boar bursts out of the undergrowth and heads for Arjuna who immediately fires an arrow. Śiva does the same and the animal is hit twice. Each of the archers claims to have been the first to wound the beast. Unable to agree on the matter, they start fighting and the god successively destroys all the hero's arrows. The conflict - but is this a "true" conflict? - ends in the victory of Śiva who, compressing Arjuna's limbs, reduces them to a *piṇḍa*, literally a "ball (of rice)", a sacrificial oblation.

In Biardeau's opinion, this episode is dominated by the symbolism of consecration. The fight with the Kirāta turns the hero into a sacrificer (1978: 159). But in this context, Hiltebeitel adds, "Arjuna... becomes 'one' with Śiva" (1980b: 159). The idea was implicit from the very beginning: god and hero hit a target at the same time and, here again, "Arjuna is one with Śiva in his destructive role." (*ibid.*)

2. In Arjuna's case, the last year of exile is also particularly suggestive. The warrior appears before Virāṭa disguised as a eunuch, a dance and music teacher named Bṛhannaḍā (or Bṛhannalā): "[N]early everything about his disguise", Hiltebeitel stresses, "holds hints of identification with Śiva" (*ibid.*: 154). A master of dance, Arjuna is a replica of Śiva Naṭarāja. Dressed and adorned in feminine fashion, he recalls Śiva *ardhanārīśvara* (the lord who is half woman). Finally, having adopted a name derived from Bṛhannara (the "great Nara"), the "epitome of manhood", he is (also in Biardeau's view) an impersonation of Mahāpuruṣa (1978: 189). But Bṛhannaḍā is feminine, and "a name in the feminine gender meaning the 'great man' implies Arjuna's completeness and echoes the homage to Śiva as the Puruṣa who is male, female, and eunuch" (Hiltebeitel 1980b: 157).

II

In the Sanskrit *Mbh*, Ekalavya, the *niṣāda*, has nothing in common with Jaras, the hunter who eventually kills the *avatāra*. But the Oriya *Mbh* fuses the two characters: Jārā, who seeks out Droṇa as a *guru*, is the Śabara who, at the end of the *dvāpara yuga*, accidentally causes Kṛṣṇa's death. The two episodes described by Sāraḷā Dāsa are perfectly symmetrical. Here is the first:

Jārā, the unexpected pupil
(Oriya *Mbh*, *Ādi parba*, I, 62, 68)

Jārā presents himself before Droṇa, aiming to receive his teachings. Driyodhana (Duryodhana), the eldest of the Kauravas, asks one of his brothers, Dhuśāsana (Duḥśāsana), to remove the intruder. Dhuśāsana drags him by the hair (*bāla dhari*) but Jārā, undaunted, settles near the palace.

One day, during a hunt organised by the two groups of cousins, the Kauravas unwittingly approach Jārā's shelter, and, near the lake, surprise the Śabara's wife, Śiriyā, who had come to fetch water and bathe. Seduced by her beauty, Dhuśāsana is ready to kidnap her with the help of his brothers. In the meantime, Jārā arrives. "How can a man of the forest (*banacara loka*) have a wife with the bearing of a queen (*pātarāṇī*)?" asks Dhuśāsana. In a second, the Śabara wipes them out.

The Pāṇḍavas return to the palace with no news of their cousins. Accompanied by Karṇa[8], Bhīma and Arjuna, Droṇa looks for the Kauravas and, finding them lifeless, realises they were killed by someone who masters his own skills. Arjuna wants to discover the mysterious author of this deed and finds Jārā. Conflict is inevitable. However, their arrows meet in the air and are mutually destroyed. The duel is interrupted when Droṇa arrives. "Who taught you the science of arms?" he asks the Śabara. Jārā reveals his secret and, thanks to the power of a magic arrow (*jībanyāsa śara*, a "life-giving" arrow), brings his adversaries back to life. Droṇa is

[8] Fathered by Sūrya, the Sun, Karṇa was the first child conceived by Kuntī before her marriage to Pāṇḍu. Abandoned at birth (as an illegitimate son), he later joined the Kauravas. Arjuna killed him in the fratricidal war between the Pāṇḍavas and the Kauravas.

> not satisfied: "If you see yourself as my disciple, you must pay for my services (*guru dakṣinā*)." Jārā is willing to pay whatever is asked and Droṇa claims the thumb from his right hand.

The link established by Sāraḷā Dāsa between Jārā (the Śabara) and Droṇa (a partial reincarnation of Bṛhaspati) has surprising resonances. Long ago, when gods and *asuras* fought for the lordship of the world, the former had chosen Bṛhaspati as their chaplain (*purohita*), whilst the latter entrusted a similar role to Śukra (Kāvya Uśanas). Śukra, a son of Bhṛgu, endowed as such with the exceptional power of the Bhārgavas, possessed the "knowledge of revivification" (*mṛtasaṃjīvinī vidyā*). "The relationship between Śukra and the asuras", Goldman writes, "is one of the most provocative and puzzling aspects of Bhārgava myth" (1971: 124):

> That Bhṛgus should show hostility for the gods on some occasions is strange, but that one of the greatest of the Bhārgava sages should regularly champion the asuras, the forces of chaos and evil – in short, of adharma – against the divine personifications of dharma is perplexing and has no non-Bhārgava parallel in the literature" (*ibid.*: 124-125).

Śukra's superior knowledge does bring about an unbalanced relationship between the gods and *asuras*. Yet, this does not lead to "real" opposition. From the dualistic perspective adopted by Goldman, the "intimate cooperation" between Śukra and Kaca (Bṛhaspati's son) is also baffling. Once, the gods exhorted Kaca to meet the *asuras' purohita* and to obtain from him the *mṛtasaṃjīvinī vidyā*. Kaca complied and asked his father's "enemy" to accept him as his pupil. Well received by Śukra (and by Śukra's daughter, Devayānī, who fell in love with him), Kaca aroused the anger of the *asuras* who then killed him. Śukra brought him back to life and the "demons" killed him again. Moreover, to get rid of him, they burned his body and mixed the ashes with Śukra's wine. Drinking this and learning that the young man now lies inside his belly, the chaplain seems helpless: Kaca's deliverance would mean his own death. Faced with the dilemma of losing either her lover or her father, Devayānī is inconsolable. There is however one solution. Before "giving birth" to Kaca, Śukra communicates to him the *mṛtasamjīvinī vidyā*, thus assuring his own revivification by his "son". We find here a new example of "mutual creation": the teacher becomes the "mother" of his pupil who, in turn, becomes the "mother" of his teacher. Being both progenitor and progeny, Śukra is clearly a replica of the demiurge.

Kaca is sucessively Bṛhaspati's and Śukra's son.[9] Far from expressing sheer antagonism, the chaplain of the gods and the chaplain of the demons collaborate in the same process. This episode (illustrating, after all, a remarkable proximity between Śukra and Bṛhaspati) throws new light on the relationship between Jārā and Droṇa (according to Sāraḷā Dāsa). During the war, Droṇa fights on the side of the "demonic" Kauravas, a role symetrical to the one he had played under the identity of Bṛhaspati: in short, he is then in the place previously occupied by Śukra. This inversion explains the apparent similarity between Jārā (the rejected pupil) and Kaca (the welcome disciple), both acquainted with the "knowledge of revivification":

Śukra and Kaca (in the classical tradition)	**Droṇa and Jārā (in the Oriya *Mbh*)**
Śukra, the chaplain of the *asuras*...	Droṇa, a reincarnation of Bṛhaspati, the gods' chaplain...
...is visited by Kaca, who wants to become his pupil.	...is visited by Jārā, who wants to become his pupil.
Kaca is well received.	Jārā is rejected.
Sacrificing himself, Śukra becomes Kaca's "progenitor".	Sacrificing himself, Jārā is eventually recognised as a pupil (i.e. a "son") of Droṇa.
Kaca obtains the "science of revivification" to favor the gods.	Jārā uses the "science of revivification" to bring the Kauravas back to life.

FIG. 45

[9] On the symbolic relationship between Śukra and Kaca, see also Dumézil 1971: 160-161; and Malamoud 1989: 81-82.

Let us now reconsider the following episodes, which clearly anticipate Draupadī's humiliation after the first dice game:

1. Dhuśāsana expells Jārā, the Śabara, dragging him by the hair;
2. Dhuśāsana is about to kidnap the Śabaruṇī, Siriyā (Śrī, symbol of sovereignty).

In the Oriya *Mbh*, Draupadī *is not* an *explicit* manifestation of Śrī (as in the classical text) but an incarnation of Durgā. Śrī is represented here by the Śabaruṇī, whose beauty and bearing so surprised the Kauravas. The comparison is revealing:

Sanskrit *Mbh*:
Explicitly identified with Śrī, Draupadī (Kṛṣṇā) is dragged by the hair by Duḥśāsana and displayed before the Kauravas as a symbol of conquered sovereignty.

Oriya *Mbh*:	
Jārā is dragged by the hair by Dhuśāsana.	A symbol of sovereignty, Śiriyā is the Kauravas' object of desire and Dhuśāsana tries to make off with her.

FIG. 46

The Śabara's reaction to the Kauravas' harsh behaviour vis-à-vis Śiriyā evokes, on the one hand, Kṛṣṇa's protection of the insulted Śrī-Draupadī; it anticipates, on the other, the ultimate destruction of the Kauravas by the Pāṇḍavas, explicitly supported by the *avatāra*. Moreover, from the classical to the vernacular *Mbh*, Draupadī's role breaks up into the episodes featuring Jārā and Śiriyā. The Śabara and Śabaruṇī are here much more than just husband and wife: they evoke Kṛṣṇa and Kṛṣṇā (Draupadī).

An intimate, if reserved relationship between the *avatāra* and the Pāṇḍavas' wife is already suggested by the Sanskrit text. The vernacular traditions are still more expressive. Referring to the hostility of Śiśupāla (King of Cedi) towards Kṛṣṇa, during Yudhiṣṭhira's *rājasūya*, certain Tamil "street dramas" claim that, in throwing the *cakra* which decapitated the Sovereign, the *avatāra* cut his own finger. Draupadī (here Kṛṣṇa's younger sister) immediately stanches the blood with an endpiece of her saree:

> Delighted with her show of compassion, [Kṛṣṇa] promises that should she ever need help, he will find a way to return her favor in kind. The allusion is of course to his replenishment of her sarees in "Dice Match and Disrobing" (Hiltebeitel 1988: 226).

The links between Kṛṣṇa and Kṛṣṇā are fraught with hidden feelings. The repertoire of Tamil professional reciters includes a motif also known from the Oriya *Mbh*, the disclosure of Draupadī's fondness: "Like the five senses, although I have five husbands, yet still I would like to have one other man for my great husband, my great heart longs" (*ibid.*: 288). "I have five husbands (*pañcupati*), it is true; but Arjuna is the one I prefer (*yekāmātra arjunare mohora adhika pīrati*)", she declares according to Sāraḷā Dāsa (*Vana parva*, I: 24). Sometimes, her preference is wholly unexpected, Karṇa being her clandestine love (*yemāne thānte mohora karṇe bole mati*). In the Tamil context, Hiltebeitel observes, the confession may imply "an allusion to a secret affection Draupadī is said to have for Karṇa" - or even for Kṛṣṇa (*ibid.*: 288-289).[10]

Sacrificing his thumb, and having been dragged by the hair, Jārā is implicitly associated not only with Kṛṣṇa but also with Kṛṣṇā, his *feminine* counterpart. The Śabara's self-amputation is quite significant:

[10] *Cf.* also Hiltebeitel 1999: 164.

the restriction of the archer's ability and power is a symbolic castration, a crucial event in Sāraḷā Dāsa's text. Destroying the parity between Jārā and Arjuna as regards the handling of weapons, the incident re-establishes, on another plane, the rivals' identification, or even their consubstantiality. Jārā does lose part of his capacities when he pays his debt; but, by doing so, he becomes a true disciple of Droṇa and strengthens his ties with Arjuna in a kind of symbolic brotherhood.

A similar motif of self-flagellation, now related to Śiva, can be found in another episode of the great epic (*Mbh* III, 81). Having cut himself on a sharp blade of *kuśa* grass, Maṅkaṇaka sees that the wound exudes a vegetal sap. He rejoices in this discovery and begins dancing; his frenetic steps cause a cosmic disturbance which spreads throughout the whole Universe. Śiva asks him: "Why are you so happy?" The Ṛṣi proudly displays the sap dripping from his hand. Then, cutting in turn his own thumb, Śiva displays the white ashes falling from the wound. Ashamed, Maṅkaṇaka stops dancing.

W. D. O'Flaherty sees in this story a manifestation of Śiva "in the role of the ascetic, opposed to the dance" (1980: 135). But the sage is a replica of Śiva Naṭarāja, whose dance produces the cyclical "destruction" of the cosmos. The wound the latter inflicts on himself is therefore a duplication of that causing Maṅkaṇaka's joy. In any case, the self-flagellation of the thumb appears in both Śiva's and Jārā's stories as a means of eliminating excessive energy. Suggested by the tale of Maṅkaṇaka, Jārā's Śaivite undertones were already implicit in the parallelism between the duel in which Arjuna and Jārā destroy each other's arrows (Oriya *Mbh*) and that of Arjuna and Śiva hitting simultaneously the same target (Sanskrit *Mbh*).

III

Ramanujan compared the dynamics of epic structures to crystal growth. Sāraḷā Dāsa offers many illustrations of this analogy: his narrative is an "open-ended system" where, like crystal strata, new episodes are regularly inserted in strategic places. Intimately related, but unfolding at different moments of the epic, the two fights between Arjuna and Jārā play symmetric roles. We have described the first; let us now focus on the second. Droṇa's unexpected pupil reappears here in the role of the unhappy tribal hunter who killed Kṛṣṇa. As we will see in the text below, Jārā is a new name for the Śabara to whom the image of the *avatāra* has been entrusted.

The death of Kṛṣṇa
(Oriya *Mbh, Mūṣaḷī parba*, 3-5)

[After the war (ending in victory for the Pāṇḍavas), Kṛṣṇa finds an isolated spot in the forest to rest. While hunting, Jārā took Kṛṣṇa's left foot for an antelope's ear, and hit it with an arrow. Mortally wounded, the *avatāra* calls for Arjuna. The Śabara departs immediately and returns in the company of the hero. Their meeting is highly dramatic. Kṛṣṇa had once given Arjuna one sixteenth (*kalā*) of his own essence, granting him special powers. He can only die after he recovers that fraction of himself. Arjuna will then be deprived of a considerable privilege. He therefore refuses to approach his dying friend]:

"I have become impure", says Arjuna, "my body is impregnated with sin" (*Arjuna bolanti mlecha papa aṅga mora*). The *avatāra* insists - "At least reach out your bow to me" - and the hero finally yields. As soon as the bow brushes Kṛṣṇa's body, he expires.

Inconsolable, Arjuna turns to Jārā, accusing him of his friend's death. It is in vain that the Śabara tries to explain himself. The two men then begin a fight to the death but, having lost part of his energy, Arjuna is unable to defeat his rival. The men's arrows meet and disintegrate in the sky. They then remember Droṇa, their common tutor (*bicārile duhīkari atanti guru droṇa*). At that moment, a heavenly voice states that there is not the least difference between them, and that they should stop fighting; it also announces that Jārā will commit himself to the worship of Kṛṣṇa on the Blue Mountain.

> The duel ends and Kṛṣṇa's body is burned. The celestial voice is heard again: the fire must be extinguished and the *avatāra*'s body consigned to the ocean.

Recovering the fragment of energy which he had given away, Kṛṣṇa abolishes the superiority Arjuna had formerly held over Jārā. The final duel is, therefore, an exact replica of the first, an eloquent manifestation of parity and balance.

It is not by chance that, refusing to approach the dying *avatāra*, Arjuna declares he has taken on the impurity of a Mleccha (a man from a tribal community). This term would be appropriate to Jārā, with whom the hero again identifies himself. Arjuna and Jārā are a single soul (*yeka ātmā*), and the reuniting of the two characters is crucial during the last moments of Kṛṣṇa's life: wounded by the Śabara's arrow, the *avatāra* expires when his body is brushed by Arjuna's bow.

The bow and arrow, symbolising perfect unity, evoke the convergence of Arjuna and Jārā. But they also display the consubstantiality of Jārā and Kṛṣṇa, of the archer's *wounded hand* and the *foot* he hits – an expression of the transcendent oneness of the "aggressor" and his "victim", of "life" and "death".

As we have recurrently seen, the momentary "concealment" of Kṛṣṇa (or Viṣṇu) is both a repetition of the original self-sacrifice and the promise of his next manifestation. Hence, the hunter's arrow is not just a means of destruction; it gives Kṛṣṇa the new form he adopts during the *kali yuga*. Jārā's "lethal" weapon and his *jībanyāsa śara*, the "giving life" arrow which allowed the Kauravas a second birth, are after all one and the same. From this point of view, the Śabara replicates Mārkaṇḍeya's action (in the *EzV*): partially destroying the banyan, the sage determines its reappearance on the Puri shores. As Mārkaṇḍeya – and the Bhārgavas in general – Jārā is a "master of death and life".

Let us now turn to the motif of Kṛṣṇa's death, according to the *Deula Tolā*.

The death of Kṛṣṇa
(*Kṛṣṇa Dāsa*, *DT*, Fragment 2)

Abandoning themselves, at the end of the *dvāpara yuga*, to consumption of the *kadamba*'s[11] inebriating juice, men no longer recognise each other. One day, approaching Kṛṣṇa while he is in repose, and mistaking the *avatāra*'s left foot for the ear of an antelope, Jārā shoots it with an arrow. Kṛṣṇa has time to reveal the reasons behind the hunter's action: "You have just avenged your father, Vālin, whom I unjustly killed. This is why you wounded me – you are not to blame (*teṇu tu māilu tora kiçi doṣa nāhī*). But go and find Arjuna."

Arjuna hurries there with his brothers. Kṛṣṇa dies and the Pāṇḍavas want to proceed with the burning of his body. A heavenly voice recommends, however, that they consign it to the ocean, from where it will emerge in the form of a sacred trunk (*dārubrahma*).[12]

Who was Vālin? What injustice did he suffer?

The story unfolds at the end of the *tretā yuga*, when Sītā, Rāma's wife, has been carried off by Rāvaṇa. Having usurped the place of his brother (Vālin), Sugrīva became the King of a monkey tribe. He will help Rāma (previous *avatāra* of Viṣṇu) if, in return, he promises to free him from Vālin. The *avatāra* agrees, thus committing a treacherous act for which he will be punished.

Another account by Sāraḷā Dāsa establishes a relationship between the death of Kṛṣṇa and Vāmana's three strides.

The death of Kṛṣṇa
(Oriya *Mbh*, *Vana parba*, II: 6)

[At the beginning of the *tretā yuga*, Vāmana appears before Bali, and asks for the space corresponding to three of his strides. Suddenly growing in stature, he covers, in just two strides, the earth and the upper world. His big left toe breaks the world's egg, causing the (aerial) waters of the Ganges to descend in impetuous streams].

---

[11] *Nauclea Cadamba*, *Anthocephallus Cadamba*.

[12] A very similar narrative was produced in the 18th century by de Polier and republished by Dumézil (1986: 308). *Cf.* also Dubuisson 1986: 37-40.

In homage to Viṣṇu-Vāmana, Brahmā pours the water of the Ganges over his left foot, aiming to gather up and then absorb some holy drops. The water, however, mysteriously disappears and this is seen as the result of a magical act (*māyā*). Humiliated, Brahmā decides to avenge himself and makes a plan to fire an arrow into Viṣṇu's foot.

Shortly afterwards, Brahmā meets Viṣṇu, accusing him of sexual incontinence: that, intoxicated by the *kadamba* juice, he had seduced countless married women (*paradārā*). Furious about the accusation, Viṣṇu kicks Brahmā with his left foot (*brahmākaī bāmapāde prahārile*). Brahmā curses him: "May an arrow strike your left foot (in like fashion)".

A little later, Brahmā surprises a Śabaruṇī. Overcome by desire, he makes love to her (*nirjana dekhi dhātā śrungāra kale içā*). Discovered by her husband, they are shot with an arrow. Yama approaches the dying Brahmā and condemns him to an earthly existence, during which he must make amends for his wrongs. Conceived by a Sabaruṇī, Brahmā will hit Kṛṣṇa's left foot with an arrow. Jārā, the Śabara, is thus a manifestation of Brahmā himself (*se jārā śabara pratakṣe kauśika brahmā*).

The death of the *avatāra* had long been premeditated by Brahmā, into whom, this time, Jārā is assimilated. Viṣṇu-Vāmana tricks Brahmā and, at the right moment, Brahmā (under the Śabara's identity) shoots Viṣṇu-Kṛṣṇa with an arrow (paying back the insult of Viṣṇu-Vāmana). This is the outcome of events going back to the beginning of the *tretā yuga* – and, in order to grasp the story's underlying meaning, the reader has to follow a strange labyrinthine loop. Looking for a pretext to take revenge on Vāmana, Brahmā accuses Viṣṇu of sexual incontinence – a crime of which he himself, shortly afterwards, will be guilty. Viṣṇu, in turn, attacks Brahmā but, in doing so, he reveals himself as a victim: accused by the demiurge of being lascivious, he kicks him. Wounded, in the meantime, by the hunter whose wife he had carried off, Brahmā is forced into a human existence and, in the form of a Śabara, finally hits the foot that hit him. Condemned, the better to punish, he sees his own sanction assimilated into that of Viṣṇu.

This intricate sequence is the expression of a backlash, the *choc en retour* which Louis Renou identified in the *RV*. The deceiver inevitably ends up becoming the victim of his own deception [*le trompeur est puni... par une sorte d'action directe de sa tromperie même* (1939: 231)].

Here are the last two versions of Kṛṣṇa's death set side by side:

Oriya *Mbh* (Sāraḷā Dāsa)	*Deula tolā* (Kṛṣṇa Dāsa)
[At the beginning of the *tretā yuga*,	[At the end of the *tretā yuga*,
Vāmana humiliates Brahmā].	Rāma treacherously kills Vālin].
Brahmā accuses Viṣṇu of licentious practices, brought on by drinking too much *kadamba* juice.	Excessive drinking of *kadamba* juice leads to the careless act of Jārā, a tribal hunter.
In response, Viṣṇu kicks Brahmā, who decides to avenge himself.	
Brahmā, in the form of a tribal hunter (Jārā), hits Kṛṣṇa's foot, causing the *avatāra's* death (end of the *dvāpara yuga*).	Jārā, a descendent of Vālin, hits Kṛṣṇa's foot, causing the *avatāra's* death (end of the *dvāpara yuga*).

FIG. 47

As we see, it makes absolutely no difference whether the final action is triggered at the "beginning" or at the "end" of the *tretā yuga*; whether the aggressive act is attributed to Vāmana or Rāma, whether the victim of this act is Vālin or Brahmā. Above all, it is irrelevant whether the juice of the *kadamba*, the cause of Kṛṣṇa's death, is drunk by Jārā, the accidental *aggressor*, or by the *victim of the aggression*, Viṣṇu himself.

The excessive consumption of the *kadamba* juice induced, at the end of the *dvāpara yuga*, a kind of collective delirium: men no longer recognised each other and, in the eyes of the Śabara hunter, even the foot of the *avatāra* was confused with the ear of an antelope. This episode could illustrate a passage from the *Kulārṇava Tantra* (VIII, 68-71) describing the states of intoxication caused by both rituals and excessive wine:

> Seized by delusion, the men embrace other men. The women are confused and ask their husbands such questions as: "Who are you, who am I, who are these other people, why are we here, is this a garden, or our home, or an inner courtyard?" (Quoted by McDaniel 1989: 109).[13]

This blurring of boundaries also occurs between cosmic cycles. Aimed at God, the act of the Śabara manifests the mystic exhilaration which comes from total surrender. At the end of the *dvāpara yuga*, Kṛṣṇa's death implies a return to transcendent unity – and this is when "aggressor" and "victim" blur into each other. In short, Jārā *is* Kṛṣṇa: the "inadvertent violence" of the tribal hunter and the god's "disappearance" are part of the same game (*līlā*). The divine, Kinsley writes, expresses its essential nature "by playing with itself, making love to itself, inciting itself to abandon itself in itself" (1975: 73). From this perspective, the drunken hunter – indifferent to superficial distinctions – is again comparable to Mārkaṇḍeya, discovering that "dissolution" and "recreation" are mere effects of Viṣṇu's *māyā*.

The death of God is here equivalent to ecstatic bliss. But death is not the only illusive "appearance" produced by the *kadamba*'s inebriating juice. In one of the most famous episodes in the *Bhāgavata Purāṇa* (X, 22), Kṛṣṇa comes across a group of shepherdesses (*gopīs*) who bathe in the waters of the Yamunā. He gathers up the clothes they left on the banks, climbs to the top of a *kadamba* and invites the young women to join him, overcoming their modesty and shyness. The clothes they are tricked out of obviously symbolise *māyā*. But the story stresses, in particular, the importance of adulterous love in Kṛṣṇaite Vaiṣṇavism.

---

[13] Madness and mysticism frequently interweave. This may be illustrated by the devotional group of the Bāuls (the "mad" ones) and the Vaiṣṇava-sahajiyā cult of Bengal. In Dimock's words, "The Bāul cannot help his madness; he is maddened by the sound of Kṛṣṇa's flute, and, like a Gopī, caring nothing for home or for the respect of the world, he follows it ..." (1966: 252). See also McDaniel 1989: "Madness and ecstasy are intimately connected in Bengali Vaiṣṇavism. The highest ecstatic state is Rādhā's *mahābhāva*, which includes incoherent speech, irrational behavior, and all possible emotions experienced intensely and simultaneously. Rādhā's divine madness is a state so passionate and extreme that it is even a mystery to Kṛṣṇa, Rādhā's beloved and Lord (1989: 29).

Significantly, the lovers impersonated by Kṛṣṇa and the shepherdesses meet in the proximity of a tree whose relation to wine and erotic passion is well known.[14] In Tantrism, wine and erotic passion are a path to transcendent reality.[15] The *kadamba*, which causes "death" and stimulates "eroticism", is particularly revealing in this context. As Coomaraswamy pointed out, "from the concept of love (*kāma*) as a fire, and Agni having 'five missiles', comes the iconography of Kāmadeva, the god of love, as an archer" (1989: 150, note 7). The "violence" of the drunken hunter, shooting his *lethal* arrow, corresponds to the *passionate behaviour* inspired by God. They are equivalent manifestations of an ecstatic trance.

* * *

In a wall niche of the great Jagannātha Temple, there is a Vāmana Trivikrama whose left foot, pointing to the sky, carries an image of a four-faced Brahmā. There he stands, outlined in brushstrokes by the *Citrakāra* (painters) of the Puri region:

[14] A Kuṣāṇā-period sculpture (today in the Lucknow Museum) depicts a woman "holding a goblet of wine" under the branches of a *kadamba* (Gupta 1996: 198 and 23, plate 17). Another (Mathura, 2nd century) shows a man and two women near the tree in question: "The man is drunk and the women are naked except for the jewellery they are wearing" (*ibid.*: 198 and 25, Plate 20). A further example (Bhubaneshwar: Brahmeśvara, 11th century) sets a pair of lovers near the *kadamba* (ibid.: 198 and 27, plate 23).

[15] The *pañca makāra*, the "five M's" - *māṃsa* ("meat"), *matsya* ("fish"), *mudrā* ("fried cereals"), *maithuna* ("sexual union") and *madya* ("wine") - are the epitome of transgressing "orthodox" Hindu practices.

FIG. 48. Vāmana Trivikrama

The temple's image was reproduced by K. C. Mishra (1971: Plate 30).[16] Biardeau stressed its peculiarity, the *avatāra*'s left leg being *abnormally vertical*. The raised leg "makes us think of the lotus stem emerging from Viṣṇu's navel" – a credible interpretation since, in this case, "Vāmana Trivikrama displays, at the tip of his vertically stretched left foot, a small four-faced Brahmā apparently sitting in the corolla of a lotus" (1976a: 199, *author's translation*).

[16] *Cf.* Starza also 1993: Plate 16.

Vāmana's left leg certainly represents the lotus stem (i.e., the umbilical cord), thus underlying the *intimacy* of the relationship between Brahmā and Viṣṇu (united by ambiguous ties). But this is not all. According to Sāraḷā Dāsa, Viṣṇu's left foot is the instrument of an attack on Brahmā – who strikes back, making it his target. With remarkable concision, the temple's image expresses a *double* backlash: Viṣṇu conceives Brahmā who conceives Viṣṇu... who attacks Brahmā who attacks Viṣṇu. This symbolic *consubstantiality* reflects, after all, the relationship between Vāmana and Bali, whose *antagonism* is generally taken for granted.

CHAPTER NINE

THE SACRIFICER'S ALTER EGO

I

We find in Sāraḷā Dāsa two versions of the Indradyumna myth. Here is the first:

The story of Indradyumna
(Oriya *Mbh, Vana parba*, II: 6)

Indradyumna, son of Gāla Mādhaba, sends a number of his Brahmins on a secret mission – a search in the four directions of space for the image of Viṣṇu. One of them, Vasu (or Vasukara), arrives at the Blue Mountain. Tortured by hunger (*bibhokṣite*), he finds a village of tribal hunters (Śabaras). A Śabaruṇī welcomes him and explains that her husband, Jārā, has left for the forest. She gives him a clay pot and some rice. Jārā returns shortly afterwards, bearing on his shoulders an antelope (*mruga*) he has just caught. As soon as they recognise the hidden resemblance of their names, the two men celebrate a friendship pact.

Staying in the village, Vasu notices that Jārā often goes off on his own, supplied with food and water. He questions the Śabaruṇī about her husband's behaviour and she talks openly about Viṣṇu's image: "We keep secretly a stone image of the god" (*gupate aci āmbhara pāsāṇa debatāye*).

The Brahmin desires to visit the deity. Jārā starts by refusing his request. However, swayed by his wife, he ends up allowing the journey on one condition – Vasu should go blindfolded. Bringing from the village a handful of seeds, the Brahmin discreetly drops them along the way.

* * *

Once he knows the idol had been discovered, Indradyumna gathers his army and heads towards Orissa, guided by Vasu. On arriving at the Blue Mountain, he learns that the icon has disappeared. He suspects the Śabara, and swears vengeance. That night, Viṣṇu appears to him in a dream. The god forbids the King to punish the Śabara, his devoted worshipper (*tu tāhākaī dukha na dia ho indradyumana rāye / aneka pūjā̃ hoilā āmbhanta dharma sabhāye*), and foretells his own reappearance on the coast in the form of a tree trunk.

> On the following day, the trunk (*dāru*) is identified on the shore – a weird piece of wood, so extraordinarily heavy that it cannot be lifted by either the King or his men. Placing themselves respectively on the right and left of the log, the Brahmin and Śabara – and they alone – are able to carry it to the mountain peak, and, finally, to set it within the recently built temple.
>
> The carving of the *dāru* is entrusted to an old artisan – Viṣṇu (*puruṣa uttamā*). Indradyumna anxiously awaits the results of his work. When the King can no longer hear the sound of the tools, he orders that the temple doors be opened. At that moment, the artisan disappears, leaving the images unfinished forever. Only the Brahmin and Śabara remain in the temple side by side.

The matrimonial alliance between the Hindu priest and the Śabaruṇī is omitted here, replaced by a ritual friendship pact between Vasu and Jārā.[1] Even so, the first meeting between the Brahmin and the tribal woman is filled with sexual allusions. In her husband's absence, she satisfies the stranger's hunger by giving him a clay pot and rice, a rather untypical behaviour which may be seen as a metaphor for a clandestine sexual relationship: in rites and myths, the pot is frequently a symbol of the female organ (*cf.* Biardeau 1971-72: 53).

Becoming, later on, a mediator between her husband and the new-comer, the Śabaruṇī eagerly adopts the latter's perspective. She reveals to him the existence of Viṣṇu's image – until then a well kept secret – and, overcoming her husband's intransigence, she persuades him to bring their guest into the presence of the god. The three characters seem to indulge in an incestuous relationship, as conceived by Françoise Héritier. In Héritier's opinion, some of the prohibitions decreed by many kinship systems should be interpreted in terms of a

---

[1] Even today, a pact of ritual friendship is often celebrated due to the recognition of some common identity, such as having the same name: "A man who is bound to give help in all contingencies, both those arising from social obligations and those which are purely economic, is the ritual friend, the *maitro*. This is a relationship entered into during boyhood or adolescence with a person of another caste. It is a solemn bond, contracted before a Brahmin and cemented and publicized by a feast, but the reasons for picking a particular person are often trifling. The most frequent one is coincidence of name" (Bailey 1957: 84).

symbolic regulation of *identity* and *difference*. Hence, a "second definition of incest" is required: the prohibition does not concern blood relatives of a different sex, but "kinsfolk of the same sex sharing the same sexual partner" (1979: 219, *author's translation*). Of course, there is no "true" consanguinity between the Brahmin and the Śabara. They do, however, celebrate a pact defining them as *maitra* - and, like biological affinities, ties of ritual friendship are sacred and indestructible.

Such ties reappear in the second version by Sāraḷā Dāsa (*Mūṣaḷī parba*), where homonymy as a sign of soul kinship (*ātmā abheda*) is more convincingly presented: here, Jārā is also known as Vasu (*jārā śabara nāma hoye basu śabara boli*). The intimacy between the Brahmin and his host's wife is equally emphasised: they are themselves united by ritual friendship (*śabara maitra helā śabaruṇī maitruṇī*). The Śabaruṇī places herself again on the side of the stranger, resolutely praising him to her husband: "He is more than life to us" (*prāṇahū adhika se aṭanti āmbhara*), she says.

It thus falls to the Śabaruṇī to strengthen - in the most ambiguous terms - the connection between host and guest. This is not wholly surprising. Hospitality, as Jamison has remarked, "is inextricably linked with sexuality and fertility in ancient India in both ritual and narrative literature... And the woman, the wife, is in certain ways the embodiment of this linkage" (1996: 144).

There are also deep Vedic reminiscences in the equivocal relationship between the Brahmin and the Śabara. The *ŚB* (I, 7, 3, 1-4) declares that, when the gods ascended to heaven through a sacrificial performance, Rudra[-Śiva] was left behind, his share of the sacrifice having been denied to him. Rudra's "marginality" has here a metaphysical meaning. His "acceptance of humiliation was an act of asceticism", the pure "gesture of detachment of the Great Yogi" (Kramrisch 1988: 62). This apparent disqualification coexists sometimes with the most exorbitant prerogatives. According to the *Maitrāyaṇī Saṃhitā* (IV, 2, 12), Prajāpati had once desired his own daughter, Uṣas (the Dawn). Uṣas turned herself into a female antelope and, to chase her, the demiurge adopted the form of the male. Rudra was charged with the punishment of this ignominious action, but, trying to appease him, Prajāpati granted him the status of *paśupati*: "Lord of the Animals" (i.e. "Lord of Sacrificial Victims"). Since Prajāpati is the paradigmatic sacrificial victim, one may conclude that Rudra-Śiva – the *mṛga vyādha*, the antelope hunter – acquires in this way an amazing ascendancy over the demiurge himself (Kramrisch, *ibid*.)

Most of Jārā's denominations – *byādha* "hunter", *mruga byādha* "antelope hunter", Śabara or Kirāta – have been applied to Rudra-Śiva. The god's relationship with the Oriya (black) antelope hunter thus deserves particular attention.

Let us first note that the habitat of the black antelope (*krusna murga, antilope cervicapra*) is the *jāṅgala*. The word *jāṅgala* may refer either to an inhospitable territory or to the privileged domain of Hindu kingdoms (Zimmermann 1982: 199), the location appropriate for sacrifice, to which the black antelope is obliquely related.

Now, the symbolic web of Vedic sacrifice is suddenly recreated when, returning from the jungle, Jārā is confronted with an insinuation of illicit sex in the unexpected proximity between the Śabaruṇī and the Brahmin. In this context, the Hindu priest evokes the incestuous demiurge, and Jārā, carrying a hunted antelope, is a replica of the threatening Rudra-Śiva. However, the virtual conflict turns into identification when the two men recognise that they share the same name. Who then is the agressor? And who is the victim? The Unity of the Supreme Being may again be hinted at under the interwoven identities of guest and host – Śiva and Viṣṇu in the form of Hari-Hara, one might say.

II

Who is who in Indradyumna's story? This is an idle question since, as we have seen, everyone has in everyone else their own alter ego. Consider the following episode from Kṛṣṇa Dāsa.

The story of Indradyumna
(*Kṛṣṇa Dāsa, DT*, Fragment 3)

Returning from heaven, Indradyumna meets Gāla Mādhaba, who had been ruling the country in the meantime and credits his own father with the building of the temple. In order to resolve the conflict between the two Sovereigns, Brahmā invites them to produce their respective witnesses. The crow argues in favour of Indradyumna, but Gāla Mādhaba contests the legitimacy of her declaration: "You are lying" (*miça kahu*). Also summoned as witnesses, the tortoises flee as soon as they realise the true builder is present. Pressed by the demiurge, they finally explain that, in the past, Indradyumna gave them the arduous task of carrying on their backs the stones needed for building. Their testimony is irrefutable: Gāla Mādhaba acknowledges the legitimacy of his rival to whose authority he now submits.

We know that Akūpāra is:

- the victim of the King's sacrifices, the animal walled in at the base of the "fire altar", and
- the reptile who carried Mount Mandara on his back, during the churning for the *amṛta*.

Akūpāra therefore plays a key role in episodes suffused with architectonic symbolism (the Vedic "fire altar" and the Cosmic Mountain being technical and metaphorical antecedents of the Hindu temple):

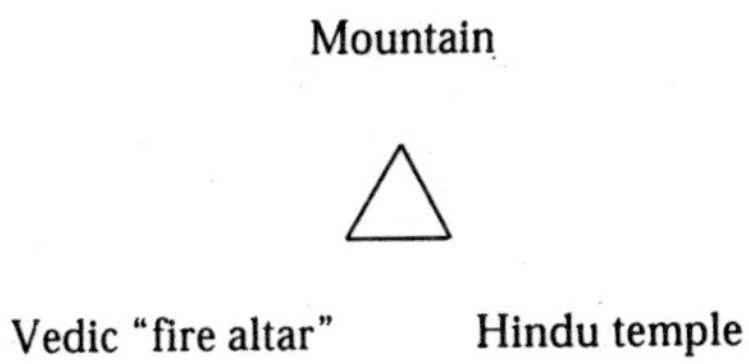

FIG. 49

It is thus not fortuitous that the terrified reptiles described by Kṛṣṇa Dāsa so strongly recall the faint-hearted Akūpāra in Indradyumna's presence (classical *Mbh*):

Kṛṣṇa Dāsa: A group of tortoises carry the stones for the temple

△

Mbh, III, 191: Akūpāra lies buried under the bricks of the "fire altar"

Mbh, I, 16: Akūpāra carries the mountain on his back

FIG. 50

An oral tradition states that hard work imposed on the labourers who carried the stones for the Jagannātha Temple eventually transformed them into tortoises (*cf.* Chapter 4, note 7); another, recorded by Russell and Hira Lal (1916, IV: 503), identifies the Śabara as the carriers of the huge stones. Since the Tortoise, Viṣṇu's second *avatāra*, is also the reptile whose form was assumed by Prajāpati in his demiurgic role (*ŚB* VII, 5,1,5), a remarkable homology is posited here between the Demiurge, the Tortoise and the Śabara:

Tortoise

△

Śabara — Demiurge (Viṣṇu, Prajāpati)

FIG. 51

In classical sources, Mount Mandara is the weighty rod used for the churning operation of *devas* and *asuras*. This *heavy stone implement*, which prompted the emergence of different beings and valuable goods (including *amṛta*) from the ocean, is transformed (by vernacular tradition) into *heavy wood*, the raw material for the sacred image that itself comes up out of the sea:

The story of Indradyumna
(Kṛṣṇa Dāsa, *DT*, Fragment 4)

> Viṣṇu manifested in the form of a *dāru*, the banyan trunk left on the shore. Its weight was such that Indradyumna's entire army was unable to remove it. There was only one solution: to call the Brahmin and the Śabara who, on either side of the *dāru* (*eka pākhe bidyāpati brāhmaṇa dhailā/ āu eka pākhe basu śabara dhailā*), raised and placed it on a golden cart, built for the purpose.

We find the same motif in the first version of the Oriya *Mbh*: having discovered the *dāru* on the Puri beach, Indradyumna realises he is incapable of moving it. It falls to the Brahmin and the Śabara, set to the right and left of the trunk respectively, to raise and carry it.

In the symmetrical positions of the two men – placing an apparently immovable *dāru* on the peak of the Blue Mountain (or on the golden cart, a multiform of the temple) – we recognise a transformation of the collaborative effort of *devas* and *asuras*, as they set themselves on either side of Mount Mandara (classical *Mbh*). One would say that the weight of the mountain – which only Indra could set on the Tortoise's back – has been transferred to the *dāru*, before which Indradyumna is now powerless. The vernacular tradition reorganises the main features of the classical scheme by permuting their respective positions:

The Churning of the Milky Ocean:	The story of Indradyumna:
Indra is the only god able to move Mount Mandara.	Indradyumna is unable to lift the *dāru*.
Indra puts Mount Mandara on the back of the Tortoise.	Indradyumna forces the tortoises to carry on their backs the stones for the building of the temple.
Working together, gods and demons use Mount Mandara as the pestle in the churning.	Brahmin and Śabara join forces to set the *dāru* on the peak of the Blue Mountain.

FIG. 52

The temple is the pretext for the quarrel between Indradyumna and Gāla Mādhaba, each claiming the privilege of a prior right to the monument over that of his rival. The reader or listener to the story knows (but Gāla Mādhaba does not) that Indradyumna appears in Puri at two distinct moments, separated by an immense temporal void. Indradyumna is right to assert that he has preceded Gāla Mādhaba, who alleges - not unreasonably - that he preceded Indradyumna. Ironically, arguing that the temple had been built by his own father (Kṛṣṇa Dāsa, Fragment 3), Gāla Mādhaba places himself in the role of son of Indradyumna, the true builder. A close relationship between the two Sovereigns is thus suggested. In this connection, the two versions by Sāraḷā Dāsa are revealing. The first roundly postulates the characters' affinity: Gāla Mādhaba is Indradyumna's father. The second is even more emphatic:

The story of Indradyumna
(Oriya *Mbh*, *Mūṣaḷī parba*, 8-10)

Sovereign of a far off kingdom, Gāla Mādhaba (or Gālaba) sends a number of his priests in search of the ancient image of Viṣṇu. Particular features distinguish one of these Brahmins - Vasu (Vasudeba, Vāsudeba). He has long hair, and carries a sacred umbrella, the Vedas and various other manuscripts, a water jar, a ceremonial spoon and a bundle of *kuśa* grass. Jārā (or Vasu), the leader of a Śabara community, welcomes him warmly. Recognising the kinship of their souls, the two men celebrate a ritual friendship pact (*kirāta boilā bipra mora maitra hoiba*).

One day, the wife of Jārā alludes to the cult of the sapphire in the stranger's presence. She herself overcomes her husband's resistance and he finally agrees to lead his guest, blindfolded, to the blue stone.

Returning to Malwa, Vasu describes in detail the outcome of his expedition. Guided by the Brahmin and accompanied by a powerful army, Gāla Mādhaba sets off but, on arriving, he learns that the image has disappeared. He accuses the Śabara of having tricked him and wipes out part of the tribal community. Jārā proclaims the innocence of his subjects and destroys, with a single arrow, half the enemy army. The battle is interrupted by the setting sun. That night, Gāla Mādhaba sees in a dream Viṣṇu condemning his actions and foretelling the imminent extinction of his lineage (*aho gālaba rājā tora na rahiba baṃśa*). Viṣṇu also advises him to build a temple on the peak of the Blue Mountain, where the god will soon reappear with Jārā's descendents at his side (*ye jārā śabara baṃśa thiba mora kati*).

[Gāla Mādhaba was unable to carry out the mission entrusted to him. From this moment onwards, the story focuses on Indradyumna, son of Madhukeśara].

Instructed by a sage (*muni*) on various sacred matters, Indradyumna hears of Gāla Mādhaba. The difficulty of his task, explains the *muni*, was the great height of the Blue Mountain which, formerly, had even obstructed the horses pulling the chariot of the Sun. The sage also tells him that a certain Śabara, Jārā, accidentally fired an arrow at Kṛṣṇa, mortally wounding him; and that, in time, the body of the *avatāra* would rise from the ocean in the form of a *dāru*.

Indradyumna decides to take on the task Gāla Mādhaba had been unable to carry out. He orders a temple built on the mountain peak. As for the image, it is carved by Jārā, helped by Brahmā in the guise of a Brahmin. The two men remain together within the building over several days, but, when he can no longer hear the sound of tools, Indradyumna orders the opening of the temple doors. The Brahmin disappears, mysteriously assimilated into Subhadrā. Jārā, however, remains beside the images: he is the ancestor of the Daitās (*jārā śabara baṃśa hoile dayitā*).

Many actions usually attributed to Indradyumna are here imputed to Gāla Mādhaba – who, like him, sends his Brahmins in search of the sapphire, organises the military expedition to the Blue Mountain, and is faced with the disappearance of the image. Unjustly accusing the tribal community, he decides to attack it, provoking Viṣṇu's wrath and, as a result, the extinction of his line.

The texts we have been considering insist on the intrinsic frailty of Gāla Mādhaba, whose arguments are shown to be irrelevant, and whose decisions are summarily revoked. However, the King's humiliation reaches its peak in Sāraḷā Dāsa's second variant, where he is turned into an "end-of-cycle" Sovereign – tactless, deprived of progeny, subjugated by all sorts of calamities. Yet, the "end" of a cycle merges into "new beginnings". Like the primordial mountain confronted by Indra at the dawn of time, Nīlagiri is an obstacle to Gāla Mādhaba's action at the ebb of a cosmic period. But an *apparent* difference must be stressed. Whilst, in the Vedic myth, Indra receives the *help* of Viṣṇu, whose strides separate sky and earth, in the Oriya tradition the god imposes on Gāla Mādhaba *an impossible task*: the building of a temple on the very top of an incredibly high mountain.

Gāla Mādhaba is a tragic character, identified with the obnoxious effects of the sun at the end of the hot season (*mādhava* is an ancient name for one of the summer months, the current *vaisākha*, April-May). A swift comparison with the *DT* clarifies this association:

The story of Indradyumna
(*Kṛṣṇa Dāsa*, *DT*, Fragment 5)

During Indradyumna's stay in Brahmā's heaven, the temple of Puri disappeared under the sand. One day, before Indrayumna's return, Gāla Mādhaba goes antelope hunting. As chance would have it, his horse stumbles over the pinnacle of the temple emerging from the dry sand. Excavations are carried out and reveal the monument in all its splendour.

Above the bulb-shaped dome of an Orissan temple, the *śikhara*, a large ribbed wheel can be seen. This is the *āmalaka*, to which we will shortly return. On it rests the finial, the upper part of which is the *kalaśa*:

FIG. 53. The finial of the temple

A rich symbolism is attached to the *kalaśa*, the "cupola". The term commonly designates a "water-pot", a "pitcher". Placed right on the top of the monument, this round, golden jar with the form of a flame also represents the sun.[2] Significantly, the Tamil *kalacam* – applied, like Sanskrit *kalaśa*, to both the "cupola" and "water-pot" – is synonymous with *akkiṉikampam* (Sk. *agniskambha*), the "fire-post" (Hiltebeitel 1991: 160). The upper part of the finial, in which water and fire seem to cohere, is thus an appropriate symbol for the seasonal conjunction brought about by Gāla Mādhaba: acting as a hunter at the "end" of summer, he announces the "beginning" of the monsoon, the unburied temple being itself a promise of renewal.

There are several sacrificial implications in this seasonal transition. The half-buried finial alludes to self-flagellation in terms akin to those studied by Hiltebeitel in Tamil Nadu.[3] Evoking a fire-post, the *kalaśa* represents, in a nutshell, the firewalking area as a metaphor for the world "destroyed" and "recreated" by the flames of *pralaya*. It stands for the Vedic *yūpa*, and epitomises the inherent violence of sacrifice.

---

[2] *Cf.* Kramrisch 1946: 355, note 192.

[3] *Cf.* Hiltebeitel 1991, Chapter 6.

As noted by Hiltebeitel,

> The regular unpointed yūpa is suitable for ordinary sacrifices, in which violence, particularly cutting and impalement, is carried out and represented away from the yūpa... But pointed, the yūpa becomes a symbol (though still not a means) of impalement (*ibid.*: 139).

In Gāla Mādhaba's episode, the shaft emerging from the sand is a pointed *yūpa.* The sudden end of the animal's roaming before this *kalaśa-yūpa* marks the right place and time for the Horse's (and the King's symbolic) immolation. In short, the Horse's motionless stance in front of the finial evokes the sacrifice of Prajāpati – for the stallion is Prajāpati's theriomorphic manifestation. But Prajāpati is the Sun (also represented by the stallion). Hence, the interruption of the Horse's trajectory by the pinnacle of the Jagannātha Temple has to be compared with an episode concerning Sūrya in the Oriya *Mbh*:

Kṛṣṇa Dāsa	**Sāraḷā Dāsa 2nd version**
During a hunt, Gāla Mādhaba's horse stumbles over the pinnacle of the buried temple.	The path of the horses pulling the chariot of Sūrya, the Sun, is interrupted by the Blue Mountain, whose excessive height "explains" why Gāla Mādhaba was unable to build the temple.

FIG. 54

Hidden *in the depths of the earth*, the temple seems to be the opposite of the mountain, *excessively close to the sky*. But this is a mirroring effect rather than real antinomy. The *kalaśa*, at the top of the buried monument, reproduces the star at the top of the high mountain, just as Gāla Mādhaba – moving in a hunting-chariot similar to Sūrya's vehicle – is a replica of the Sun. Now, if Sūrya is represented by both the *kalaśa* and Gāla Mādhaba, the inescapable conclusion is that of a symbolic connection between the King and the *kalaśa*:

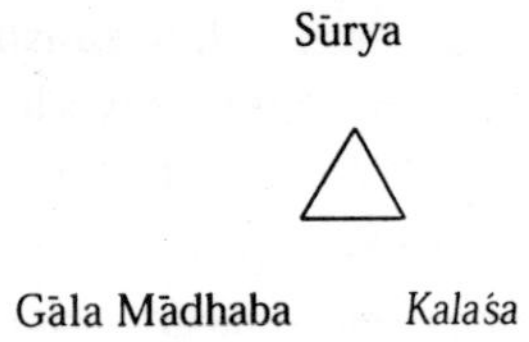

FIG. 55

Identified with the upper element of the finial – the protruding object which interrupts his (or his Horse's) trajectory – Gāla Mādhaba is... his own opponent. This is not unexpected, the sacrificer being also the sacrificial victim *par excellence*. The metaphoric self-immolation of Gāla Mādhaba reproduces after all that of Indradyumna in the *BrP.*

* * *

Indian myths have familiarised us with the motif of the antelope hunter running after his prey in an arid, sterile landscape. The *Mbh* (I, 73) tells us that, one day, after an exhausting antelope chase, King Yayāti attempted to quench his thirst. He found only a completely dry well and, at the bottom, a Brahmin girl, Devayānī, whose *despair* – as much as the aridity of the landscape – may be understood as a sign of socio-cosmic crisis.

This story presents a number of remarkable analogies with Kṛṣṇa Dāsa's text, for example the empty well corresponding to the "water-pot" hidden in dry sands (*śukhilā bāli*). According to the classical tradition, Yayāti rescues Devayānī by pulling her out of the well; in the Oriya myth, Gāla Mādhaba brings the temple out of the netherworld. A critical situation is thus overcome, in both contexts, by an ascent leading to transition from darkness to light: Devayānī's passage from the gloomy bottom of a waterless well to sunshine is equivalent to that of the *kalaśa* itself, from the chthonic world to open sky.

The King of our stories (Yayāti, Gāla Mādhaba) has to cope, simultaneously, with dryness and obscurity: the hot season ends at summer's solstice, when, having reached its greatest altitude and its northernmost point, the sun seems to lose part of its strength and days begin to shorten. This new evidence of cosmic crisis calls for a renewed form of communication between above and below, and this is precisely when Gāla Mādhaba plays a key role.

We have stressed the identity relationship between the *kalaśa* emerging from a heap of dry sand, and the sun shining above the Blue Mountain peak. The Hindu temple with its golden cupola is sometimes explicitly compared to the Cosmic Mountain, retaining and immobilising the sun:

> The golden Kalaśa, a "high seat", on the summit of the god's dwelling, looks as if it were the sun's orb that had arisen on the lordly mountain of sunrise. The Kalaśa is likened to the sun and the temple is "the Mountain where the Sun rests at midday". Meru, the support of the Sun, and "the one Sun that never leaves the Meru" (Aitareya Brāhmaṇa, XIV. 6.44) are symbols of the ultimate state of illumination of the Sādhaka for whom the sun neither rises nor sets (Kramrisch 1946: 355).

Digging the soil and revealing the *kalaśa* – in some sense a hidden sun – Gāla Mādhaba provokes an immediate effect on the *celestial* vault. This is a reinvigorating action, the *kalaśa* being a "jar of the nectar of deathlessness" (*ibid*.: 273).

In other words, the King is the healer who overcomes Sūrya's vulnerability at the time of the summer solstice. Being identified with the weakened and reinvigorated Sun, he is also assimilated to the *kalaśa-yūpa*, the aggressive but revitalising sacrificial post (Fig. 55). An expression of self-regeneration, Gāla Mādhaba's action dramatises both sacrificial death and rebirth.

In this connection, the symbolism of the *āmalaka* is highly significant. Like the upper perforated brick in the Vedic fire altar to which it corresponds *mutatis mutandis*, the *āmalaka* ensures a passage to the sky. It is a *muktidvāra* or "door of liberation", an entrance to heaven (*ibid.*: 354). Briefly, the removal of dry sand around the finial opens a passage to the upper world where Indradyumna still remains in Brahmā's presence. This decisive step seems to hasten Indradyumna's descent and, therefore, the very consecration of the temple.

* * *

Prevented, according to the second version by Sāraḷā Dāsa, from building the temple of Jagannātha on the top of the Blue Mountain, Gāla Mādhaba is credited with the rediscovery of the buried monument, a fact leading to the consecration ceremony, in Kṛṣṇa Dāsa's *DT*. One might be tempted to speak, *on one hand*, of the failure of a project; *on the other*, of a glimmering of hope and renewal. The contrast is misleading. Gāla Mādhaba does not represent first the *wrong*, then the *right* side of a process. As with *every* character in the story, he is one and the other simultaneously. The same should be recognised about his relationship with Indradyumna. Shall we say that the second version by Sāraḷā Dāsa projects onto Gāla Mādhaba the "negative" – and *only* the "negative" – aspects usually attributed to the first stage of Indradyumna's trajectory? Is it not true that, bringing the temple to light, Gāla Mādhaba (as portrayed by Kṛṣṇa Dāsa) initiates a "regeneration" process? In the same way, the highest forms of emulation between the two Sovereigns combine with the ultimate expression of consubstantiality. Indradyumna's true rival is Gāla Mādhaba – who is, it might be said, Indrayumna through the looking glass.

III

Like the ambiguous relationship between the Brahmin and Śabara, the one between Gāla Mādhaba and Indradyumna is reminiscent of the Churning motif:

The story of Indradyumna (Kṛṣṇa Dāsa):	The churning of the Milky Ocean for the *amṛta*:
The temple (metaphor for the original Mountain) both separates and brings together Indradyumna and Gāla Mādhaba, watched by Brahmā.	Mount Mandara both separates and brings together *devas* and *asuras*, watched by Brahmā.

FIG. 56

Here there are again remarkable mirror effects, the main characters in the story reflecting each other as *stone* and *wood*, main elements of the mythical landscape. Although occupying symmetrical positions, Brahmin and Śabara join hands in an episode revolving around an uncommonly heavy piece of *wood*: the trunk out of which the sacred image will be carved. Conversely, the "constructive contest" of the two Sovereigns is triggered by the *stone* temple.

Indradyumna's witnesses according to the *DT*, the tortoises represent basic features of an architectonic structure (Vedic altar or Hindu temple) symbolically related to the Cosmic Mountain. They play a function akin to that ascribed to Akūpāra in the classical *Mbh*. The Churning for the *amṛta* is thus a central motif, contributing decisively to the overarching structure of the story of Indradyumna. It is however clear that the main elements of the Milky-Ocean theme incessantly decompose and reorganise in new patterns:

1. In Oriya, or in Orissa-related accounts, the Cosmic Tree, which emerges from the ocean as a heavy trunk (*dāru*), replaces the Cosmic Mountain (of the classical tradition);
2. The mountain placed on Akūpāra's back (*Mbh*) seems to crumble into a mound of stones which, transported by a group of tortoises, are used in the building of the temple-mountain (*DT*).
3. The excessive weight of Mount Mandara (*Mbh*) is transferred to the *dāru* which will be set on the peak of the Blue Mountain or on the golden cart, homologous to the temple-mountain (Indradyumna myth).
4. Carrying the uncommonly heavy *dāru*, Brahmin and Śabara play a role identical to that of *devas* and *asuras*, moving the Cosmic Mountain (in the classical tradition).
5. In vernacular narratives, the tortoises occupy a place similar to that of Akūpāra (in the classical *Mbh*). As the main witnesses for Indradyumna, they put an end to the quarrel between the two Sovereigns.
6. Both united and separated by the temple (a multiform manifestation of the Cosmic Mountain), Indradyumna and Gāla Mādhaba are watched by Brahmā; their function replicates that of *devas* and *asuras* who, watched by Brahmā, move the Cosmic Mountain as if it were a churning rod.

In the sequence sketched out above, the essential features of the mythical landscape permanently change their relative positions. The Cosmic Mountain, *supported* by the Tortoise (in the classical *Mbh*), turns into the *support* of the equally heavy *dāru* (in the Oriya myth, where the Blue Mountain top becomes the appropriate location for the tree trunk). *Supporting object* and *object supported*, the mountain is also, alternately, the *passive material* calling for Indra's creative intervention (in the Vedic myth), and the *active instrument* (in the Churning of the Milky Ocean); both an *obstacle* to creation and an *agent* of creation. This expresses the very nature of the "demiurgic" process, the constant interchange of "agent" and "action", "interior" and "exterior", "container" and "content".

The same conclusion may be drawn from the plasticity of the characters and the intermingling of the narratives. The relationship between Gāla Mādhaba and Indradyumna has just been considered in the light of the Churning motif. Let us now look at it from another perspective. Gāla Mādhaba's initial "animosity" towards Indradyumna further suggests the initial "resistance" of the Śabara to the Brahmin's project. The parallelism is reinforced by the well known homology between mountain and temple: Gāla Mādhaba refuses to acknowledge Indradyumna's rights over the Jagannātha Temple just as the Śabarā tries to prevent the Brahmin from getting to the Blue Mountain peak. This brings us back to the Purāṇic motif of "Vāmana's three strides":

Bhāgavata Purāṇa:
Vāmana covers the earth.
Vāmana covers the sky and aerial space.
Vāmana moves downwards. This third stride consecrates the *avatāra*'s supremacy over the "demon".

FIG. 57

The *avatāra*'s trajectory is, as shown, a paradigm of the Brahmin's path (Kṛṣṇa Dāsa):

The Brahmin's journey	
1st movement:	The Brahmin reaches the sacred tree.
2nd movement:	He climbs to a high branch.
3rd movement:	Returning to the ground, he meets the Śabara again and abrogates his privileges.

FIG. 58

Indradyumna's trajectory follows the same pattern:

The Sovereign's journey	
1st movement:	Indradyumna climbs the Blue Mountain.
2nd movement:	He ascends to Brahmaloka.
3rd movement:	Returning to Puri, he surprises Gāla Mādhaba and annuls his prerogatives.

FIG. 59

In other words, Gāla Mādhaba – Indradyumna's alter ego – is a replica of the Śabara who is both a reproduction of the "demon" (Bali/Vṛtra) and the Brahmin's alter ego.

PART IV

FROM MYTH TO RITUAL

CHAPTER TEN

THE COSMIC PILLAR

I

In the Purāṇic texts, the concealment of the sapphire is claimed by Yama. A different explanation of the same event is given by Kṛṣṇa Dāsa:

The story of Indradyumna
(*Kṛṣṇa Dāsa, DT*, Fragment 6)

On learning of the sapphire's discovery, Indradyumna is exultant. He leaves Malwa and goes to the Blue Mountain. He believes he is close to achieving his aims and cannot contain a proud boast (*garba*): "Only I shall ensure the rituals [of Viṣṇu] during the *kali yuga*," (*kali yuge pūjā karāibi parā muhī*). The image disappears at once.

Indradyumna's arrogance here is the immediate cause of the blue stone's disappearance. A similar description is found in the Hunter version.

The story of Indradyumna
(Hunter, Fragment 1)[1]

When the king... reached the Blue Mountain, [his] heart swelled within him, and he cried, "Who is like unto me, whom the Lord of the World has chosen to build his temple, and to teach men in this age of darkness to call on his name?" But the Lord Jagannath was wroth at the king's pride, and a voice was heard from heaven saying, "O king! Thou shalt indeed build my temple, but me thou shalt not behold. When it is finished, then thou shalt seek anew for thy god". At that same moment the blue image vanished from off the earth.

Skanda Purāṇa; Brahma Purāṇa	*Deula Tolā*; Hunter
The disappearance of the sapphire is claimed by Yama.	The disappearance of the sapphire is the result of Indradyumna's arrogance.

FIG. 60

[1] Hunter 1872, I: 91.

This implicit homology between Yama and Indradyumna, the exemplary King of Orissa, is hardly surprising. The Indian god – as well as his homonym in Iranian tradition (Yama or Yima) – has obvious affinities with royalty. He is a model of the perfect sovereign in the epic literature, a genuine incarnation of *dharma*. From the time of the Vedas, he is also the King of the Dead, a role not recorded in Iran probably due to the monotheism of the Zoroastrian reform: "For the prophet", as Bruce Lincoln points out, "there could be no lord in heaven but Ahura Mazdā (the 'Wise Lord')..." (1991: 38).

The Avesta states that the end of Yama's glorious existence is the consequence of "an enormous sin" (Dumézil 1971: 247) – a display of pride according to some sources: "I am Sovereign of the entire world"; "Is there any other god but me?"; "Who dares say there is [another] king than me?" (*ibid.*: 283). Such demonstrations of arrogance have no equivalent in Indian narratives concerning Yama. However, Dumézil sustains that characters akin to the Iranian god appear in the *Mbh* "under other names" (*ibid.*: 250). Yayāti, ancestor of the Pāṇḍavas, could be one of them; he instituted the main structures of social life (*ibid.*: 259) and was rewarded with a place in heaven. But this privilege was temporary.

Yayāti: the fall from heaven
(*Mbh* I, 81-88)

Asked, one day, by Indra about his religious merits, Yayāti answers: "I don't see anyone who, in this respect, can be compared to me". Punished for his pride, the Sovereign leaves heaven and seeks the company of virtuous men on earth who might recognise him, helping him to re-establish his former privileges. He happens upon the place where his four grandsons (Aṣṭaka, Pratardana, Vasumanas and Śibi) are performing a royal ritual. They are willing to give up their accumulated rights to their grandfather. Five celestial chariots then appear to carry Yayāti and his grandsons to heaven.

Certain aspects of the Iranian tradition are easily recognised in this story; its analogy with the myth of Indradyumna is even more striking. Falling from and returning to his heavenly dwelling, Yayāti evokes King Indradyumna, who was himself forced to leave heaven, according to the classical *Mbh* (*cf.* Chapter 4). Both were forgotten and had to reconfirm their prestige of old by performing a royal ritual:

Yayāti (classical *Mbh*)	**Indradyumna (classical *Mbh*)**	**Indradyumna (*DT*; Hunter)**
Because of his pride...	Due to destructive time...	Because of his pride...
... Yayāti falls from heaven and is forgotten.	...Indradyumna falls from heaven and is forgotten.	... Indradyumna causes the hiding of the sapphire (in the lower world).
He joins in a royal ritual (*vājapeya*)...	He performs an *aśvamedha* (a sacrifice implying the building of a "fire altar").	He orders the Jagannātha Temple to be built (the temple is here conceived as a replica of a "fire altar", a structure whose construction was necessarily associated with an *aśvamedha*).
...and returns to heaven...	He returns to heaven...	He ascends to Brahmaloka.
...after confirmation of his prestige.	...after confirmation of his prestige.	Renovation of the temporal cycles: beginning of the *kali yuga*.

FIG. 61

In the stories sketched above, "pride" and "time" produce the same effects: a downward movement (the King's fall; the sapphire's displacement from the Blue Mountain peak to the underworld), followed by an upward movement (the King's return to heaven or his ascension to Brahmaloka).

It is not irrelevant that the question inducing Yayāti's arrogance ("Who would you compare yourself with in terms of ascetic merits?") was asked by Indra, by whom a similar fault – with similar consequences – had been committed:

Indra's arrogance
(*Mbh,* I, 189)

During a sacrifice carried out by the gods, Yama busied himself with the killing of the animal victims. Neglected, the human beings multiplied and became immortal. The other gods complained to Brahmā, who tranquilised them: Yama would soon resume his functions.

Returning to the banks of the Ganges, where the sacrifice was taking place, the gods saw a golden lotus float by on the current. To discover its origin, Indra went upstream and met Śrī, who had come to bathe. She was crying, and her tears, falling into the river, turned into golden lotuses. The goddess led him to the top of the Himalayas where, oblivious to their surroundings, Śiva and Pārvatī were playing dice. Indra twice announced his presence: "I am Lord of the Universe." Śiva stared at him and transformed him into a tree trunk. At the end of the game, Śiva asked Śrī to bring Indra into his presence with the idea of teaching him a lesson in humility. Her touch made him fall, but he was forced by Śiva to get up and move a stone blocking the entrance to a grotto. Within, the King of the Gods came upon four replicas of himself. Like him, they had behaved arrogantly. The five Indras will be reborn among men, becoming the putative sons of Pāṇḍu.

There are again several analogies between this story and that of Indradyumna:

Indra Classical *Mahābhārata:*	Indradyumna *Skanda Purāṇa:*	 Kṛṣṇa Dāsa; Hunter:
Yama temporarily suspends his functions as God of Death.	Yama sees his prerogatives as God of Death suspended in the Puruṣottama kṣetra.	
Yama's intervention is linked to Indra's journey to an Himalayan peak in the transition between two cosmic periods.	Yama's intervention is linked to Indradyumna's journey to the Blue Mountain peak in the transition between two cosmic periods.	
Indra behaves arrogantly.	Indradyumna acknowledges the decrease of his merits, despite having just performed an *aśvamedha.*	Indradyumna behaves arrogantly.
As a result of his misdeed, Indra takes on the form of a pillar.	After his display of arrogance (or as a result of the decrease of his merit), Indradyumna commits himself to building the Jagannātha Temple.	

FIG. 62

Indra's bluster has commonly been seen as a thoughtless and imprudent gesture, an insult to Śiva. Commenting on Śrī's sadness, Hiltebeitel wrote:

> [T]he "ill-fortuned" (*mandabhāgya*) Śrī... is weeping because... her husbands – four former Indras whom the fifth... is now carelessly imitating – have insulted Śiva by their folly and pride and have been forced to lie dormant in a cave (1976: 96).[2]

Śiva is time "in its destructive form", Biardeau writes in turn, and "Indra realises this to his own cost when he disturbs Śiva and Pārvatī's game to claim his sovereignty in untimely manner" (1976b: 144-145, *author's translation*).

To assert that Indra's claim to sovereignty is untimely (*à contre-temps*) contradicts the very logic of the narrative. The myth displays some of the features of the *rājasūya* – a ritual of royal consecration which clarifies the motif of the proud sacrificer – and, from this perspective, Indra's performance is perfectly adjusted to and synchronised with Śiva's action.

The enthronement ceremonies of the *rājasūya* included a dice game, "a cosmogonical rite intended to bring about the recreation of the universe and the birth of the king" (Heesterman 1957: 153). Don Handelman and David Shulman stressed the "creative" purpose of this game, ensuring the transition from indifferentiation to manifest reality:[3] "Without the game, there would be no time, perhaps no space as well... – in short, no world as we know it..." (1997: 5-6).

[2] Weeping at the source of the Ganges, Śrī has been further described by Hiltebeitel as "the very antithesis of what one would expect if he were looking for the goddess of Prosperity" (1976: 171). But tears are "a seed substitute" (O'Flaherty 1980: 40). They symbolise, in this context, the monsoon rains, fertility and future prosperity: transforming themselves into golden lotuses, they hardly could be seen as an expression of impoverishment. In fact, the ambiguity of the goddess is later acknowledged by Hiltebeitel (2001: 167).

[3] "The highest level of the cosmic whole, that of no-time and no-space... is a nonhuman level, since human beings are partial creatures of time and space. On this plane, there are no rips in the cosmic weave, no gaps that open through time

Subtle ties unite the gamblers not only with time in its "destructive form" but also with the reconstruction of temporality.[4] Both aspects are interwoven in the symbolism of the *rājasūya*:

> In order to be reborn the consecrated has to pass through death just as the sun and the moon have to pass invisibly to the east, where they reappear. In this respect the dicing pavilion may be compared to the consecration hut, which is considered the womb of the dīkṣita, where he is to behave as if dead (Heesterman 1957: 153).

The *rājasūya*, Heesterman has noted, "is often equated to the slaying of Vṛtra" (*ibid.*: 23, note 33) – an event which, according to the *ŚB* (V, 2, 3, 7), brought Indra universal dominion. This was a demiurgic act: by eliminating Vṛtra's "resistance", the King of Gods released the waters and, making the movement of the stars possible, secured the start (or restart) of temporal cycles. Thus the self-assertive pronouncement by which Indra recalls his demiurgic intervention – "I am Lord of the Universe" – does not contradict the purpose of Śiva who, playing dice, introduces a new *yuga*. Śiva and Indra do not oppose each other: their seeming divergence is an expression of the deepest complicity.

It is also in the light of the royal consecration that we can understand Indra's trials – namely, his transformation into a pillar (a *sthāṇu*), and his loss of energy. In the course of the *rājasūya*, a bow and three arrows (allusive to the weapons that ensured Indra's victory over Vṛtra) were placed by the *adhvaryu* in the hands of the *yajamāna*. Then the *adhvaryu* raised the arms of the sacrificer, a ritual sequence which may

---

into space – indeed, into spaciousness. However, in cosmogonic terms, one level below, as it were, the cosmic self begins to divide, taking the form of the androgyne, a male with a female half. It is at this level that the dice game first appears, in processes of cosmic externalization and self-alienation of the deity – as a module that generates cosmic fragmentation" (1997: 75-76).

[4] As Sylvain Lévi observed long ago, the basis of the ancient game of dice seems to have been a "combination of four terms..., kali 1, dvāpara 2, tretā 3, krita 4," which, later, would be the origin of the names for the four ages of the world (1920: 12, *author's translation*).

> be interpreted as the cosmogonic act of raising the axis mundi; and so we see the king, when receiving the unction, standing erect with raised arms on the throne, as the personification of the cosmic pillar resting on the navel of the earth (the throne) and reaching up to the sky (Heesterman 1957: 101).

In Vedic conception, royal consecration and vulnerability intertwine: "He who is being anointed with the rājasūya (ceremony) suffers a loss in power and strength" (*ibid.*: 23). This probably refers to the primordial self-immolation of Prajāpati. A similar role is sometimes allotted to Indra – the danger inherent to the sacrificer's performance being clearly illustrated in the myth summarised above. Right at the moment of his consecration, Indra is emptied, deprived of energy by the contact of Śrī, the embodiment of sovereignty.

II

The weakening of the Divine King provoked by Śrī appeared strange to Hiltebeitel:

> Śrī's touch is gratuitous, perhaps an anachronism in this myth; whatever its meaning, its effects are unrecorded. The theme of Indra's first contact... with Śrī and the kingship she represents has, it seems, been reinterpreted as a lesson in divine priorities. The king of the gods learns that he is not the lord of the universe (1976: 172).

But Indra's depletion of energy and his transformation into a pillar are intrinsic to cosmic "regeneration" (and royal consecration).

In the expression which describes "Indra as a pillar" (*sthāṇu*), Hiltebeitel rightly sees a pun on one of Śiva's names – Sthāṇu (1976: 170). However, the pun itself remains obscure if we do not admit that the whole narrative underlines the gods' *identification*, rather than their opposition. Let us consider the reasons for Śiva's metamorphosis into a *sthāṇu*, according to an Orissan tradition. A 10th century Ekapāda Bhairava – a fierce one-legged Śiva – is enshrined in a Kuṇḍeśvara small temple (in the vicinity of Jagatsinghpur, Cuttack district). Although half erased, a feminine visage – Pārvatī's – may be seen, imprinted on the knee of Ekapāda Bhairava's single leg. This image is related to the following story, narrated by local Brahmins.

Śiva and Pārvatī
(oral version, 1)

> Long ago, in order to get access to the inebriating sap of the date-palm tree (*khajuri*), it was enough to make an incision at the base of the trunk. Śiva would drink it abundantly. On one occasion, intoxicated and stirred by desire, he approached Pārvatī before sunset and tried to possess her. Indignant, she determined that, from then on, the *khajuri* sap would flow back to the tree-top. Furious (*bhairava*), Śiva confronts Pārvatī. She kneels before him and grabs hold of the god's legs which stick together. At that moment, he is transformed into a pillar, a one-legged figure (*ekapāda*). Simultaneously, the *liṅga* rises to the sky.

This short narrative betrays obvious Tantric features. Like Kṛṣṇa, Śiva indulges in excessive drinking and trangresses conventional morality, the *khajuri* (*phoenix dactylifera*) playing here a role comparable to that of the *kadamba* (see Chapter 8). The god's lascivious behaviour has unexpected consequences. Pārvatī induces the return of the sap and, by doing so, suppresses Śiva's sexual desire. An equivalence between sap and semen[5] is thus posited by the text.

The vital juice stored in the top of the tree evokes the common belief that semen may be accumulated in the head (Carstairs 1958: 84). The "return of semen" is supposed to stimulate concentration; moreo-

[5] The assimilation of semen with the intoxicating sap of the *khajuri* reminds us of the link between semen and *soma*: "Because of its intoxicating and ecstatic effects on men and gods the soma is the divine drink *par excellence*, the 'nectar', to which those who partake of it owe physical strength, a long life, security against death and disease. It is not surprising that the preparation of this juice was identified... with sexual intercourse" (Gonda 1965: 47).

ver, it "stands, on the physiological plane, for a transcendence of the phenomenal world" (Eliade 1958: 270). Hence, the movement of the sap calls to mind the ascension of the *kuṇḍalinī*, although, from this perspective, Pārvatī's intervention appears paradoxical. She forces the sap of the palm-tree to flow back, inhibiting Śiva's sexual impulse; but, the very ascent of the liquid, reproducing the rising of the serpent and its arrival at the *sahasrāra* (the seventh *cakra*), is a return to Oneness – and this is symbolised precisely by divine sexual intercourse (*maithuna*). We are entitled to assume that, *apparently rejecting* the god's erotic behaviour, she *fully accepts* his allure, their *separation* anticipating, after all, their mystical *encounter*. The myth suggests the interplay between tangible and intangible levels of reality: the inexpressible *maithuna*, realised at the highest and most subtle centre of energy – the *sahasrāra cakra* – is first represented through the sexual harassment of the goddess by the lecherous god.

The lovers' separation seems to deny their ultimate state of bliss and undividedness. However, even here, the "first" and "last" moments of the unfolding process are indiscernible. Quarrel arises when Śiva consumes the sap of the *khajuri*. But since the sap is homologous to the god's semen, Śiva feeds off his own substance. In other words, the "cause" of chaos and fragmentation is also an expression of integrity and oneness.

Tantrism claims that, *before* ascension, the *kuṇḍalinī* is coiled around the *liṅga*; obstructing its opening, it prevents the flowing of vital energy. Imprinted on the knee of Ekapāda Bhairava, the goddess' face is a simile of the serpent's head. In short, the leg-pillar replicates the *liṅga*, whilst the arms of the goddess, encircling it, stand here for the *yoni* (the female organ). Again, this is a prefiguration of the mystical intercourse of *puruṣa* and *prakṛti*, the fusing of the legs foretelling the return to Unity.

* * *

When Pārvatī imprisons the god's legs, his phallus rises into the sky. This is a symbol of both virility and continence. As O'Flaherty wrote,

> [A]lthough the erect phallus is of course a sign of priapism, in Indian culture it is a symbol of chastity as well. Śiva is described as ithyphallic... and this condition is often equated with a state of chastity: 'He is called *ūrdhvaliṅga* because the lowered *liṅga* sheds its seed, but not the raised *liṅga*' [*MhB*, with the commentary of Nilakantha (1862), XIII. 17: 45-6]. The basic Sanskrit expression for the practice of chastity is the drawing up of the seed (*ūrdhvaretas*), but, by synecdoche, the seed is often confused with the *liṅga* itself, which is 'raised' in chastity" (1973: 9-10).

Thus, in the myth and iconography of Śiva, creation and annihilation, sexuality and abstinence coexist as two sides of the same coin. Even under the form of Bhairava, Śiva is not merely an agent of cosmic "destruction", as becomes clear in the epilogue of a second version of the myth:

Śiva and Pārvatī
(oral version, 2)

> When he realises that Pārvatī had reversed the course of the *khajuri* sap, Śiva begins the Tāṇḍava dance. In the violence of his performance, his legs lose their articulation and are about to separate from his body. It falls to Brahmā to bring them together, keeping them united, immovable as a *sthāṇu*.

A "delirious outburst precipitating havoc" (Zimmer 1946: 171), Tāṇḍava, Śiva's dance in the transition between cosmic cycles, is simultaneously an act of creation. At the frenetic height of this destructive-creative motion, the disjunction of the lower members reenacts Prajāpati's sacrifice, the origin of the Universe. But this time it is Śiva who assumes the "demiurgical" role, and Brahmā who ensures the "recomposition" of the fragmented body. Gathering the dispersed members of Bhairava (-Prajāpati) through the action of Brahmā (-Prajāpati), the Supreme Being recreates himself. The one-legged god is the Pillar which allows a continuous flow of energy between heaven and earth. He is the *axis mundi*, image of ultimate harmony and wholeness.

Śiva's "reprehensible" behaviour is twice rebuked. First, when Pārvatī makes the *khajuri* sap flow back; secondly, when the god is immobilised, subjected somehow, to a lesson of humility. Śiva is thus "punished" at the very moment he decides to "punish"; moreover he is "humiliated" by a "humiliated partner" – Pārvatī (or Brahmā), who bows before him in submission. By limiting Bhairava's action, Pārvatī (or Brahmā) acknowledges, after all, his infinite power: the agent of punishment (or humiliation) and the object of his action eventually blur.

* * *

The same blend of "opposite" features – including acquisition and loss of prestige, arrogance, and humility – appears in the story of Indradyumna. In the *SkP*, the King of Malwa performs an *aśvamedha* – a royal consecration ceremony equivalent to a "demiurgic" process – and builds the Jagannātha Temple, itself a multiform of the *axis mundi*, and, of course, a sign of unchallenged authority. Yet, construction of the monument is a visible sign of the *yajamāna*'s vulnerability: Indradyumna admits the decrease of his religious merits after his ritual performances.

Explicitly introducing in this context the double motif of the King's pride and his humiliation, the *DT* and Hunter versions are still more eloquent:

SkP	*DT*; Hunter
Indradyumna leaves Malwa during the *kṛta yuga* and arrives in Orissa (at the start of the *kali yuga*).	
After performing an *aśvamedha*, Indradyumna is affected by an unexpected loss of religious merit.	Indradyumna's display of arrogance is immediately punished: the image disappears.
Building of the Jagannātha Temple.	

FIG. 63

The motif of the "sacrificer's humiliation" is also illustrated by Gāla Mādhaba, unable to erect the temple on the peak of the Blue Mountain (Sāraḷā Dāsa, 2nd version). Here again, he corresponds to Indradyumna, helpless before the uncommonly heavy *dāru* lying on the shore (Sāraḷā Dās, first version; Kṛṣṇa Dāsa, Hunter). Being a replica of the *yūpa*, the *dāru* is not only an epitome of royal authority, but also an expression of the sacrificer's powerlessness. As a symbol of the new cult, established at the threshold of the *kali yuga*, it brings to mind the *sthāṇu* into which Indra has been transformed when, playing dice, Śiva and Pārvatī prepared a new cosmic cycle.

CHAPTER ELEVEN

THE DEMIURGIC ROLE OF A ROYAL SWEEPER

I

The *yajamāna*'s vulnerability is concomitant with that of the sun. In this connection, the relationship of Gāla Mādhaba with the *kalaśa*, the hidden sun which he unburies (and to which, therefore, he gives birth), is particularly significant. Healing the weakened sun of the summer solstice, the King heals himself and his kingdom. The deep symbolism of the transitional period between the hot and rainy seasons is also underlined by the *Mbh*.

As we have seen, the dice game between Śakuni and Yudhiṣṭhira leads to the proscription of the Pāṇḍavas. The basic rules of social life are then suspended, the heroes' sexual relations with Draupadī being interrupted while they remain in the forest: "This half 'savage' and 'sterile' existence", writes Biardeau, "corresponds to a period of latency" (1976b: 153) which evokes the initiation (*dīkṣā*) of the sacrificer, his return to a foetal state. More evocative yet is the place where the Pāṇḍavas and Draupadī spend the thirteenth year of their exile – the kingdom of the Fish (*Matsya*), ruled by Virāṭa (*Virāṭa parvan*).

The name of Virāṭa is related to that of Virāj,[1] the undifferentiated demiurge in whom male and female are somehow fused,[2] the Person "in whom God and matter are one" (Gonda 1970: 25). Virāṭa is thus a metaphor of primordial, formless reality. The same idea applies to his kingdom: Matsya, Hiltebeitel points out, "has both cosmogonic overtones (e.g., the Matsyāvatāra) and hints of chaos (the *matsyanyāya*: 'the big fish eat the little fish')" (1980b: 150).

Like the twelve months of the year, the twelve years in the forest are an expression of totality.[3] But what could be the meaning of the thirteenth year? For van Buitenen, it represents "the hinge between

---

[1] *Cf.* Biardeau 1976b: 208, note 1.

[2] *Cf.* Coomaraswamy, "The Vedic Doctrine of 'Silence'" (1937), in Coomaraswamy 1977, II: 2: 205, note 15.

[3] *Cf.* Biardeau 1976b: 151-152.

one completed term and the next one, with the liminality that in European folklore is associated with the Eleven Nights" (1978: 4). In his opinion, such transition was marked by a celebration similar to the current Holī (held at the full moon of *phālguna*, February-March), the appropriate context for the "licentious side of the masquerade of *The Book of Virāṭa*" (*ibid.*: 5). However, Hiltebeitel observes that "a connection specifically with Holī, or with Phālguna month..., breaks down". The disclosure of the heroes' identities "at the year's end occurs during *grīṣma*, the hot season (May-July)" (1980b: 148, note 5). This brings us closer to the summer solstice.

The thirteenth year of the Pāṇḍavas' exile is not merely a link between two independent totalities. A synthesis of the "dissolution-recreation" process, this thirteenth year of exile is a *time beyond time*, homologous to the *space beyond space* represented by Virāṭa's chaotic realm. Referring to the symbolism inherent in different expressions of totality, Held was the first to stress that, in India, "the number of the whole is obtained by continually adding one to the whole already obtained" (1935: 123). The formula was rephrased by Heesterman: the *final* number "not only exceeds, but also encompasses" the whole produced by the preceding numbers (1957: 13). Equally accepted by Kuiper (1962) and Gonda (1965), this interpretation is supported by many instances: "there are thirty-three gods; Prajāpati is the thirty-fourth", states for example the *ŚB* (IV, 5, 7, 2) (Gonda 1965: 124).

More than just a *conclusion after the conclusion* – or a *beginning before the beginning* – the thirteenth year of exile is the higher plane in which the opposition between "beginning" and "end", and between "past" and "future" seems to be suppressed. This idea is further corroborated by a most significant episode. When Arjuna renounces his eunuch's disguise, the Kauravas surprise him and rejoice. They believe that the end of the stipulated time has not yet been reached and that the Pāṇḍavas should be condemned to a new banishment. Nevertheless, Bhīṣma reminds them that, due to the increasing divergence between the solar and lunar years, the calendar is cyclically corrected by the addition of an intercalary period: what the Kauravas considered part of the thirteenth year was already a temporal interpolation.

Some of the motifs converging in the last period of exile emphatically express the demiurgic process:

Mahābhārata (*Virāṭa parvan*)

- The thirteenth year of exile – a synthesis of the "dissolution" (*pralaya*), time beyond time. This intermediate period corrects the difference between the lunar and solar years.
- The Kingdom of the Matsya (= water; primordial chaos; foetal state corresponding to the initiation of the sacrificer).
- Transvestism: Arjuna in the role of eunuch (identified with Śiva *ardhanārīśvara* and the demiurge as androgynous).

FIG. 64

The Oriya *Mbh* relates the thirteenth year of the Pāṇḍavas' exile to the "sandalwood festival" (*candana yātrā*), a ceremony which was first held, thanks to the initiative of Yudhiṣṭhira, and under his direction, during the heroes' stay at Virāṭa's court.[4] This festival is divided into two twenty-one day periods – *bāhāra candana* (or "exterior" *candana*)

[4] The *Mbh* is a fundamental source of reference for countless local traditions. Various regions of the province claim the privilege of having sheltered the Pāṇḍavas at some time or other. The temples of Mahendragiri (Ganjam) commemorate the arrival of the heroes. The same is true in the Bramhagiri area (near Chilika Lake): the temples of Yudhiṣṭhireśvara, Bhīmeśvara, Arjuneśvara, Nakuleśvara and Sahadeveśvara mark the different places where each of the Pāṇḍavas stopped to pay homage to Śiva.

and *bhitara candana* (or "interior" *candana*) - set between the third day of the bright fortnight of *baiśākha* (April-May) and the penultimate day of *jyeṣṭha* (May-June).

Described by Sāraḷā Dāsa as a "spring celebration" (*basanta utsaba*), the *candana yātrā* overlaps the end of spring and the beginning of summer.[5] As commonly accepted today, the summer's end coincides with the end of *jyeṣṭha*, the eve of its last day marking the conclusion of the *bhitara candana*.

- ***bāhāra candana***

The images representative of Jagannātha (Mādana Mohana) and his wives, Lakṣmī and Sarasvatī, are placed on a palanquin and carried in procession. They are accompanied by Balabhadra (Rāmakṛṣṇa) and the "five Pāṇḍavas" (or "five Śivas"[6]). When the images reach the Narendra Tank, they are put in two boats: the first, reserved for Mādana Mohana and his wives, also carries a group of *devadāsīs* (dancers of the temple), musicians and Brahmins; the second follows with Rāmakṛṣṇa and the Pāṇḍavas. A joyful atmosphere is created by the musicians and *devadāsīs*:

> On the boat of Mādan Mohan and his wives, the devadasis take turns dancing and singing. The dances performed at that time combine pure dance and expressive dance and song (*abhinaya*). The devadasi... sings; the drummer accompanies her. The songs sung at this time are called "boat songs" (*cāpa gīta*) and are characterized by the mood of erotic love (*srungāra rasa*). On the boat of Rāmakrisna and the five Śivas young boys dressed as women dance (Marglin 1985: 103-104).

[5] Traditionally, the year has six seasons (of two months), spring (*basanta*) occupying *caitra* (March-April) and *baiśākha* (April-May); and summer (*grīṣma*), *jyeṣṭha* (May-June) and *āṣāḍha* (June-July).

[6] Each of them - Yameśvara, Lokanātha, Mārkaṇḍeśvara, Kopalāmocana, Nīlakaṇṭha - also has a temple in Puri.

The scene is dominated by a sensuous aura which evokes the Pāṇḍavas' sojourn in the court of Virāṭa. Sāraḷā Dāsa also resorts to suggestive images when describing the *candana yātrā* introduced by Yudhiṣṭhira in the Matsya kingdom (*Virāṭa parba,* 15): groups of women dance to the music of all manner of instruments, and crowds rush to the banks of the Kṛṣṇā river, to the place where the image of Viṣṇu (Cakradhara) has been taken. Specially built boats slide into the water, the whole country indulging in a pleasant celebration.

As noted, the name of Virāṭa is identified with that of Virāj. Now, Virāj is one of the ancestors of Jārā. According to Sāraḷā Dāsa (second version), the Śabara was the son of Jarāja, who was the son of Virāj, who was the son of Ajapati, who was the son of Ajara:

Ajara → Ajapati → Virāj → Jarāja → Jārā.

Preceded by Ajapati and Ajara (< *a-ja*, "not born", "not subject to old age", "undecaying"), and followed by Jarāja and Jārā (whose names suggest "decrepitude", "old age"), Virāj is placed right at the core of Jārā's genealogical structure. Graphically displaying her/his primordial, vital ambiguity, Virāj symbolises, to be sure, the inexhaustible source of renewal, the eternal movement from "life" to "death" and "death to life"...

- ***bhitara candana***

The "interior" *candana* takes place within the Jagannātha Temple, where the effects of the hot season are mitigated through water and sandalwood (applied over the images).

- ***naba kalebara***

The increasing discrepancy between lunar and solar years demands the introduction of a leap month. This thirteenth month (*puruṣottama māsa*, "month of Puruṣottama") is, in fact, an extra *āṣāḍha*, inserted between the first and second fortnight of the regular *āṣāḍha*:

1st fortnight of the regular *āṣāḍha* (June-July)

Supplementary *āṣāḍha* (*puruṣottama māsa*)

2nd fortnight of the regular *āṣāḍha*

FIG. 65

The *naba kalebara* occurs in a year with two *āṣāḍhas*. The ceremonies (described in detail by Tripathi[7]) start back on the tenth day of the bright fortnight of *caitra* (March-April). A group of ritualists, which includes Brahmins, Pati Mahāpātra,[8] Daitās and Viśvakarmās (carpenters), gathers inside the temple. One or two days later, the party moves towards the village of Kākaṭpur, on the banks of the Prācī river (about 50 km north-east of Puri). After getting directions from the goddess Maṅgalā[9] as to the location of the *nīm* trees, the ritualists enter the forest and begin a search which may last several days. South of each of the trees eventually identified, a cluster of huts is built, a *Śabara palli* or "Śabara village", the residence of the Daitās. To the west, a sacrificial pavilion (*yajñaśālā*) is erected, conceived in the image of the *prācīnavaṃśa*, the sacrificer's enclosure in Vedic ritual: a rectangular space with four entrances set according to the cardinal points, within

7 Tripathi 1978b.

8 See Chapter 6, note 9.

9 Maṅgalā, a manifestation of Durgā, has an important temple in Kākaṭpur.

which an altar (*vedi*) occupies a central place. The Brahmins, Pati Mahāpātra and Daitā Pati, stay here during the night.[10]

To the north of the sacrificial pavilion, an *aṅkurārpaṇa* ("offering of sprouts") is performed: from the west to the east, various seeds are scattered on the ground; their germination marks the beginning of a fire sacrifice (*yajña*). On the last day of the *vanayāga* (the "forest sacrifice"), a gourd, representing a sacrificial animal, is taken to the tree, cut in half and fragmented into small pieces. The fragments are then crushed and offered to the protective divinities of the ten directions. Taking up an axe of gold and another of silver, Pati Mahāpātra and Daitā Pati pretend to chop down the trunk. It is, however, the Viśvakarmās who actually bring it down. The *dārus* are then carried to Puri; they must enter the precinct of the Jagannātha Temple before the end of *jyeṣṭha*.

The preliminary activities of the *naba kalebara* thus close when the "sandalwood festival" also comes to an end on the penultimate day of *jyeṣṭha*. The following day (*snāna pūrṇimā*) is dedicated to the *snāna yātrā*, the "bathing festival".

• snāna yātrā

Although a very short ritual (a one-day ceremony at the end of the summer), the *snāna yātrā* is an important event, fraught with cosmogonical innuendos. On the final morning of *jyeṣṭha*, the images are withdrawn from the inner sanctuary (*bhitara pokhariā*) and taken to a platform (*snāna maṇḍapa*) in the temple precinct, near the eastern door of the outer wall (see Fig. 2). Brahmins and Daitās pour 108 jars of water over them[11] – in Marglin's words a "veritable drenching" (1985: 249). This is a dramatisation of the *pralaya*, the "literal dissolu-

[10] Daitā Pati, the leader of the Daitās, is a representative of the mythical Viśvāvasu.

[11] In the *naba kalebara* years, the *dārus* taken from Kākaṭpur are brought to the bathing platform and share in the ablutions.

tion of the features painted on the face of the deities" being accompanied "by a dissolution of the normal boundaries both spatial and social" (*ibid.*: 270). As a matter of fact, the distance habitually set between Brahmins and Daitās is now replaced by proximity and cooperation. The ritual scenario itself changes: the *snāna maṇḍapa* "is raised so that the images placed on it are visible from the street" (*ibid.*: 248); the very location of the platform, close to the temple's main entrance, "makes it clear that the images are on public display" (*ibid.*). At this moment, no boundaries seem to exist between "exterior" and "interior".

After the bath, the King of Puri (or a Brahmin replacing him) sweeps the *snāna maṇḍapa*, a ceremony known as *cerā pahārā*.[12] Finally, enormous masks of Gaṇeśa are carried to the place and fitted on the images of Jagannātha, Subhadrā, Balabhadra and Sudarśana. This is an obvious return from apparent multiplicity into essential unity.[13] From the same perspective, the meeting of Gaṇeśa – the elephantine god – and the King of Puri – a "Lord of Elephants", a Gajapati[14] – is highly significant.

A symbol of rain, the elephant (the "king's clouds") appears in India as the "quintessentially appropriate royal animal" (Courtright 1985: 28). Besides, Gaṇeśa is a deity of thresholds. Bringing the monsoon, he ensures fertility and, hence, royal authority at the threshold of socio-cosmical recreation (when *pralaya* is dramatically evoked).

---

[12] *Cerā* is not only the "excrement" but also a "malevolent spirit", a "bad nature" (*asat prakrutika*). In the ritual context of Puri, the word rather designates the perfumed and purifying water with which the king sprinkles the ground.

[13] This is not exceptional in any way. Vaiṣṇavism and Śaivism converge, in multiple forms, in the Jagannātha cult. From the Tantric point of view, Jagannātha *is* Kālī at the moment when the morning meal is consecrated to him; and he is identified with (Śiva) Bhairava during the rituals at the end of the day which represent the sexual union of the god with Bhairavī (Marglin 1985: 197); he is also identified with Rudra-Śiva during the *naba kalebara* (Mishra 1971: 153).

[14] The expression "Lord of Elephants" refers particularly to the sovereigns of the Sūrya dynasty (founded in the 15th century by Kapilendra). The title, however, was known long before that: "the earliest inscriptional reference in Orissa to a 'lord of elephants' (*dviradādhipati*) is to be found in an epigraph, which probably belongs to the 11th century" (Mukherjee 1953: 3, note 7).

We have just seen that, in the course of the ceremonies, Jagannātha-Viṣṇu disappears under the mask of Gaṇeśa. However, his birthday coinciding with the *snāna yātrā*, his reappearance is also guided by Gaṇeśa. The King of Puri is himself a *calanti Viṣṇu* – a "walking Viṣṇu", an embodiment of Jagannātha. Not surprisingly, the *snāna yātrā* is held when the Elephant-faced god grants lordship to the Lord of Elephants, in some sense giving birth to him. But there is more about the demiurgic symbolism which pervades the connection between Gaṇeśa and the royal sweeper.

Most Purāṇic narratives state that Gaṇeśa was created with no direct involvement of a progenitor (sometimes without a progenitrix). His story is a perfect illustration of creation from dirt and pollution:

> In the post-Vedic myths, when parthenogenesis among females takes place, the model used is usually not the female substance (milk) but the male substance (semen – for which... other substances are frequently substituted). The goddess Pārvatī produced Skanda from her own spittle, and Gaṇeśa was born from the water in which she washed herself after she had made love with Śiva, water mixed with her own seed..., or from the rubbings of her body when she anointed herself in the bath... The female seed is thus equated with dirt (O'Flaherty 1980: 37).

Some episodes in the story of Gaṇeśa are reminiscent of the Vedic demiurgic myth which, of course, underwent important modifications. For example, Prajāpati's dismembering and recomposition are reenacted by the severing and reconstructing of Gaṇeśa's body (decapitated and brought back to life with the head of an elephant).[15]

Gaṇeśa also seems to have inherited Prajāpati's sexual ambiguity. Created by Pārvatī to become her quarters' doorkeeper – so the story goes (*ŚP* II, 4, 13-17) – he is like "a eunuch guarding the women of the harem" (Courtright 1985: 111). In this context, Courtright con-

[15] The sacrificial symbolism appears in many aspects of Gaṇeśa's story. On the analogy between the reconstruction of Gaṇeśa's body and the Vedic *agnicayana*, see Courtright 1985: 54-55; on the presence of the Milky-Ocean motif in the myth of Gaṇeśa, see *ibid.*: 61.

tends, the goddess "imitates the mythical male creator, who by creating out of or off of his body imitates the female procreative powers. Here the woman masquerades as the man who masquerades as the woman" (*ibid.*: 54).

The bath and the regenerative power of dirt, main features of the myths about Gaṇeśa, enlighten the strong links between the god and the King of Puri – who also *creates out of dirt* at the outset of a new socio-cosmogonical cycle. But now, the King of Puri himself mimics Pārvatī. The eternal reverberation inherent in creation is expressed through a pattern of endless repetitions. Masquerading as the goddess who masquerades as the first man who masquerades as a first woman, the royal sweeper is a replica of the androgynous demiurge. Hence, reversibility rules the relationship between God and King. The Elephant-faced god bestows royal authority upon the Lord of Elephants who, in turn, appears as a male counterfeit of the mother of the Elephant-faced god...[16]

* * *

At the end of the morning of the *snāna yātrā*, a cooked meal is prepared and offered to Jagannātha and his brothers. The ablutions, however, cause an outbreak of fever among them; as a consequence, the icons are placed in the "outer sanctuary" (*bāhāra pokhariā*) and remain there for a period called *anasara* (or *mahā anasara*).

- ***Anasara* (or *mahā anasara*)**

During the (dark) fortnight of *āṣāḍha*, the regular services of the temple are interrupted, the musical instruments fall silent, and activity in the temple kitchens drops dramatically.

[16] "[T]he king's renewal of his kingdom", Ronald Inden writes, "also meant the renewal of the macrocosmic level of the universe itself. Thus is the cycle completed: the king renews the gods, and they in turn renew the king" (1978: 34).

On this occasion, the Brahmins have no access to the "outer sanctuary": only the Daitās and a "half-brahmin" (Pati Mahāpātra) can then visit them: "Although the Pati Mahāpātra is there to do the offering," Marglin writes, "it is said that the offering is done in 'tribal fashion' (*śabarī pūjā*)" (1985: 250). The peculiar behaviour adopted by the Daitās during *anasara* is underlined by the same author:

> [They] take up residence in that area and bring raw food such as fruits and milk and milk products. They peel the fruits, taste them first to ascertain if they are ripe, and then they offer them to the deities. The peels are not thrown outside but remain on the floor. This is said to be the same type of worship that their ancestor, the tribal chief Viśvābasu, performed in the forest. The *daitās*, as the blood relatives of Jagannātha, sleep and eat right there with their kinsmen.
>
> They also administer an herbal medicine which has been prescribed and prepared by the temple doctor (*baidya*). This man is a brahmin and cannot himself enter the place where the deities are suffering (*ibid.*: 251).[17]

The *anasara* represents a return to the Śabara world, the everlasting source of renewal. The images (whose paintwork has suffered in the ablutions) are then gradually restored. The "opening of the eyes" (*netrotsaba*) marks the end of this "rejuvenation" process: it takes place on the first day of the bright fortnight.

In the *naba kalebara* years, the suspension of common temple activities lasts for three fortnights (the leap month being added to the first fortnight of the *regular āṣāḍha*). The period is now called *mahā anasara* (or "great *anasara*"):

---

[17] The "rules" of the *Śabarī pūjā* evoke Tantric conceptions, namely those inherent in the cult of Mātaṅgī, a goddess "closely identified", in Kinsley's words, with "Śavareśvarī (mistress of the Śavaras)" (Kinsley 1997: 219). As the author points out, some texts "describing her worship specify that devotees should offer her *ucciṣṭa* [leftover food] with their hands and mouths stained with *ucciṣṭa*; that is, worshipers should be in a state of pollution, having eaten and not washed" (*ibid.*: 215).

1st fortnight of regular āṣāḍha (extra āṣāḍha) | 2nd fortnight of regular āṣāḍha

mahā anasara

FIG. 66

After the ablutions on the last day of *jyeṣṭha*, the *dārus* are taken to the interior of a provisional pavilion – to which, apart from the artisans, only the Daitās and Pati Mahāpātra have access. The carving of the new images is shrouded in mystery: outside, the Brahmins recite the *Puruṣa sūkta*, the famous Vedic prayer evoking the self-sacrifice of the Supreme Being.

Once finished, the new images are set opposite the old ones and, on the night of the *regular āṣāḍha* new moon, Daitās and Pati Mahāpātra transfer the "vital substance" from the latter to the former. The gods "die" at that moment; the Daitās weep and mourn for Jagannātha.

During the second fortnight of the *supplementary aṣāḍha*, the new images are given "flesh" and "bone". Then, they are painted by the Citrakāras. The final detail, however, is entrusted to temple Brahmins, who, on the first day of the bright fortnight of the *regular aṣāḍha*, add the pupils (*netrotsaba*) (Tripathi 1978a: 263).

The *anasara* (or *mahā anasara*) is followed by the "car festival" (*ratha yātrā*).

• The *ratha yātrā*.

Three large wooden cars (*ratha*) – the building of which began around two months earlier[18] – are set before the temple's eastern entrance to receive the images on the second day of the bright fortnight

[18] On the third day of the bright fortnight of *baiśākha* (April-May).

of *āṣāḍha*.[19] Sprinkled with water from the Ganges, the floor of the vehicles is then swept by the King of Puri. In the evening of the same day, the cars travel along the *Baḍa Dāṇḍa*, the "Main Road" separating the temple of Jagannātha from that of Guṇḍīcā. As in the past, the journey takes place amidst, in Mitra's words, "a frenzy of religious excitement" (1875, II: 134).

Meanwhile, in the great temple, Lakṣmī feels abandoned. Four days after the beginning of the *ratha yātrā*, she sets off in search of her husband: placed on a palanquin, her image is carried, at midnight, by Brahmins accompanied by a group of *devadāsīs*. Resorting to sorcery, she overcomes Jagannātha's indifference (Marglin 1985: 257-258). The god leaves the temple of Guṇḍīcā on the tenth day of the fortnight, after a new *çerā pahārā* performed by the King.

Still hurt by her husband's desertion, Lakṣmī returns to the main temple and orders that the doors of the sanctuary be shut. The King arranges a meeting between the couple and, on the following day, *devadāsīs* and Daitās, representing Lakṣmī and Jagannātha respectively, simulate the dialogue of reconciliation (Mishra 1971: 137).

The *ratha yātrā* is, to some extent, a replica of the temple's consecration and the establishment of the cult described by the myth. Contributing to the effort to re-establish harmony between Jagannātha and Lakṣmī, and thus reopening the shrine, the King of Puri reproduces Indradyumna's – and Indra's – demiurgic action.

The conclusion of the "car festival" coincides with the beginning of Viṣṇu's periodic sleep: for four months, matrimonial alliances are suspended and social life seems vulnerable.[20]

---

[19] The Sudarśana pillar is placed in Subhadrā's car.

[20] "During this four month period", Inden wrote, "the gods slept and the king, along with the entire state apparatus, suspended normal administrative and warrior functions. The king retired to a retreat outside his capital and after putting an image of Viṣṇu to sleep, devoted himself to the keeping of a four month vow (*cāturmāsya*) and the performance of a number of rituals. The purpose of these rituals was to regulate the rains and to prevent society from being overwhelmed by demons, enemies, flood, famine, and disease during the anxiety-laden night of the rainy season" (1978: 59).

According to Tripathi, the *naba kalebara* is "unique in many respect in the field of Hindu religious worship" (1978a: 223) – "as unique as the icons themselves" in Eschmann's opinion (1978b: 266). Its supposed specificity was sought among the tribal populations of Orissa, namely in the Khond ceremonies accompanying the buffalo sacrifice and including the erection of a wooden post. Yet, the Khond rituals "were not held at regular intervals". To account for the periodicity of the *naba kalebara*, new arguments were needed. Tripathi refers to the Muslim invasions of Orissa (1568):

> It is obvious that the removal of the deities from the sanctum, their transport and concealment, etc., must often have caused severe damage to their wooden figures necessitating very frequently, if not every time, their total renewal. ... It was most probably in this turbulent period... that the ceremony of Navakalevara attained a more or less regular character (1978b: 229).

Complying with the tribal thesis, Stietencron shared a similar point of view.[21] Consequently, the relationship of the *naba kalebara* to the periodical reorganisation of the luni-solar calendar has been undervalued, if not ignored.

A new perspective comes into view when we place the *naba kalebara* within the web of myths and rituals to which it undoubtedly belongs:

---

[21] In his opinion, "The renewal of the images as well as their relation to priests and ritual techniques from the upper Mahanadi valley and possibly of Khond origin may... essentially relate to the late 16th century" (1978b: 66).

Naba kalebara: ritual and mythological connections.

- **Transition from the hot to the rainy season.**

Diverse ritual actions unfold at the end of the hot season. Like those described by Sāraḷā Dāsa (as regards the Matsya kingdom), the current ceremonies of the *candana yātrā* include aquatic references: merry-making in the Narendra tank ("exterior" *candana*) or in the Kṛṣṇā river (Oriya *Mbh*).

- **Sexual ambivalence.**

The transvestism of the young men accompanying the "five Pāṇḍavas" ("exterior" *candana*) is comparable to that of Arjuna in the court of Virāṭa (*Mbh*).

- ***Pralaya***

On the last day of summer, the painting done on the wooden images is washed away (the icons are concealed beneath the mask of Gaṇeśa). These signs of "dissolution" evoke some of the motifs associated with the Pāṇḍavas' last year of exile (*Mbh*).

- **"Destruction" and "recreation"**

The "death" and "rebirth" of the gods call to mind the Pāṇḍavas' "disappearance" and "reappearance" during the thirteenth year of exile (*Mbh*).

- **Leap period**

The extra *āṣāḍha* of the *naba kalebara* corresponds to the extra period following the Pāṇḍavas' reclusion at the court of Virāṭa (*Mbh*).

FIG. 67

The most important sequences of the *naba kalebara* are spread between the end of the hot season and the beginning of the rainy one. The same temporal references are found in the myth of Indradyumna, whose characters oscillate continuously between "destruction" and "recreation". Provoking a kind of *pralaya*, the disappearance of the blue stone occurs when the Hindu priest leaves Malwa; conversely, Indradyumna's arrival in Orissa initiates a new era. The King's journey starts in *jyeṣṭha*, the last month of summer; it ends when seeds germinate under the rain.

The transition between the hot and the rainy seasons is also the appropriate moment for the felling of the sacred tree – the banyan, cut down by the Sovereign, according to the myth (*BrP*), or, in current rituals, the *nīm*, collected from the groves of Kākaṭpur.

Similar spatial coordinates are adopted in myth and ritual. Built in the woods on behalf of the Daitās during the *naba kalebara*, the *Śabara palli* is an allusion to the ancient mythical landscape; the carrying of the *dārus*, the secrecy surrounding the work of the artisans, and the installation of the new images also reproduce familiar aspects of the narrative. Finally, the Brahmin and Śabara of the mythical accounts are replaced, in present-day rituals, by temple priests and Daitās, Indradyumna's role as *yajamāna* being played by the King of Puri.

II

Indra's propping up of the sky with his *vajra* is often imitated by Indian Kings through rituals of erecting a banner, a bamboo pole or a post – similes of the *axis mundi*. Such ceremonies are "a reiteration of the creation and must as such have inaugurated the new year, that is, a new life in a renovated world" (Kuiper 1979: 130). In Hopkins' opinion – accepted by Dumézil (1971) and Kuiper (1979) – the festival of Indra would occur, in former times, "after the rains had ceased and when New Year's was celebrated" (1915: 126).[22]

The intervention of the King of Puri as a sweeper (in the *çerā pahārā*) is itself a commemoration of the new year. According to Mitra, this is precisely its main purpose: "to wash off the accumulated dust and soot of the year" (1875, II: 131).

The *snāna yātrā* is a crucial moment. In the cycle of annual rites, this is the first time the Sovereign appears (directly or vicariously) as the temple's hereditary sweeper. Held at the *jyeṣṭha pūrṇimā* (*jyeṣṭha*'s full moon), the ceremony marks the birth of Jagannātha and, as often said, the beginning of the new year.[23] The second ritual appearance of the royal sweeper takes place at the opening of the *ratha yātrā*. It presented, in the past, dramatic overtones unknown today. Here is Mitra's testimony:

> When the images have been seated on their thrones in their respective cars, they are richly dressed and ornamented for the occasion ... After this the Rājā ... comes in a large procession, with led horses, elephants, palankins and other paraphernalia. When about a hundred yards in front of the foremost car, he descends from his vehicle and walks barefoot, and, as the hereditary sweeper of the temple, sweeps the ground before the cars with a jewelled broom, and worships the images in due form with flowers and incense. Then, descending from the last car, he successively holds the cables attached to the three cars and emblematically drags them, the actual operation of dragging being afterwards performed by a body of 4,200 coolies, called Kālābetiyās (*ibid.*: 132).

In conducting this ceremony, performed on the verge of the rainy season, the King reproduces Indra's demiurgic action. A reconfirmation of royal authority, the ritual provides new evidence on the relationship between powerfulness and vulnerability: walking barefoot,

---

[22] Despite lack of agreement over the precise date of the Indian New Year, the rainy season was, in the post-Vedic period, the great caesura of the calendar (Kuiper 1979: 135).

[23] The *Puruṣottama mahātmya* of the *SkP* sets the New Year on the *phālguna* full moon.

sweeping the ground like an Untouchable, and pretending to move the huge wooden cars, a gruelling task indeed, the Sovereign behaves like a humble Kālābetiyā.

But who are the Kālābetiyās and what is their role? Included by N. Patnaik among the *sebakas* of the Puri temple, their only function is to "drag the Cars" (1977: 51). According to Elwin, they are "'black-backed' Saoras [who] pull the car of Jagannath at the great festival" (1955: 29). This information is taken directly from Russell and Hira Lal, who used the form Kālāpithia ("Black Backs") and described them as Śabaras, "employed to drag the car of Jagannāth" (1916, IV: 504).

God's temporary "residence", the "car", *ratha*, replaces the temple which, in turn, occasionally adopts its shape.[24] Hence, the Kālāpithias (< *kāla*, "black"; *pithā*, "back") correspond to the mythical Tortoises, stone carriers in the *DT*, and to Akūpāra bearing the primordial Mountain on its back (according to the Sanskrit tradition). Akūpāra is also, as we know, the walled-in reptile of the Vedic "fire altars" erected by Indradyumna. The painful reminiscences of its task are underlined by the classical *Mbh*, and references to the indelible marks of fire on its shell are found in the *Kaumārikākhaṇḍa* of the *SkP* (see Chapter 4, note 3).

Every year, in the course of the Car Festival, the Churning of the Milky Ocean is reenacted by the Kālāpithias, whose name and function refer simultaneously to the Vedic *agnicayana* and to Hindu temple-making. But their role implies much more than just an allusion to Viṣṇu's second *avatāra*. Dragging the *rathas*, they remind us of the strenuous act of Indra, who removed the Mount Mandara and placed it on the back of the Tortoise. Briefly, they reassert the essential homology between Indra and Viṣṇu. Moreover, the apparent divergence between *devas* and *asuras* is transcended. It is clear that, from the temple of Jagannātha to that of Guṇḍīcā, and from the latter back to the former, the coming and going of the *rathas*, pulled by thick ropes,

[24] As is the case in Koṇārak.

cannot fail to symbolise the rotary movement of the Cosmic Mountain, around which the serpent Vāsuki was coiled. The replacement of the "serpent" by the "rope" is ironic here, since their obvious likeness commonly evokes the *trompe-l'oeil* effects produced by *māyā*. One is tempted to conclude that the Kālāpithias (with whom the King of Puri identifies himself) do "hold the strings" in more than a literal sense. Establishing a secret link between Indra and Viṣṇu, and between "gods" and "demons" (in the episode of the *amṛtamanthana*), their ritual task further emphasises the symbolic convergence between the Sovereign and the multitude of devotees (who also pull the cars). The Kālāpithias do represent the intangible point where *all* the actors in the drama come together in harmony.

CHAPTER TWELVE

SWEEPING THE GROUND, BEHOLDING THE SKY

Uṣas, the Vedic personification of Dawn, is commonly seen as a friendly goddess, prodigal of wealth. But she also displays a gloomy facet:[1] *RV* II, 15, 6, for example, states that Indra destroyed her car with the *vajra*, apparently alluding to the god's battle with Vṛtra. The fact that she is often linked with the "primordial hill opened by Indra" suggests that she "was conceived as a reiteration of the cosmogonical process" (Kuiper 1960: 225). This is not incompatible with Bergaigne's point of view, according to which the goddess who became the object of Indra's animosity would be the "indolent" Dawn of the summer solstice.[2]

In post-Vedic texts, Uṣas is replaced by Aruṇa, a male divinity whose birth brings us back to the Churning of the Milky Ocean:

Aruṇa's birth
(*Mbh*, I, 14-30)

Prajāpati had two daughters, Kadrū and Vinatā, both wives of the sage Kaśyapa (literally a "tortoise"). Kadrū wanted to give birth to a thousand serpents; Vinatā longed for two sons who would surpass those of her sister in strength and courage.

Kaśyapa satisfied their desires. Kadrū conceived a thousand serpents. But Vinatā, seeing that her sons were late in coming into the world, took matters into her own hands and broke the shell of one of the eggs. Aruṇa was therefore premature - only the upper part of his body had time to develop. He vented his fury on his mother: "Because of your act," he told her, "you'll become a slave." Advising Vinatā to wait patiently for the full development of her second embryo, Aruṇa ascended into the sky where he became charioteer of the Sun. A long time later, Garuḍa was born. He is the king of birds, Viṣṇu's vehicle.

---

[1] Uṣas' duplicity has often been stressed. *Cf.* Coomaraswamy 1935a; Kuiper 1960; Dumézil 1973; Oguibénine 1988.

[2] *Cf.* Dumézil 1973; Oguibénine 1988: 133-134.

One day, Vinatā and Kadrū approached Uccaiḥśravas, the horse recently created from the Ocean of Milk. Vinatā stated that the animal was completely white; Kadrū argued that its tail was black. Vying with each other, they struck a wager as to which of them would become her sister's slave, but left close examination of Uccaiḥśravas to the following day. Kadrū, in the meantime, ordered her children to coil themselves around the horse's tail, simulating black plaits. At first the serpents refused – and were condemned to destruction during a sacrifice. Seeking to avoid this condemnation, the serpents eventually submitted. Thus Vinatā lost the bet and became her sister's slave.

The serpents later agreed to free Vinatā if Garuḍa would bring them the gods' elixir of immortality. With Viṣṇu's consent, Garuḍa complied with this request, but Indra recovered the *amṛta* in a lightning strike.

Prajāpati is an incestuous god. The same is true of Kaśyapa, a *prajāpati* himself. His marriage with the demiurge's two daughters leads to "incest" as defined by Françoise Héritier – the excessive conjunction of kinsfolk of the same sex sharing the same sexual partner. The sisters further illustrate the symmetrical excesses – extreme similitude or disastrous divergence – sometimes attributed to Prajāpati's initial action. Kadrū conceives a *large number of identical creatures*; Vinatā gives birth to *two dissimilar beings*. Moreover, Kadrū's serpents are *chthonic* characters, *demoniacal, black, and poisonous*; the sons of Vinatā are *celestial* characters, *allies of the gods, bright and luminous*, directly or indirectly *associated with the search for amṛta*. In spite of this, the actors in the drama (the mothers as well as their children) are united by an ambiguous relationship. Their "antagonistic complicity" may be illustrated by the episode of Uccaiḥśravas' decisive transformation. In order to become a perfect symbol of unity – a subtle intermingling of "life" and "death", "light" and "darkness" – the stallion, whose unspotted *whiteness* is a reflection of *amṛta*, the elixir of eternity, has to be tainted by the *black* reptiles, previously converted into perishable beings by Kadrū's anathema.

"Throughout the *Mahābhārata*", O'Flaherty writes,

> snakes are the shadows of horses. The horse is the right animal to sacrifice, the animal on which one rides triumphantly up to heaven... The snake is the wrong animal to sacrifice, the animal that drags one down into the underworld" (1986: 16).

In Aruṇa's birth story, the serpents become part of Uccaiḥśravas, the horse finally transformed into a black and white animal. This perverse, if creative symbiosis obviously implies the partners' common nature. "A blurring of boundaries sometimes occurs in the categories of snakes and horses. Generally, snakes are the enemies of horses, but there is also a confounding of snakes and horses" (*ibid.*: 20). Uccaiḥśravas is thus a metaphor for the "reconstructed" Universe", a "recomposition" achieved as a result of the sisters' "false divergence." This episode recalls the symbolism of the *aśvamedha* (and, of course, that of the *agnicayana*: the "fire altar", the reconstituted body of Prajāpati, demanded the alternation of perishable and imperishable features). A replica of the demiurge, the horse destined for sacrifice was chosen according to a group of criteria among which colour was particularly important. A passage from the *ŚB* observes that the stallion should display all colours - because colour is "everything" and the *aśvamedha* is "everything"; another source mentions the need for a combination of white and black because the horse was born from the eye (white and black) of Prajāpati (*ŚB* XIII, 4, 2, 2-3). Be that as it may, the animal should not be of a single colour: he is, like the creator, a manifestation of plurality.

Interdependent threads interweave in the story of Aruṇa. Kadrū does not hesitate in condemning her own sons when they refuse to submit to her will - and it is through their condemnation that she attains ascendance over Vinatā. The Universe's sacrificial "reconstruction" - symbolised by the hybrid figure of a white horse with a black, serpentine tail - is therefore deeply rooted in Kadrū's deceptive behaviour, in the unfair condemnation she inflicts on her children and sister. Eventually, the snakes now turned into perishable beings become "perfect partners" of Vinatā's sons, again a highly meaningful relationship in the myth.

The motif of children cursed by their mother apparently inverts that of a mother (Vinatā) cursed by her son (Aruṇa). But the outcome of these actions is the same. Playing a crucial part in the drama of "creation", both Kadrū's curse directed towards her sons, *and* Aruṇa's imprecation directed towards his mother lead to the social disqualification of Vinatā, the deceived partner.

The conflictual relationship between mother and children (particularly that between Vinatā and Aruṇa, the Dawn) is associated with the sun's movement (and its periodic vulnerability). Guilty of causing Aruṇa's physical imperfection, Vinatā is a new example of the offender offended: she is victim of her own impatience – the creator's thoughtless haste.

* * *

Kadrū and Vinatā convey "distinct" attitudes towards temporality, symbolised by the "opposition" between the *swift birth* of the serpents and the *delayed birth* of Aruṇa and Garuḍa:

Prajāpati

Kadrū | Vinatā

A thousand serpents (swift birth) | Aruṇa and Garuḍa (belated birth)

FIG. 68

But the gestation of Aruṇa and that of Garuḍa also contrast:

Vinatā

Aruṇa (interrupted gestation) | Garuḍa (long gestation)

FIG. 69

The reiterative structures of "creation" are again illustrated by the homology between Vinatā's sons and Prajāpati's daughters. Moreover, "creation" is now the outcome of the interplay between solstices. The Sanskrit story of Aruṇa is, among other things, a reenactment of the "indolent" Uṣas' Vedic motif. Provoking the premature birth of her son, Vinatā induces his appearance during the summer solstice. The Oriya *Mbh* (*Vana parba*, II, 6), however, points in another direction. To heal her own infertility, Vinatā holds a ritual in *māgha* (January-February): a "road sweeping" ceremony (*dāṇḍa cerā pahārā*):

> *dāṇḍa cerā pahārā se kalā / aruṇa garuḍa beniputra se pāilā* ("she swept the roads and obtained her two sons, Aruṇa and Garuḍa").

Occuring now around the time of the winter solstice (formerly associated with the beginning of the new year),[3] the birth of Aruṇa, as portrayed by Sāraḷā Dāsa, *is not delayed*. "Creation" is thus related to Aruṇa's appearance at the time of either the summer or the winter

[3] "[A]fter a system of six seasons had been formed ..., the winter ended with *śiśirā*, and New Year's day... fell on the eighth day of the second half of Māgha, that is, January-February or formerly December-January... This is, accordingly, round about the winter solstice, which fell on the new moon of Māgha" (Kuiper 1979: 134, note 102).

solstice, depending on the source. These apparently different perspectives are, of course, firmly connected.

Ritual sweeping, equated again to a "demiurgic" intervention, is here reintroduced by the Oriya *Mbh*. The same text further reveals the persistent association between road sweeping and royal consecration. A good example of this link can be found in a well-known episode of Kuntī's adolescence. Let us first recall its Sanskrit version.

Kuntibhoja, Kuntī's adoptive father, had received a visit from Durvāsas, a strict and irascible Brahmin who intended to stay some time in the palace. Kuntibhoja asked his daughter to take care of their guest. The princess gladly accepted her father's request. For a whole year, she served Durvāsas with zeal, patiently accepting his fickleness and his slightest whim. Highly pleased, at the end of his visit he gave her a magic formula that would allow her to summon any god, bonding him to her own will, and even to conceive children with him.

In Jamison's opinion, this story illustrates the recurring theme of the humiliated host, the "value attached to yielding without complaint to any demand of a guest, no matter how bizarre or painful" (1996: 169). But the humiliated host is here a King, a character whose submissiveness is endowed with ritual overtones. Kuntabhoja's demeaned condition is explicitly emphasised by the Oriya *Mbh*, which brings up again the *ṭerā pahārā* motif.

How Kuntī obtained her magic formula
(*Sāraḷā Dāsa, Mbh, Ādi parba*, I, 28)

Durbāsā (= Durvāsas), an ascetic of great merit, decided to settle in the kingdom of Kuntabhoja (= Kuntibhoja), a Sovereign with no male offspring. Becoming the humble servant of the ascetic, Kuntī offers to sweep, every day, in the dawn light (*rātra prabhātare*), the courtyard of the house, and then to wash it with *ṭerā*. At the end of his stay, Durbāsā promises Kuntabhoja numerous male descendants and grants Kuntī the magic formula (*mahā mantra*) that will also come to guarantee the birth of Pāṇḍu's putative sons.

Kuntabhoja is a Sovereign devoid of male descendants. But thanks to the symbolic efficacy of her procedure, Kuntī, the compliant sweeper to whom the King's humiliation is transferred, guarantees the renewal of the exhausted kingdom. Ensuring the continuity of her father's line, she prefigures the role she will play later on as wife of the impotent Pāṇḍu.

II

In Vedic times, the broom was an important ritual instrument, "always wandering from one priest to the other".[4] Often associated with the sacrificer's wife, it bears a creative symbolism: "the ritual broom, a male sexual symbol, is thrown in her lap or put between her thighs with the explanation that she will thus conceive a son" (Jamison 1996: 48; *cf.* also: 59-61).

Even today, the use of a broom is supposed "to drive out poverty" (Crooke, II: 190). Such is the case in many villages around Puri, where ritual "road sweeping" (*dāṇḍa pahārā*) is performed yearly. The ceremony is carried out during the last five days of *kārtika* (October-November) and *mārgaśira* (November-December). Before sunrise, the ritualists – pubescent girls and married women who have still not conceived (or whose children have not survived) – leave their homes without washing. This is highly significant, since ritual efficacy depends, in this context, on the creative power of "dirt" and "impurity" (O'Flaherty 1980).

With brooms made out of *vajra mūli* branches (*sida cordifolia; pinicillaria spicata*) the ritualists diligently sweep the village streets. They also strike a tuft of pandanus – *kiā* (*pandanus odoratissimus*) – three times with their improvised tools. This "aggression" is probably

[4] Eggeling, referring to the sacrificial ceremonies of Brahmanism (1963, I, 84, note 2).

a dramatisation of sexual intercourse, the masculine role being played by girls and women:[5] the bundle of *vajra mūli* branches (literally: the "root of the *vajra*") seems to replace – and feminise – Indra's phallic weapon, the *vajra*.

After bathing in a brook or lagoon, the female road sweepers go to a small clay temple, where a *tulasi* branch[6] is sprinkled with drops of milk. Milk is not only a female equivalent of semen; like semen itself, it is sometimes considered a sufficient means of procreation:

> Side by side with conventional observations on where babies come from, the Vedas suggest that a man can create without a woman, a woman without a man. Semen by itself is fertile; milk by itself is fertile (*ibid.*: 32).

Each of the ritual five days of *mārgaśira* is explicitly associated with one of the five Pāṇḍavas; and the day of the full moon, when ceremonies end, is called *pāṇḍu pūrṇimā* (the full moon of Pāṇḍu). Evoking the King's sexual impotence, and the birth of the heroes ensured by Kuntī (as a sweeper, according to Sāraḷā Dāsa), the *daṇḍa (çerā) pahārā* appears again as a means of healing.

From ethnography and Orissan vernacular traditions, two main conclusions may thus be drawn regarding *çerā pahārā* performances:

1. Rituals emphasise the creative power of female road sweepers. In this context, women sometimes play the role of men ("dirt" being a symbol of female parthenogenesis).

2. Road-sweeping ceremonies are related to cosmogonic creation and, hence, to royal consecration.

---

[5] The "Pandanus plant", Gupta remarks, "is indigenous to the coastline of India but is depicted mainly on the temples of Orissa, Andhra Pradesh, Uttar Pradesh and Rajasthan. The plant is quite inhospitable with its prickly leaves and in spite of it, the depiction of the tree is associated with either an amorous couple standing under it or a *vrikshaka* [*a nymph*]" (1996: 135).

[6] A recurrent object of feminine worship, the *tulasi* (*ocimum sanctum*) is considered a manifestation of Śri-Lakṣmī: "The plant is held in such great reverence that the Hindu marriage season is declared open only after a special *puja* is performed in front of the *Tulasi* plant on the eleventh day of *Kartika*" (Gupta 1996: 131).

This helps us to understand the ritual intervention of the King during the *ratha yātrā*: sweeping for a renewed world, removing the "dust and soot of the year", he takes hold of the very symbol of female fertility. It is in the burlesque role of an "impure" and "feminised" male that he appears in the ceremonies of the summer solstice. A synthesis of masculine and feminine attributes, he is the replica of the androgynous demiurge, a mirror image of Arjuna at the court of Virāṭa.[7]

III

The royal *çerā pahārā* marks the arrival of the rains and announces the progressive shortening of the days (summer solstice): the world will gradually dive into a "nocturnal" existence, symbolised by Viṣṇu's "cosmic sleep", during which marriage ceremonies will be suspended. As a sweeper, the Sovereign betrays the *yajamāna*'s vulnerability – a fact which seems to reflect seasonal weakness: the royal *çerā pahārā* takes place in a moment when "darkness", "sickness" and "social destitution" converge.

Summer solstice:
Darkness: shortening of the days. Vinatā forces the appearance of Aruṇa (the Dawn), causing him physical imperfection (Sanskrit *Mbh*). Viṣṇu's sleep.
Matrimonal alliances are suspended.
"Illness" (or "death") of the gods.
"Social destitution" (the King of Puri appears as a ritual sweeper).

FIG. 70

[7] *Cf.* O'Flaherty 1980: 26.

The rituals performed on the last days of *kārtika* (after Viṣṇu's sleep has come to an end) and repeated at the end of *mārgaśira* (around the time of the winter solstice) themselves enhance the chances of conception:

Winter solstice:
Light: days grow longer.
Pregnancy is stimulated; rituals of *kārtika* and *mārgaśira*; Vinatā recovers her own fertility (Oriya *Mbh*).

FIG. 71

From Fig. 70 to Fig. 71, the nature of Vinatā's influence seems to have changed. The summer solstice (Fig. 70) is "disruptive" and brings about Aruṇa's deformity; conversely, the winter solstice (Fig. 71) is "mild" and allows a recovery from infertility. But summer and winter solstices, like physical disorder and healing techniques, are related aspects of a single process, ruled by the subtle interplay of *rasas*.

The *rasas* are essential nutrients of Ayurvedic medicine diffused in the fat of animals and sap of plants (Zimmermann 1982: 21). Beginning at the critical period of the summer solstice, their "emission" ends during the winter solstice. From then on, "the Sun captures the *rasas*" (*ibid.*: 47), and beings become debilitated until a new crisis peak is reached at the time of the next summer solstice. Men will then again face poverty and disease, and the gods of Puri will "sicken" or "die." According to the *Deula Tolā*, this is the moment when the *kalaśa*, the finial of the temple, is found by Gāla Mādhaba. Homologous to Yayāti's empty well, the "water-jar" half-buried in the sand is a symbol of scarcity; but, like the well, it is also a promise of prosperity, the announcement of a new start. Revealing the finial of the Jagannātha Temple – the "hidden sun" – Gāla Mādhaba rescues the star that has been hurt, as it were, by darkness (Chapter 9). But, by scratching the soil's surface, he also prefigures the action of the King of Puri, who sweeps the ground during the summer solstice rituals. The dissipation of "creative" energy is insinuated by the King's appearance in the "degraded" status of a sweeper. As one may expect, however, this is just half of the story. Sweepers, in rituals and mythical accounts, are endowed with amazing capacities. Sweeping the road, according to the Oriya *Mbh*, Vinatā suppresses her own infertility, and in doing so gives birth to the Dawn, the Sun's charioteer.[8]

The King of Puri seems to be inspired by Gāla Mādhaba and, of course, by Vinatā. In order to renew the exhausted world, he acts – during the most dangerous period of the Sun's yearly movement – as both a sweeper and a magic healer.

IV

The relationship between summer and winter solstices is perfectly illustrated by the Vedic Gavāmayana (the "cow path"), a *soma* sacrifice lasting for one year and aiming to reinvigorate the Sun (Jamison 1991). In some respects, the ritual itself and its mythical context are remarkably close to the overall symbolism of the Jagannātha cult.

The Vedic rituals held on the day of Visuvant (the summer solstice) are reminiscent of passages from the *Saṃhitās* and *Brāhmaṇas* about the weakening of the Sun (Vivasvant) who, attacked by Svarbhānu, had lost his brightness. The premature birth of Vivasvant is also referred to in this context. According to the *ŚB* (III, 1, 3, 3), Aditi conceived seven perfect children but the eighth, the Sun, "was

[8] In this connection, it is not irrelevant that Sūrya, the Sun, is the first god summoned by Kuntī when she gets the magic formula of Durvāsas.

a mere lump of bodily matter, as broad as it was high": he was named Mārtāṇḍa (the one coming from a "dead egg").

It is sometimes specified that this defective conception was caused by Aditi's impatience. As reward for strictly accurate ritual procedures, she had been given three pairs of twins; one day, however, out of desire for new offspring, she committed an error, eating the offerings destined for the gods (instead of the leftovers). Her wish came true, but her child was born prematurely. Deciding to reanimate this "lump of matter", Aditi's first sons reshaped their brother in the form of a man. The remaining fragments of this activity turned into an elephant... (*ŚB* III, 1, 3, 4)

Inextricably interwoven in this narrative, maternal aggression, female parthenogenesis, and botched birth are also important motifs in myths and rituals of Puri. Gaṇeśa, who plays a decisive role in *snāna yātrā* ceremonies – Jagannātha's birthday, on the eve of the New Year –[9] was born without direct intervention of Śiva, his father; according to some accounts, he was a victim of his mother's offence. Additionally, Courtright remarks, his "elephantine appearance recalls that of the elephant made up of pieces left over from the creation of Mārtāṇḍa" (1985: 57):

> The story of Mārtāṇḍa and the elephant-shaped leftover, and that of the birth of Gaṇeśa are connected... by the theme of the agression of the mother against the son. Aditi condemns Mārtāṇḍa to mortality and formlessness by cheating the gods out of their rice offerings.... The theme of maternal aggression in the myths of Gaṇeśa is more veiled; but it is there – as [may be] seen in the myth where Pārvatī curses Gaṇeśa to be ugly (*ibid.*)

[9] Gaṇeśa came into the world without Śiva's involvement, according to the majority of myths. Some versions state, nonetheless, that he was born in Śiva's mind: "What is common to all the myths of Gaṇeśa's origins is that he is *never* born from the sexual union of his mother and father in their divine forms as Śiva and Pārvatī" (Courtright 1985: 42).

The same motifs recur in classical and vernacular stories about Vinatā. Like Aditi, she is an impatient mother, provoking the physical awkwardness of her child (Sanskrit *Mbh*); like Aditi and Pārvatī, she is an agent of unilateral creation (Oriya *Mbh*). Furthermore, maternal aggression, miscarriage, and physical deformity are linked with sacrifice, fertility rituals, and solstitial polarity.

Mārtāṇḍa's congenital debility required the beneficial intervention of a Ṛṣi named Atri, who was himself born prematurely – in Jamison's opinion, the reason for his special capacity to reinvigorate the Sun:

> If I am correct, Atri's botched birth is not merely coincidentally similar to the sun's, but is the episode that empowers him to engage with the sun. It gives him potential power over the life of the sun greater than that possessed by the ordinarily much more powerful gods (Jamison 1991: 243).

To the same extent as Atri's premature birth, Aruṇa's coming into the world also anticipates the sun's origins. A misshapen creature in the classical *Mbh*, Aruṇa is led by his mother to become the forerunner of the star, whose daily appearance he stimulates. Her impatience here is connected with the vulnerability of the sun, threatened by darkness at the *summer solstice*. But Vinatā is not always an impatient mother. In the Oriya *Mbh*, she conceives Aruṇa, the Dawn (thus securing the regular trajectory of the sun) at the time of the *winter solstice*. This is when she performs the *dāṇḍa pahārā*: sweeping the ground, she beholds the sky.

This mirroring relationship between below and above is further enhanced by royal authority. Rescuing the Sun by means of the road-sweeping rituals of the summer solstice, the King of Puri guarantees fertility on earth. Like Gāla Mādhaba and Indradyumna in the myth, he is endowed with implicit healing capacities. The vernacular narratives in which the sterility of Indradyumna's wife is a central theme clarify this symbolic connection.

The story of Indradyumna
(Hunter, Fragment 2)[10]

... Then the king, with his army and 5000 male elephants, tried to drag the block [of timber] with crimson cords to the temple; but he could not, until, chidden for his presumption by lord Jagannath in a vision, he summoned Basu the fowler to his aid.

Thereafter the king gathered together all the carpenters in his country, and gave them lands and villages as the price for fashioning the block into an image of lord Jagannath. But when they put their chisels on the wood, the iron lost its edge; and when they struck them with their mallets, the mallets missed and crushed their hands; till at last the lord Vishnu came down in the form of an aged carpenter, and by signs and wonders declared his power unto the king. Him the king shut up alone in the temple with the block, and swore that no man should enter for twenty-one days, sealing the doors with his own seal. But the queen longed to see the face of the god, that he might redeem her life from barrenness. So she persuaded her husband; and he, opening the door before the end of the promised time, found the three images of Jagannath, and his brother and sister, fashioned from the waist upwards. But Jagannath and his brother had only stumps for arms, while his sister had none at all, and even so they remain to this day.

The King's haste – in fact, that of his sterile wife – is homologous to Vinatā's in the classical *Mbh*: deciding to break the egg shell prematurely, she became responsible for Aruṇa's physical incompleteness (only the upper part of his body having been formed). There is here a striking analogy: the Jagannātha Temple, broken into because the images' gestation seemed too slow, corresponds to the egg, slow to hatch. Moreover, the queen's sterility (in the myth of Indradyumna) is a replica of Vinatā's in the Oriya *Mbh*: the healing rituals she performs are, somehow, reproduced by the King of Puri in the *ratha yātrā*.

Aruṇa's deformity is, of course, comparable to Jagannātha's which, in turn, is equivalent to that of the Sun (= Prajāpati). We know that "the length [of Jagannātha's figure] should be the same as the breadth

[10] Hunter 1872, I: 92-93.

of his arms" (Starza 1993: 120), a fact which accounts for one of the god's names: *cakrakrti* ("round" like the *cakra*). This expression is similar to the one adopted by the *ŚB* to describe the formless nature of Mārtāṇḍa, "a mere lump of bodily matter, as broad as it was high". In short, the image of Aruṇa (the Dawn) reflects itself onto and is reflected back by that of Jagannātha-Viṣṇu, who is identified with Prajāpati (the Sun).

The iconography of Jagannātha, Indradyumna's myth, and all the ceremonies held around the Puri temple weave an intricate pattern of sacrificial symbolism:

Oriya *Mbh*:	**Seasonal rites:**
Vinatā, a sterile woman, performs the *dāṇḍa çerā pahārā* to guarantee her fertility.	***End of the rainy season:*** Young pubescent and sterile women, perform the *dāṇḍa pahārā* to guarantee their fertility. ***End of the dry season:*** The King of Puri performs the *çerā pahārā* to inaugurate a new cycle of fertility.
	This ritual performance identifies the King with an Untouchable.
Sanskrit *Mbh*:	**Indradyumna's story:**
The hasty mother breaks the egg she has produced,	Encouraged by his sterile queen, Indradyumna breaks into the temple he has built,
disturbing the gestation process, and condemning to imperfection...	
...Aruṇa's body,	...Jagannāth's image,
of which only the upper part has developed.	of which only the upper part had been sculpted.
As a result, Vinatā condemns herself to slavery.	

FIG. 72

Indradyumna is usually held responsible for the incompleteness of Jagannātha. However, beneath Indradyumna's eagerness, and his interruption of the artisan's labour, one recognises the anxiety of his wife. The sterile queen calls to mind the greedy Vinatā. But Vinatā, causing Aruṇa's deformity and condemning herself to slavery - as if emptied of creative energy - evokes the royal sweeper of Puri, and also Prajāpati, destroying and recreating forever. The "unusual" incompletely carved images of the great temple are a reminder of this circle of eternal becoming.

CODA

CHAPTER THIRTEEN

BEYOND THE WHOLE: AN IMPLICATE ORDER

Coincident with Jagannātha's birthday, the *snāna yātrā* is said to mark the transition from the old to the new year:

"End" of the hot season; "end" of the old year

Snāna yātrā ("bathing festival") Jagannātha's birthday

"Beginning" of the monsoon; the new year

FIG. 73

Damaging the paintwork of the wooden icons, the abundant ablution of the *snāna yātrā* is a sign of cosmic dissolution (Marglin 1985: 270). But all the following ritual events likewise evoke decay and annihilation.

The days after:

• The *anasara* is a caesura in the temporal flow: the gods fall "ill", the kitchens are inactive, there is silence in the temple area. In the *naba kalebara* years, the reenactment of a *pralaya* becomes particularly visible: the (*mahā*) *anasara* implies the "death" and "rebirth" of the deities, the renewal of the icons, the adjustment of the calendar.

• The end of *anasara* (or *mahā anasara*) is linked to the beginning of the *ratha yātrā* (the "Car festival"). Temporality is again suspended, as suggested by the closing of the sanctuary and withdrawal of the main deities.

• Immediately following the "Car festival", the "sleep of Viṣṇu" represents the "end" of a *yuga* and, hence, is again a dramatic representation of the great dissolution. The Supreme Being "not only burns the world but, as the earth becomes flooded with water, also sleeps upon the serpent Śeṣa" (Gonda 1954: 89). The "cosmic sleep" runs from the tenth day of the bright fortnight of *āṣāḍha* (June-July) to the eleventh day of the bright fortnight of *kārtika* (October-November). Matrimonial alliances are adjourned.

• Performed by pubescent girls and barren women during *kārtika* and *mārgaśira*, the *dāṇḍa çerā pahārā* seems to put an end to a state of crisis and infertility – as if, until then, the Universe had been submerged in the all-pervading night of a *pralaya*:

> *snāna yatra [pralaya]* → *anasara* (or *mahā anasara*) *[pralaya]* → *ratha yātrā [pralaya]* → "cosmic sleep" *[pralaya]*...

We are faced here with an "accumulation of false beginnings", as Malamoud would have it. Time, from this perspective, means never-ending renewal.

As Frédérique Marglin perceptively recognises, the *snāna yātrā* – the "starting point" in the above string of rituals – marks the apparent transition from illness to rejuvenation, or from "death" to "life", by introducing "almost all the themes which will be later developed" (1985: 271). For example, the passage of the images from the "inner" to the "outer" sanctuary – an operation carried out on the morning of that day – prefigures their ultimate transfer, during the *ratha yātrā*, to the exterior of the temple precinct. In the same way, the first intervention of the King (or his surrogate) as a sweeper discreetly announces similar performances days later before the crowd. Marglin resorts to a western metaphor: the *snāna yātrā* is like "a musical overture" (*ibid.*: 272). But let us pause here for a moment.

The "bathing festival" is much more than an *anticipation* of future events. A typical hide-and-reveal ceremony, its double-sided structure is stressed from the very beginning. Its *temporal* ambiguity – the ablutions fall betwixt and between two "cycles" – corresponds to a *spa-*

tial divide ("inside" and "outside" the temple precinct; the "inner" and "outer" sanctuaries, *bhitara* and *bāhāra pokhariā*). At the end of the hot season, a similar relationship insinuates itself between the two halves of the "sandalwood festival" (*bāhāra* and *bhitara candana*).

The days before:

• The "sandalwood festival" – *candana yātrā* – is associated with the thirteenth year of the Pāṇḍava's banishment, when the heroes and Draupadī "hide" and "reveal" themselves. This last year of exile, spent among the Matsya, is already conceived as a *pralaya*. There is a clear parallelism between the disguise of the heroes (in Virāṭa's court) and the hiding of the wooden images under Gaṇeśa's mask (in the *snāna yātrā*). The sudden lack of differentiation among the four icons is a return to transcendent Unity, that is to Reality as symbolised in the Indradyumna myth by the banyan fig tree before it splits into four parts. Furthermore, Gaṇeśa's hermaphroditism evokes Arjuna's sexual ambivalence. It refers to the undifferentiated world as it was prior to Prajāpati's self-sacrifice. Like the Pāṇḍava's thirteenth year of exile – neither a "conclusion after the conclusion" nor a "beginning before the beginning" – the *snāna yātrā* takes us to the highest plane where time and non-time are indiscernible:

... candana yātrā [pralaya] → *snāna yātrā [pralaya]...*

The "bathing festival" is a one-day ceremony. But despite (or due to) its short duration, a vast array of mythical references cohere in it.

We may conclude that, like Gaṇeśa himself, the *snāna yātrā* points forwards and backwards, simultaneously. The *overture* which announces "the main themes of the symphony to follow" (Marglin 1985: 272) is also a *coda*, an epitome of the whole. As an instant suspended between "past" and "future", the one-day ritual is an imperceptible point of infinite implication.

BIBLIOGRAPHY

1. Oriya texts

Dārubrahma gitā (by Jagannātha Dāsa). Cuttack, 1953.

Deula Tolā (by Kṛṣṇa Dāsa). Bhubaneshwar, *no date.*

Mādaḷā Pāñjī. Ed. by A. B. Mahānti. Bhubaneshwar, 1969.

Mahābhārata (by Sāraḷā Dāsa). Ed. by A. B. Mahānti. 15 vols. Bhubaneshwar, 1968-1970.

2. Sanskrit Texts and Translations

Aitareya Brāhmaṇa. Ed. and trans. by M. Haug. 2 vols. Bombay, 1863.

Bhāgavata Purāṇa. Ed. by P. R. Śāstrī. Varanasi, 1962.
- Trans. by N. Raghunathan. 2 vols. Madras, 1976.

Brahma Purāṇa. Ed. by N. Āpte. Poona, 1895.
- Trans. by a Board of Scholars. *AITMS.* 4 vols. New Delhi, 1985-1986.

Chāndogya Upaniṣad. Ed. by V. P. Limaye, R. D. Vadekar. Poona, 1958.
- Trans. by R. Hume. Oxford, 1931.

Kūrma Purāṇa. Ed. by A. S. Gupta. Benares, 1971.
- Trans. by G. V. Tagare. *AITMS.* 2 vols. Delhi, 1981-1982.

Mahābhārata. Ed. by V. S. Sukthankar et al. 19 vols. Poona, 1933-59.
- Trans. by K. M. Ganguli. 12 vols. Delhi, 1970 (1884-1896);
- Trans. by J. A. B. van Buitenen. 3 vols. (Books 1-5). Chicago, 1973-1978.

Maitrāyaṇī Saṃhitā. Ed. by L. von Schroeder. 4 vols. Leipzig, 1883-1886.

Manu Smṛti. Ed. by J. H. Dave. 5 vols. Bombay, 1972-82.
- Trans. by G. Bühler. *SBE.* Delhi, 1964.

Matsya Purāṇa. Ed. by N. Āpte. Poona, 1907.
- Trans. by A Taluqdar of Oudh. Allahabad, 1916.

Nārada Purāṇa. Ed. by S. Sarma. Bareli, 1971.
- Trans. by G. V. Tagare. *AITMS.* 5 vols. Delhi, 1980-1982.

Ṛg Veda Saṃhitā. Trans. by H. H. Wilson. 7 vols. Delhi, 1977 (1850-1888).

Satapatha Brāhmaṇa. Trans. by J. Eggeling. *SBE.* 5 vols. Delhi, 1963 (1882-1900).

Śiva Purāṇa. Ed. by J. Miśra. Bombay, 1965.
- Trans. by a Board of Scholars. *AITMS.* 4 vols. Delhi, 1973.

Skanda Purāṇa. Bombay, 1910.
- Trans. by G. V. Tagare. *AITMS,* Part 1-7. Delhi, 1992-1995.

3. Other references

ACHARYA, P. K.

1934: *A Dictionary of Hindu Architecture.* Oxford.

ASSAYAG, J.

1998: "La construction de l'*objet* en anthropologie. L'indianisme et le comparatisme de Louis Dumont", in *L'Homme*, 146: 165-189.

AUBOYER, J.

1960: *Khajuraho.* The Hague.

AVALON, A. (See WOODROFFE, Sir J.)

BAILEY, F. G.

1957: *Caste and the Economic Frontier. A Village in Highland Orissa.* Manchester.

1960: *Tribe, Caste, and Nation. A Study of Political Activity and Political Change in Highland Orissa.* Manchester.

BAILEY, G.

2003: "The Purāṇas. A Study in the Development of Hinduism", in Sharma, A. (ed.): *The Study of Hinduism*: 139-168.

BAKKER, H.

1991: "The Footprints of the Lord", in Eck, D. L., F. Mallison (eds.): *Devotion Divine*: 19-37.

BANERJEA, J. N.

1941: *The Development of Hindu Iconography.* Calcutta.

BANERJI, R. D.

1930-1931: *History of Orissa, from the Earliest Times to the British Period.* 2 vols. Calcutta.

BARTH, A.

1914-1918: *Oeuvres.* 4 vols. Paris.

BÄUMER, B. (ed.)

1982: *Rūpa Pratirūpa. Alice Boner Commemoration Volume.* New Delhi.

BECK, B. E. F.

1978: "The Personality of a King: Prerogatives and Dilemmas of Kingship as Portrayed in a Contemporary Epic From South India", in Richards, J. F. (ed.): *Kingship and Authority in South Asia*: 168-191.

1982: *The Three Twins: The Telling of a South Indian Folk Epic.* Bloomington.

1986: "Social Dyads in Indic Folktales", in Blackburn, S. H., A. K. Ramanujan (eds.): *Another Harmony*: 76-102.

1989: "Core Triangles in the Folk Epics of India", in Blackburn, S. H., P. J. Claus, J. B. Flueckiger, S. S. Wadley (eds.): *Oral Epics in India*: 155-175.

BENDER, E. (ed.)
1962: *Indological Studies in Honor of W. Norman Brown.* New Haven.

BENVENISTE, E.
1937: "Expression indo-européenne de l''éternité'", in *Bulletin de la Société Linguistique de Paris*, 38, 1: 103-112.

BENVENISTE, E., L. RENOU
1934: *Vṛtra et Vṛθragna. Etude de mythologie indo-iranienne.* Paris.

BERGAIGNE, A.
1878-1883: *La Religion védique d'après les hymnes du Rig-Veda.* 3 vols. Paris.

BHARATI, A.
1965: *The Tantric Tradition.* London.

BHATTACHARYA, F.
1981: "La déesse et le royaume selon le Kālaketu Upākhyāna du Caṇḍī Maṅgala", in Biardeau, M. (ed.): *Autour de la déesse hindoue*: 17-54.

BIARDEAU, M.
1964: *Théorie de la connaissance et philosophie de la parole dans le brahmanisme classique.* Paris.
1965: "*Ahaṃkāra*, the Ego Principle in the *Upaniṣad*", in *CIS*, 8: 62-84.
1968: "Études de mythologie hindoue", 1, in *BEFEO*, 54: 19-45.
1969: "Études de mythologie hindoue", 2, in *BEFEO*, 55: 59-105.
1971: "Études de mythologie hindoue", 3, in *BEFEO*, 58: 17-89.
1971-1972: "*Brahmanes et potiers*", in *Annuaire de l'Ecole Pratique des Hautes Etudes, 5e Section: Sciences Religieuses*, 79: 31-55.
1976a: "Le Sacrifice dans l'Hindouisme", in Biardeau, M., Ch. Malamoud (ed.): *Le Sacrifice dans l'Inde ancienne*: 7-154.
1976b: "Études de mythologie hindoue", 4, in *BEFEO*, 63: 111-263.
1978: "Études de mythologie hindoue", 5, in *BEFEO*, 65: 87-238.
1981a: "L'arbre *śamī* et le buffle sacrificiel", in Biardeau, M. (ed.): *Autour de la déesse hindoue*: 215-243.
1981b: "The salvation of the king in the *Mahābhārata*", in *CIS*, 15: 75-97.
1984: "Nala et Damayantī, héros épiques" (1), in *IIJ*, 27: 247-274.
1985: "Nala et Damayantī, héros épiques" (2), in *IIJ*, 28: 1-34.
1988: "Semis de graines dans des pots: réflexions sur une forme", in Blondeau, A.-M., K. Schipper (eds.): *Essais sur le rituel*, I: 93-117.
1989: *Histoires de poteaux. Variations védiques autour de la Déesse hindoue.* Paris.
1993: "Le Brâhmanisme ancien ou la non-violence impossible", in *Puruṣārtha*, 16: 125-139.
2002: *Le Mahābhārata. Un récit fondateur du brahmanisme et son interprétation.* 2 vols. Paris.

BIARDEAU, M. (ed.)
1981: *Autour de la déesse hindoue, Puruṣārtha,* 5.

BIARDEAU, M., CH. MALAMOUD
1976: *Le Sacrifice dans l'Inde ancienne.* Paris.

BLACKBURN, S. H., A. K. RAMANUJAN (eds.)
1986: *Another Harmony. New Essays on the Folklore of India.* Berkeley.

BLACKBURN, S.H., P. J. CLAUS, J. B. FLUECKIGER, S.S. WADLEY (eds.)
1989: *Oral Epics in India.* Berkeley.

BLONDEAU, A.-M., K. SCHIPPER (eds.)
1988-1990: *Essais sur le rituel.* 2 vols. Louvain-Paris.

BOAL, B. M.
1983: *The Konds. Human sacrifice and Religious Change.* Warminster.

BOHM, D.
1980: *Wholeness and the Implicate Order.* London.
1985: *Unfolding Meaning. A Weekend of Dialogue.* London.

BONER, A.
1962: *Principles of Composition in Hindu Sculpture. Cave Temple Period.* Leiden.

BONER, A., S. R. SARMA (eds.)
1966: *Śilpa Prakāśa. Medieval Orissan Sanskrit Text on Temple Architecture* (translated and annotated). Leiden.
1972: *New Light on the Sun Temple of Konārka. Four Unpublished Manuscripts Relating to Construction History and Ritual of the Temple* (translated and annotated). Varanasi.

BONER, A., S. R. SARMA, B. BÄUMER (ed.)
1982: *Vāstusūtra Upaniṣad. The Essence of Form in Sacred Art.* Delhi.

BONER, G., L. Soni, J. Soni (eds.)
1993: *Alice Boner Diaries. India 1934-1967.* Delhi.

BOSE, N. K.
1932: *Canons of Orissan Architecture.* Calcutta.

BROWN, C. M.
1982: "The Theology of Rādhā in the Purāṇas", in Hawley, J. S., D. M. Wulff (eds.): *The Divine Consort*: 57-71.

BROWN, W. N.
1942: "The Creation Myth of the Rig Veda", in *JAOS*, 62: 85-98.
1965: "Theories of Creation in the Rig Veda", in *JAOS*, 85: 23-34.

BURNIER, R.
1950: *Visages de l'Inde Médiévale.* Paris.

BUTTERWORTH, E. A. S.
1970: *The Tree at the Navel of the Earth.* Berlin.

CALAND, W., V. HENRY
1906: *L'Agniṣṭoma. Description complète de la forme normale du sacrifice de soma dans le culte védique.* 2 vols. Paris.

CARMAN, J. B., F. A. MARGLIN (eds.)
1985: *Purity and Auspiciousness in Indian Society.* Leiden.

CARSTAIRS, G. M.
1961: *The Twice-Born. A Study of a Community of High-Caste Hindus.* Bloomington.

CASE, M. H. (ed.)
1994: *Heinrich Zimmer. Coming into His Own.* Princeton.

CASE, M., N. G. BARRIER (eds.)
1986: *Aspects of India. Essays in Honor of Edward Cameron Dimock, Jr.* New Delhi.

CHAKRAVARTI, C.
1963: *Tantras. Studies on Their Religion and Literature.* Calcutta.

CHATTERJI, S.K.
1966: *The People, Language and Culture of Orissa.* Bhubaneshwar.

COOMARASWAMY, A. K.
1927: *History of Indian and Indonesian Art.* Leipzig.
1928: *Yakṣas (1).* Washington.
1931: *Yakṣas (2).* Washington.
1934: *The Transformation of Nature in Art.* Cambridge, Mass.
1935a: *The Darker Side of Dawn.* Washington.
1935b: "Angel and Titan: An Essay in Vedic Ontology", in *JAOS*, 55: 373-419.
1942: *Spiritual Authority and Temporal Power in the Indian Theory of Government.* New Haven.
1977: *Selected Papers.* Vol. 1: *Traditional Art and Symbolism* Vol. 2: *Metaphysics* (edited by Roger Lipsey). Princeton.
1989: *What is Civilisation? and Other Essays.* Delhi.

COURTRIGHT, P. B.
1985: *Gaṇeśa. Lord of Obstacles, Lord of Beginnings.* New York.

CUNNINGHAM, A.
1854: *The Bhilsa Topes or Buddhist Monuments of Central India.* London.

DAGENS, B.
2005: *Traités, temples et images du monde indien. Études d'histoire et d'archéologie* (articles rassemblés par M.-L. Barazer-Billoret et V. Lefèvre). Pondichéry.

DANGE, S. A.
1969: *Legends in The Mahābhārata with a brief survey of folk-tales*. Delhi.

DANIÉLOU, A.
1962: *L'Érotisme divinisé*. Paris.

DAS, V.
1977: *Structure and Cognition. Aspects of Hindu Caste and Ritual*. Delhi.

DASH, G. N.
1978a: "The Evolution of the Priestly Power: the Gaṅgavaṃśa Period", in Eschmann, A., H. Kulke, G.C. Tripathi (eds.): *CJRTO*: 157-168.
1978b: "The Evolution of the Priestly Power: the Sūryavaṃśa Period", in Eschmann, A., H. Kulke, G.C. Tripathi (eds.): *CJRTO*: 209-221.

DEHEJIA, V.
1979: *Early Stone Temples of Orissa*. New Delhi.

DETIENNE, M. (ed.)
1990: *Tracés de fondation*. Louvain-Paris.

DIMOCK Jr., E. C.
1966: *The Place of the Hidden Moon. Erotic Mysticism in the Vaiṣṇava-sahajiyā Cult of Bengal*. Chicago.

DONALDSON, T. E.
1985-1987: *Hindu Temple Art of Orissa*. 3 vols. Leiden.

DONIGER, W. (See also O'FLAHERTY, W. D.)
1993a: "Echoes of the *Mahābhārata*: Why is a Parrot the Narrator of the *Bhāgavata Purāṇa* and the *Devībhāgavata Purāṇa*?" in Doniger, W. (ed.): *Purāṇa Perennis*: 31-57.
1993b: "The Scrapbook of Undeserved Salvation: The *Kedāra Khaṇḍa* of the *Skanda Purāṇa*" in Doniger, W. (ed.): *Purāṇa Perennis*: 59-81.
1994: "Speaking in Tongues: Deceptive Stories about Sexual Deception", in *Journal of Religion*, 74 (3): 320-337.
1996: "Enigmas of Sexual Masquerade in Hindu Myths and Tales", in Hasan-Rokem, G., D. Shulman (eds.): *Untying the Knot*: 208-223.
1998: *The Implied Spider. Politics and Theology in Myth*. New York.
1999a: *Splitting the Difference. Gender and Myth in Ancient Greece and India*. Chicago.
1999b: "The Dreams and Dramas of a Jealous Hindu Queen", in Shulman, D., G. G. Stroumsa (eds.): *Dream Cultures*: 74-84.
2000: *The Bedtrick. Tales of Sex and Masquerade*. Chicago.
2005: *The Woman Who Pretended to Be Who She Was. Myths of Self-Imitation*. Oxford.

DONIGER, W. (ed)
1993: *Purāṇa Perennis: Reciprocity and Transformation in Hindu and Jaina Texts*. Albany.

DUBOIS, Abbé J. A.
1825: *Moeurs, institutions et cérémonies des peuples de l'Inde.* 2 vols. Paris.

DUBUISSON, D.
1978: "La déesse chevelue et la reine coiffeuse: recherches sur un thème épique de l'Inde ancienne", in *JA*, 266: 291-310.
1986: *La Légende royale dans l'Inde ancienne. Rāma et le Rāmāyaṇa.* Paris.

DUMÉZIL, G.
1968: *Mythe et épopée. L'idéologie des trois fonctions dans les épopées des peuples indo-européens.* Paris.
1969: *Heur et malheur du guerrier.* Paris.
1970: *Du mythe au roman.* Paris.
1971: *Mythe et épopée II. Types épiques indo-européens: un héros, un sorcier, un roi.* Paris.
1973: *Mythe et épopée III. Histoires romaines.* Paris.
1979: *Mariages indo-européens.* Paris.
1986: *Le Mahabarat et le Bhagavat du Colonel de Polier.* Paris.
1994: *Le Roman des jumeaux.* Paris.

DUMONT, P. E.
1927: *L'Aśvamedha. Description du sacrifice solennel du cheval dans le culte védique d'après les textes du Yajurveda blanc.* Paris.

DUNCAN, J. S.
1990: *The City as Text: The Politics of Landscape Interpretation in the Kandyan Kingdom.* Cambridge.

ECK, D. L.
1982: *Banaras. City of Light.* Princeton.
1991: "Following Rāma, Worshipping Śiva", in Eck, D. L., F. Mallison (eds.): *Devotion Divine*: 49-71.

ECK, D. L., F. MALLISON (eds.)
1991: *Devotion Divine. Bhakti Traditions from the Regions of India. Studies in Honour of Charlotte Vaudeville.* Groningen, Paris.

EISENSTADT, S. N., R. KAHANE, D. SHULMAN (eds.)
1984: *Orthodoxy, Heterodoxy and Dissent in India.* Berlin.

ELIADE, M.
1958a: *Yoga. Immortality and Freedom.* Princeton.
1958b: *Patterns in Comparative Religion.* New York.
1964: *Shamanism. Archaic Techniques of Ecstasy.* Princeton.

ELWIN, V.
1951: *The Tribal Art of Middle India. A Personal Record.* Oxford.
1955: *The Religion of an Indian Tribe.* Oxford.

ESCHMANN, A.
1978a: "Hinduization of Tribal Deities in Orissa: the Śākta and Śaiva Typology", in Eschmann, A., H. Kulke, G.C. Tripathi (eds.): *CJRTO*: 79-97.
1978b: "The Vaiṣṇava Typology of Hinduization and the Origin of Jagannātha", in Eschmann, A., H. Kulke, G.C. Tripathi (eds.): *CJRTO*: 99-117.
1978c: "Prototypes of the Navakalevara Ritual and their Relation to the Jagannātha Cult", in Eschmann, A., H. Kulke, G. C. Tripathi (eds.): *CJRTO*: 265-283.

ESCHMANN, A., H. KULKE, G.C. TRIPATHI
1978: "The Formation of the Jagannātha Triad", in Eschmann, A., H. Kulke, G.C. Tripathi (eds.): *CJRTO*: 169-196.

ESCHMANN, A., H. KULKE, G.C. TRIPATHI (eds.)
1978: *The Cult of Jagannath and the Regional Tradition of Orissa*. New Delhi.

FABRI, Ch. L.
1974: *History of the Art of Orissa*. Bombay.

FILLIOZAT, J.
1933: "La force organique et la force cosmique dans la philosophie médicale de l'Inde et dans le Veda", in *Revue Philosophique de la France et de l'Etranger*, 116: 410-429.

GANGULY, M. M.
1912: *Orissa and Her Remains. Ancient and Medieval (Puri District)*. Calcutta.

GEIB, R.
1975: *Die Indradyumna-Legende: Ein Beitrag zur Geschichte des Jagannātha Kultes*. Wiesbaden.

GETTY, A.
1936: *Gaṇeśa. A Monograph on the Elephant-Faced God*. Oxford.

GOLDMAN, R.P.
1977: *Gods, Priests, and Warriors. The Bhṛgus of the Mahābhārata*. New York.
1995: "Gods in Hiding: The Mahābhārata's Virāṭa Parvan and the Divinity of the Indian Epic Hero", in Narang S. P. (ed.)., *Modern Evaluation of the Mahābhārata*: 73-100.

GOMES DA SILVA, J.C.
1989: *L'Identité volée. Essais d'anthropologie sociale*. Bruxelles.
1994: "Formes et énigmes: à propos d'un mythe de fondation d'Orissa", in C. Vielle, P. Swiggers, G. Jucquois: *Comparatisme, Mythologies, Langages: en hommage à Claude Lévi-Strauss*. Louvain, 143-170.

1998: "Logique du récit, logiques des savoirs", in F. Laplantine, J. Lévy, J.-B. Martin, A. Nouss (eds): *Récit et Connaissance*. Lyon: 9-21.
2003a: *O Discurso contra si próprio*. Lisboa.
2003b: "L'Anthropologue et le comparatisme", in *Cultures en mouvement*, 55: 36-39.
2006: "Objets illusoires de l'écriture", in *Écrire les Sciences Sociales, Revue des Sciences Sociales*, 36: 14-19.
2008: "A Forma sob as formas. A propósito da arte tântrica de Orissa", in Frias, S. (ed.): *Etnografia e Emoções*, Lisboa: 65-86.

GONDA, J.
1954: *Aspects of Early Viṣṇuism*. Utrecht.
1961: "Ascetics and Courtesans", in *Adyar Library Bulletin*: 78-102.
1963: *The Vision of the Vedic Poets*. The Hague.
1965: *Change and Continuity in Indian Religion*. The Hague.
1966: *Ancient Indian Kingship from the Religious Point of View*. Leiden.
1968: "Atharvaveda 11, 7", in *Mélanges d'indianisme à la mémoire de Louis Renou*. (Publications de l'Institut de civilisation indienne, 28). Paris: 301-336.
1969: *Eye and Gaze in the Veda*. Amsterdam, London.
1970: *Viṣṇuism and Śivaism. A Comparison*. London.
1982: "The Popular Prajāpati", in *HR*, 22 (2): 129-149.

GOPINATHA RAO, T.A.
1914: *Elements of Hindu Iconography*. 2 vols., 4 parts. Madras.

GUPTA, S. M.
1971: *Plant Myths and Traditions in India*. Leiden.
1996: *Plants in Indian Temple Art*. Delhi.

HANDELMAN, D.
1996: "Traps of Trans-formation: Theoretical Convergences between Riddle and Ritual", in Hasan-Rokem, G., D. Shulman (eds.): *Untying the Knot*: 37-61.

HANDELMAN, D., D. SHULMAN
1997: *God Inside Out: Śiva's Game of Dice*. Oxford.

HASAN-ROKEM, G., D. SHULMAN (eds.)
1996: *Untying the Knot. On Riddles and Other Enigmatic Modes*. New York.

HAVELL, E. B.
1908: *Indian Sculpture and Painting*. London.

HAWLEY, J. S., D. M. WULFF (eds.)
1982: *The Divine Consort. Rādhā and the Goddesses of India*. Boston.

HAZRA, R. C.
1940: *Studies in the Purāṇic Records on Hindu Rites and Customs*. Dacca.

HEESTERMAN, J. C.

1957: *The Ancient Indian Royal Consecration. The Rājasūya Described according to the Yajus Texts and Annotated.* The Hague.

1985: *The Inner Conflict of Tradition. Essays in Indian Ritual, Kingship, and Society.* Chicago.

1993: *The Broken World of Sacrifice. An Essay in Ancient Indian Ritual.* Chicago.

HEIMANN, B.

1964: *Facets of Indian Thought.* New York.

HELD, G. J.

1935: *The Mahābhārata. An Ethnological Study.* Amsterdam.

HERITIER, F.

1979: "Symbolique de l'inceste et de sa prohibition", in M. Izard, P. Smith (eds.): *La Fonction symbolique.* Paris: 209-243.

1981: *L'Exercice de la Parenté.* Paris.

HEUSCH, L.

1985: *Sacrifice in Africa. A Structuralist Approach.* Manchester.

HILTEBEITEL, A.

1976: *The Ritual of Battle: Krishna in the Mahābhārata.* Ithaca.

1977: "Nahuṣa in the Skies: a Human King of Heaven", in *HR*, 16, 4: 329-350.

1980a: "Draupadī's Garments", in *IIJ*, 22: 97-112.

1980b: "Śiva, the Goddess, and the Disguises of the Pāṇḍavas and Draupadī", in *HR*, 20: 147-174.

1981: "Draupadī's Hair" in Biardeau, M. (ed.): *Autour de la déesse hindoue*: 179-214.

1984: "The Two Kṛṣṇas on one Chariot: Upaniṣadic Imagery and Epic Mythology", in *HR* 24: 1-26.

1985a: "Two Kṛṣṇas, Three Kṛṣṇas, Four Kṛṣṇas, More Kṛṣṇas: Dark Interactions in the *Mahābhārata*", in *Journal of South Asian Literature, 20. Essays on the Mahābhārata*: 71-77.

1985b: "Purity and Auspiciousness in the Sanskrit Epics", in Carman, J. B., F. A. Marglin (eds.): *Purity and Auspiciousness in Indian Society*: 41-54.

1988: *The Cult of Draupad˜ı, I. Mythologies: From Gingee to Kurukṣetra.* Chicago.

1991: *The Cult of Draupad˜ı, II. On Hindu Ritual and the Goddess.* Chicago.

1999: *Rethinking India's Oral and Classical Epics. Draupadī Among Rajputs, Muslims, and Dalits.* Chicago.

2001: *Rethinking the Mahābhārata. A Reader's Guide to the Education of the Dharma King.* Chicago.

2003: "India's Epics. Writing, Orality, and Divinity" in Sharma, A. (ed.): *The Study of Hinduism*: 114-138.

HILTEBEITEL, A. (ed.)
1989: *Criminal Gods and Demon Devotees. Essays on the Guardians of Popular Hinduism.* New York.

HOLTZMANN, A.
1881: *Ueber das alte indische Epos.* Durlach.

HOPKINS, E. W.
1915: *Epic Mythology.* Strassburg.

HUBERT, H., M. MAUSS
1968 [1899]: "Essai sur la nature et les fonctions du sacrifice", in M. Mauss, *Œuvres*, I. Paris: 193-307.

HUNTER, W.W.
1872: *Orissa.* 2 vols. London.
1886: *The Imperial Gazetteer of India, vol. 6.* London (2nd ed.)

INDEN, R.
1978: "Ritual, Authority and Cyclic Time in Hindu Kingship", in Richards, J. F. (ed.): *Kingship and Authority in South Asia*: 28-73.

JAMISON, S. W.
1991: *The Ravenous Hyenas and the Wounded Sun. Myth and Ritual in Ancient India.* Ithaca.
1996: *Sacrificed Wife/ Sacrificer's Wife. Women, Ritual, and Hospitality in Ancient India.* New York.

JAMISON, S. W., M. WITZEL
2003: "Vedic Hinduism", in Sharma, A. (ed.): *The Study of Hinduism*: 65-113.

JOSHI, N. P.
1984: "Early Forms of Śiva", in Meister, M. W. (ed.): *Discourses on Śiva*: 47-61.

KEITH, A. B.
1925: *The Religion and Philosophy of the Veda and the Upanishads.* 2 vols. Cambridge, Massachusetts.

KINSLEY, D.
1975: *The Sword and the Flute. Kālī and Kṛṣṇa, Dark Visions of the Terrible and the Sublime in Hindu Mythology.* Berkeley.
1989: *The Goddesses' Mirror. Visions of the Divine from East and West.* Albany.
1997: *Tantric Visions of the Divine Feminine. The Ten Mahāvidyās.* Berkeley.

KHANNA, M.
1979: *Yantra. The Tantric Symbol of Cosmic Unity.* London.

KNIPE, D. M.
1975: *The Image of Fire. Vedic Experiences of Heat.* Delhi.

KRAMRISCH, S.

1946: *The Hindu Temple*. 2 vols. Calcutta.

1947: "The Walls of Orissan Temples", in *Journal of the Indian Society of Oriental Art*, 15: 178-196.

1954: *The Art of India. Traditions of Indian Sculpture, Panting and Architecture*. London.

1960: *Indian Sculpture in the Philadelphia Museum of Art*. Philadelphia.

1962: "Two: Its Significance in the ṚgVeda", in Bender, E. (ed.): *Indological Studies in Honor of W. Norman Brown*: 109-136.

1962-1963: "The Triple Structure of Creation in the ṚgVeda", in *HR*, 2, 1: 140-175; 2, 2: 256-285.

1968: *Unknown India: Ritual Art in Tribe and Village*. Philadelphia.

1981: *The Presence of Śiva*. Princeton.

KUIPER, F. B. J.

1960: "The Ancient Aryan Verbal Contest", in *IIJ*, 4, 4: 217-281.

1961: "Some Observations on Dumézil's Theory", in *Numen*, 8, 1: 34-45.

1962: "The Three Strides of Viṣṇu", in Bender, E. (ed.): *Indological Studies in Honor of W. Norman Brown*: 137-151.

1964: "The Bliss of Aša", in *IIJ*, 8, 2: 96-129.

1979: *Varuṇa and Vidūṣaka. On the Origin of the Sanskrit Drama*. Amsterdam.

KULKE, H.

1978a: "Royal Temple Policy and the Structure of Medieval Hindu Kingdoms", in Eschmann, A., H. Kulke, G. C. Tripathi (eds.): *CJRTO*: 125-137.

1978b: "Early Royal Patronage of the Jagannātha Cult", in Eschmann, A., H. Kulke, G. C. Tripathi (eds.): *CJRTO*: 139-155.

1978c: "Jagannātha as the State Deity under the Gajapatis of Orissa", in Eschmann, A., H. Kulke, G. C. Tripathi (eds.): *CJRTO*: 199-208.

KULKE, H., D. ROTHERMUND

1986: *A History of India*. London.

KULKE, H., B. SCHNEPEL (eds.)

2001: *Jagannath Revisited. Studying Society, Religion and the State in Orissa*. New Delhi.

LEVI, S.

1898: *La Doctrine du sacrifice dans les Brâhmanas*. Paris.

1920: *La Légende de Nala et Damayanti* (traduite, avec introduction, notes et vocabulaire). Paris.

LEVI-STRAUSS, C.

1958: *Anthropologie structurale*. Paris.

1964: *Le Cru et le cuit*. Paris.

1971: *L'Homme nu*. Paris.

1975: *La Voie des masques*. 2 vols. Genève.
1980: "Une petite énigme mythico-philosophique", in *Le Temps de la Réflexion*, Paris: 133-141.

LINCOLN, B.
1991: *Death, War, and Sacrifice. Studies in Ideology and Practice.* Chicago.

LINDA, M. F.
1994: "Zimmer and Coomaraswamy. Visions and Visualizations", in Case, M. H. (ed.): *Heirich Zimmer*: 119-142.

LIPSEY, R.
1977: *Coomaraswamy. His Life and Work.* Princeton.

LONG, J.B.
1975: "Life out of Death. A Structural Analysis of the Myth of the 'Churning of the Ocean of Milk'", in Smith, B. (ed.): *Hinduism. New Essays in the History of Religion*: 171-207.

MACDONALD, A.W.
1953: "Juggernaut reconstruit", in *JA*, 261: 487-528.

MAHAPATRA, G.
1979: *The Land of Viṣṇu.* Delhi.

MAHTAB, H.
1959-1960: *History of Orissa.* 2 vols. Cuttack.

MALAMOUD, Ch.
1989: *Cuire le monde. Rite et pensée dans l'Inde ancienne.* Paris.
1990: "Sans Lieu ni date. Note sur l'absence de fondation dans l'Inde védique", in Detienne, M. (ed.): *Tracés de fondation*: 183-191.
2002: *Le Jumeau solaire.* Paris.
2005a: *Féminité de la parole. Études sur l'Inde ancienne.* Paris.
2005b: *La Danse des pierres. Études sur la scène sacrificielle dans l'Inde ancienne.* Paris.

MANSINHA, M.
1962: *History of Oriya Literature.* New Delhi.

MARGLIN, F.A.
1982: "Types of Sexual Union and their Implicit Meanings", in Hawley, J. S., D. M. Wulff (eds): *The Divine Consort*: 298-315.
1985a: *Wives of the God-King. The Rituals of the Devadasis of Puri.* Delhi.
1985b: "Types of Oppositions in Hindu Culture", in Carman, J. C., F. A. Marglin (eds.): *Purity and Auspiciousness in Indian Society.* Leiden: 65-83.

MARGLIN, F. A., MISHRA, P. C.
1991: "Death and Regeneration: Brahmin and Non-Brahmin Narratives", in Eck, D. L., F. Mallison (eds.): *Devotion Divine*: 209-230.

MARRIOT, McKim
1989: "Constructing an Indian Ethnosociology", in *CIS*, 23: 1-39.

MATILAL, B.K.
1991: "Kṛṣṇa: In Defence of a Devious Divinity", in Sharma, A. (ed.): *Essays on the Mahābhārata*: 401-418.

MATILAL, B.K. (ed.)
1989: *Moral Dilemmas in the Mahābhārata*. Delhi.

McDANIEL, J.
1989: *The Madness of the Saints. Ecstatic Religion in Bengal*. Chicago.

MEISTER, M. W. (ed.)
1984: *Discourses on Śiva. Proceedings of a Symposium on the Nature of Religious Imagery*. Philadelphia.

MICHELL, G.
1977: *The Hindu Temple. An Introduction to its Meaning and Forms*. London.

MILLER, B. S.
1982: "The Divine Duality of Rādhā and Krishna", in Hawley, J. S., D. M. Wulff (eds): *The Divine Consort*: 13-26.

MILLER, B. S. (ed.)
1983: *Exploring India's Sacred Art. Selected Writings of Stella Kramrisch* (with a biographichal essay). Philadelphia.

MILLER, D. A.
1971: "Royauté et ambiguïté sexuelle", *in Annales. Économies, Sociétés, Civilisations*, 26, 3-4: 639-652.

MINKOWSKI, C. Z.
1989: "Janamejaya's *Sattra* and Ritual Structure", in *JAOS*, 109, 3: 401-420.

MISHRA, K. C.
1971: *The Cult of Jagannātha*. Calcutta.

MITRA, D.
1984: "Lakulīśa and Early Śaiva Temples in Orissa", in Meister, M. W. (ed.): *Discourses on Śiva*: 103-118.

MITRA, R.
1875: *The Antiquities of Orissa*. 2 vols. Calcutta.

MONIER-WILLIAMS, M.
1899: *A Sanskrit-English Dictionary*. Oxford.

MOOKERJEE, A.
1966: *Tantra Art. Its Philosophy and Physics*. New York.

MOOKERJEE, A., M. KHANNA
1977: *The Tantric Way. Art. Science. Ritual.* London.

MUKHERJEE, P.
1940: *The History of Medieval Vaishnavism in Orissa.* Calcutta.
1953: *The History of the Gajapati Kings of Orissa.* Cuttack.
1977: *History of the Jagannath Temple in the 19th Century.* Calcutta.
1979: *History of the Chaitanya Faith in Orissa.* New Delhi.

MUS, P.
1998: *Barabuḍur: Sketch of a History of Buddhism Based on Archaeological Criticism of the Texts.* Translated from the French by A. W. Macdonald. New Delhi.

NARANG, S. P. (ed.)
1995: *Modern Evaluation of the Mahābhārata. Prof. R. K. Sharma Felicitation Volume.* Delhi.

NAYAK, P. K.
2001: "Jagannath and the Adivasis: Reconsidering the Cult and its Traditions", in Kulke, H., B. Schnepel (eds.): *Jagannath Revisited*: 25-48.

OBEYESEKERE, G.
1984: *The Cult of the Goddess Pattini.* Chicago.

O'FLAHERTY, W. D. (See also DONIGER, W.)
1973: *Asceticism and Eroticism in the Mythology of Śiva.* Oxford.
1976: *The Origins of Evil in Hindu Mythology.* Berkeley.
1980: *Women, Androgynes, and Other Mythical Beasts.* Chicago.
1982: "The Shifting Balance of Power in the Marriage of Śiva and Pārvatī", in Hawley, J. S. and D. M. Wulff (eds.): *The Divine Consort*: 129-143.
1984a: *Dreams, Illusion, and Other Realities.* Chicago.
1984b: "Śiva Erect and Supine", in Meister, M. W. (ed.): *Discourses on Śiva*: 289-297.
1986: "Horses and Snakes in the *Ādi Parvan* of the *Mahābhārata*", in Case M., N. G. Barrier (ed.): *Aspects of India*: 16-44.
1988: *Other Peoples' Myths. The Cave of Echoes.* Chicago.

OGUIBENINE, B. L.
1973: *Structure d'un mythe védique. Le mythe cosmogonique dans le Ṛgveda.* The Hague-Paris.
1988: *La Déesse Uṣas. Recherches sur le sacrifice de la parole dans le Ṛgveda.* Louvain-Paris.

PANIGRAHI, K. C.
1961: *Archaeological Remains at Bhubaneswar.* Calcutta.
1981: *History of Orissa.* Cuttack.

PATNAIK, N.
1977: *Cultural Tradition in Puri. Structure and Organization of a Pilgrim Centre.* Simla.

POTT, P. H.
1966: *Yoga and Yantra: Their Interrelation and their Significance for Indian Archaeology.* The Hague.

PRAHARAJ, G. C.
1931-1940: *Orḍīā Bhāshākosha.* 7 vols. Cuttack.

RAJAGURU, S. N.
1968-1972: *History of the Gaṅgas.* 2 vols. Bhubaneshwar.

RAMANUJAN, A. K.
1999: *The Collected Essays of A. K. Ramanujan* (edited by V. Dharwadker). New Delhi.

RAWSON, P.
1968: *Erotic Art of the East. The Sexual Theme in Oriental Painting and Sculpture.* London.
1973a: *Tantra. The Indian Cult of Ecstasy.* London.
1973b: *The Art of Tantra.* London.

RAY, B. L.
1998: *Jagannātha Cult. Origin, Rituals, Festivals, Religion and Philosophy (A Critical Study of Sthaḷa Purāṇa, 'Nīlādri Mahodayam').* Delhi.

RENOU, L.
1939: "L'ambiguïté du vocabulaire du Ṛgveda", in *JA*, 231, 2: 161-235.
1978: *L'Inde fondamentale. Études d'indianisme réunies et présentées par Ch. Malamoud.* Paris.

RENOU, L., FILLIOZAT, J.
1947-53: *L'Inde classique. Manuel d'Études indiennes.* 2 vols. Paris.

RICHARDS, J. F. (ed.)
1978: *Kingship and Authority in South Asia.* Madison.

RICHMAN, P. (ed.)
1991: *Many Rāmāyaṇas. The Diversity of a Narrative Tradition in South Asia.* Berkeley.

ROCHER, L.
1984: "Śiva in the Purāṇas", in Meister, M. W. (ed.): *Discourses on Śiva:* 202-211.
1986: *The Purāṇas.* Wiesbaden.

ROCHER, L. (ed.)
1984: *Ezourvedam. A French Veda of the Eighteenth Century.* Amsterdam.

ROY, S. N.
1927: "The Savaras of Orissa", in *Man in India*, 7 (4): 16-58.

RUSSELL, R. V., HIRA LAL
1916: *The Tribes and Castes of the Central Provinces of India*. 4 vols. London.

SCHEUER, J.
1982: *Śiva dans le Mahābhārata*. Paris.

SCHOMER, K.
1989: "Paradigms for the Kali Yuga: The Heroes of the Ālhā Epic and Their Fate", in Blackburn, S. H., P. J. Claus, J. B. Flueckiger, S. S. Wadley (eds.): *Oral Epics in India*: 140-154.

SENAPATI, N., D. C. KUANR
1977: *Orissa District Gazetteers (Puri)*. Cuttack.

SHARMA, A. (ed.)
1991: *Essays on the Mahābhārata*. Leiden.
2003: *The Study of Hinduism*. Columbia.

SHULMAN, D. D.
1980: *Tamil Temple Myths. Sacrifice and Divine Marriage in the South Indian Śaiva Tradition*. Princeton.
1984: "The Enemy Within: Idealism and Dissent in South Indian Hinduism", in Eisenstadt, S. N., R. Kahane, D. Shulman (eds.): *Orthodoxy, Heterodoxy and Dissent in India*: 11-55.
1985: *The King and the Clown in South Indian Myth and Poetry*. Princeton.
1993: *The Hungry God. Hindu Tales of Filicide and Devotion*. Chicago.
1997: "Embracing the Subject: Harṣa's Play within a Play", in *Journal of Indian Philosophy*, 25: 69-89.
1999: "Dreaming the Self in South India", in Shulman, D., G. G. Stroumsa (eds.): *Dream Cultures*: 43-73.

SHULMAN, D., G. G. STROUMSA (eds.)
1999: *Dream Cultures. Explorations in the Comparative History of Dreaming*. New York.

SILBURN, L.
1955: *Instant et cause. Le discontinu dans la pensée philosophique de l'Inde*. Paris.
1983: *La Kuṇḍalinī ou l'énergie des profondeurs. Etude d'ensemble d'après les textes du Śivaïsme non dualiste du Kaśmir*. Paris.

SIRCAR, D. C.
1960: *Studies in the Geography of Ancient and Medieval India*. Delhi.
1971: *Studies in the Religious Life of Ancient and Medieval India*. Delhi.

SMITH, B. K.
1989: *Reflections on Resemblance, Ritual, and Religion.* New York.

SMITH, D. B.
1868: *Report on Pilgrimage to Juggernaut in 1868.* Calcutta.

SOIFER. D. A.
1991: *The Myths of Narasiṁha and Vāmana. Two Avatars in Cosmological Perspective.* Albany.

SORENSEN, S.
1978 (1904): *An Index to the Names in the Mahābhārata.* Delhi.

STAAL, F.
1983: *Agni. The Vedic Ritual of the Fire Altar.* 2 vols. Berkeley.
1990: *Rules without Meaning. Ritual, Mantras and the Human Sciences.* (Toronto Studies in Religion, vol. 4). New York.

STARZA, O. M.
1993: *The Jagannatha Temple at Puri. Its Architecture, Art and Culture.* Leiden.

STARZA-MAJEWSKI, O. M.
1983: *The Jagannātha Temple at Purī and its Deities.* Amsterdam.

STEIN, B.
1978: "All the Kings' *Mana*: Perspectives on Kingship in Medieval South India", in Richards, J. F. (ed.): *Kingship and Authority in South Asia* 115-167.

STIETENCRON, H. von
1978a: "The Advent of Viṣṇuism in Orissa: An Outline of its History according to Archaeological and Epigraphical Sources from the Gupta Period up to 1135 A.D.", in Eschmann, A., H. Kulke, G. C. Tripathi (eds.): *CJRTO*: 1-30.
1978b: "Early Temples of Jagannātha in Orissa: The Formative Phase", in Eschmann, A., H. Kulke, G. C. Tripathi (eds.): *CJRTO*: 61-78.
1978c: "The Śaiva Component in the Early Evolution of Jagannātha", in Eschmann, A., H. Kulke, G. C. Tripathi (eds.): *CJRTO*: 119-123.
1978d: "The Jagannātha Temples in Contemporary Orissa", in Eschmann, A., H. Kulke, G. C. Tripathi (eds.): *CJRTO*: 469-475.

STIRLING, A.
1846: *Orissa: its Geography, Statistics, History, Religion and Antiquities.* London.

SULLIVAN, B.M.
1990: *Kṛṣṇa Dvaipāyana Vyāsa and the Mahābhārata. A New Interpretation.* Leiden.

TARABOUT, G.
1986: *Sacrifier et donner à voir en pays Malabar.* Paris.
1990: "Sacrifice et renoncement dans les mythes de fondation des temples au Kérala", in Detienne, M. (ed): *Tracés de fondation*: 211-232.

THIEME, P.
1962: "Chess and Backgammon (Tric-Trac) in Sanskrit Literature", in Bender, E. (ed.): *Indological Studies in Honor of W. Norman Brown*: 204-216.

THOMAS, L.
1994: "The Identity of the Destroyer in the Mahābhārata", in *Numen*, 41: 255-272.

THURSTON, E.
1909: *Castes and Tribes of Southern India*. 7 vols. Madras.

TRIPATHI, G. C.
1978a: "On the Concept of 'Puruṣottama' in the Āgamas", in Eschmann, A., H. Kulke, G. C. Tripathi (eds.): *CJRTO*: 31-59.
1978b: "Navakalevara: The Unique Ceremony of the 'birth' and the 'death' of the 'Lord of the World'", in Eschmann, A., H. Kulke, G. C. Tripathi (eds.): *CJRTO*: 223-264.
1978c: "Jagannātha: the Ageless Deity of the Hindus", in Eschmann, A., H. Kulke, G. C. Tripathi (eds.): *CJRTO*: 477-490.
2004: *Communication with God. The Daily Pūjā Ceremony in the Jagannātha Temple*. New Delhi.

TUCCI, G.
1961: *The Theory and Practice of the Mandala*. New York.

VAN BUITENEN, J. A. B.
1972: "On the Structure of the Sabhāparvan of the Mahābhārata", in J. Ensink, P. Gaeffke (eds.): *India Maior. Congratulatory Volume Presented to J. Gonda*. Leiden: 68-84.

VERPOORTEN, J.-M.
1977: "Unité et distinction dans les spéculations rituelles védiques", in *Archiv für Begriffsgeschichte*, 21 (1): 59-85.

VIENNOT, O.
1954: *Le Culte de l'arbre dans l'Inde ancienne*. Paris.

VISUVALINGAM, E.
1989: "Bhairava's Royal Brahmanicide: The Problem of the Mahābrāhmaṇa", in Hiltebeitel, A. (ed.): *Criminal Gods and Demon Devotees*: 157-229.

VISUVALINGAM, S.
1989: "The Transgressive Sacrality of the Dīkṣita: Sacrifice, Criminality and *Bhakti* in the Hindu Tradition", in Hiltebeitel, A. (ed.): *Criminal Gods and Demon Devotees*: 427-462.

WILLIAMS, J. G.
1984: "Śiva and the Cult of Jagannātha: Iconography and Ambiguity", in Meister, M. W. (ed.): *Discourses on Śiva*: 298-311.

1996: *The Two-Headed Deer. Illustrations of the Rāmāyaṇa in Orissa.* Berkeley.

WITZEL, M.

1987: "On the Origin of the Literary Device of the 'Frame Story' in Old Indian Literature", in H. Falk (ed.): *Hinduismus und Buddhismus. Festschrift für Ulrich Schneider.* Freiburg: 380-414.

WOODROFFE, Sir J.

1918: *Sakti and Śākta.* Madras.

1922: *The Garland of Letters.* Madras

1931: *The Serpent Power.* London.

ZIMMER, H.

1946: *Myths and Symbols in Indian Art and Civilization.* New York.

1955: *The Art of Indian Asia. Its Mythology and Transformations.* 2 vol. New York.

1984: *Artistic Form and Yoga in the Sacred Images of India.* Princeton.

ZIMMERMANN, F.

1982: *La Jungle et le fumet des viandes. Un thème écologique dans la médecine hindoue.* Paris.

INDEX